MW00632934

The Long Way Home

Museums and Collections

Editors: Mary Bouquet, University College Utrecht, and Howard Morphy, The Australian National University, Canberra

As houses of memory and sources of information about the world, museums function as a dynamic interface between past, present and future. Museum collections are increasingly being recognized as material archives of human creativity and as invaluable resources for interdisciplinary research. Museums provide powerful forums for the expression of ideas and are central to the production of public culture: they may inspire the imagination, generate heated emotions and express conflicting values in their material form and histories. This series explores the potential of museum collections to transform our knowledge of the world, and for exhibitions to influence the way in which we view and inhabit that world. It offers essential reading for those involved in all aspects of the museum sphere: curators, researchers, collectors, students and the visiting public.

The Long Way Home

The Meanings and Values of Repatriation

Edited by

Paul Turnbull and Michael Pickering

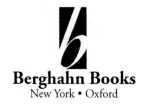

Berghahn Books
New York • Oxford

First published in 2010 by
Berghahn Books
www.berghahnbooks.com

©2010 Paul Turnbull and Michael Pickering

All rights reserved. Except for the quotation of short passages for the purposes
of criticism and review, no part of this book may be reproduced in any form
or by any means, electronic or mechanical, including photocopying,
recording, or any information storage and retrieval system now known
or to be invented, without written permission of the publisher.

Library of Congress Cataloging-in-Publication Data

A C.I.P. record for this book is available from the Library of Congress

British Library Cataloguing in Publication Data

A catalogue record for this book is available from the British Library

Printed in the United States on acid-free paper

Published in association with The National Museum of Australia Press.

ISBN 978-1-84545-958-1 (hardback)

Contents

Acknowledgements

We wish to thank the National Museum of Australia and the Australian National University's Research School of Humanities for generously sponsoring the Meanings and Values of Repatriation Conference held in Canberra in 2005. The essays in this collection grew out of that remarkable event and the conversations that began there. Our special thanks to Howard Morphy and Craddock Morton for their encouragement and support, and to Rick West, who made time despite his busy schedule then as Director of the National Museum of the American Indian to participate in the conference. We also thank Julie Ogden and the Publication Section of the National Museum of Australia for their invaluable assistance in the preparation of this book.

Introduction

Paul Turnbull

This collection of essays has its origins in conversations, stimulated by the National Museum of Australia's experiences of the repatriation of Aboriginal Australian ancestral bodily remains.

Unlike most of Australia's larger state museums, the history of the National Museum of Australia does not date back to the nineteenth century and the institution, therefore, had no interest in actively seeking to acquire human remains or Aboriginal and Torres Strait Islander peoples secret/sacred objects that are typically covered by cultural sanctions as to access. The Museum was not established until 1980 and its architecturally striking exhibition spaces, on Canberra's Acton Peninsula, were opened to coincide with the centenary of the federation of Australia in 2001.

Even so, the Museum has been actively involved in repatriation. It inherited, and has sought to resolve the fate of, Aboriginal remains that were collected by other federal institutions that have since ceased operations, notably the Australian Institute of Anatomy, which closed in the mid 1980s. More importantly, since the early 1990s, the Museum has acted as a voluntary repository for unprovenanced remains and items that have been returned to Australia by overseas museums and other scientific institutions. The goal of the Museum has been to consult with Indigenous communities with a view to having remains that have been consigned to its care returned to their community of origin, in most cases for reburial in accordance with ancestral law. Over the past two decades, staff who have been assigned to the Museum's repatriation program have assisted in the return of the remains of over 1000 Indigenous people to their ancestral communities.

I first met the director of the Museum's repatriation unit, Michael Pickering, in the mid 1990s as a result of my ongoing interest in the history of the procurement and scientific uses of Aboriginal ancestral remains. At the time, I was gathering archival evidence about the plundering of burial places in the 1930s and 1940s by George Murray Black, an engineering graduate of Melbourne University who took over the running of his family's pastoral property in South Gippsland. Black was a keen amateur anthropologist who spent his leisure time exhuming the bones of around 1800 individuals from burial places along the Murray River in northern Victoria. Until the late 1930s, the main beneficiary of his grave-robbing was the Australian Institute of Anatomy, founded in 1919 by

Colin Mackenzie, a fellow Melbourne University graduate and comparative anatomist who went on to specialise in orthopaedics, and was to direct the institute until the year before his death in 1938. Mackenzie encouraged Black to send him the remains of people who had died at some point after coming into contact with Europeans, as evidenced by their burial with coin and steel axes. But it seems clear, from correspondence between Black and Mackenzie that is held by the National Library of Australia, that the anatomist especially sought to obtain skulls with 'low foreheads with petrification' (Mackenzie 1935). My interest was in how Mackenzie's interest in such skulls was connected with contemporary thinking about the evolutionary genealogy of the human species, notably the claim by Sir Arthur Keith, at this time Britain's pre-eminent authority on ancient man, that a skull unearthed in 1925 from a large burial place on the floodplain of the Murray River was one of the most primitive human forms known to science.

The Museum's repatriation program had sought to acquire what knowledge it could of Black's successive donations to the institute through the 1930s of oil-drums packed with skeletal material. The Museum was thus able to provide me with important pieces of the intellectual jigsaw that I was trying to piece together. However, Pickering's and my discussion of this disturbing legacy to the Museum soon gave way to our talking at length about our respective involvement in repatriation, and the difficulties encountered by Indigenous people and Museum personnel in enabling remains that were deaccessioned from collections to make the journey home to ancestral country.

In my case, investigating the history of how remains found their way into Museum and medico-scientific collections had brought home to me the frustration that the Museum experienced because of the lack of evidence, in many cases of where and in what circumstances, items that had been received by the Museum after their return from overseas institutions had originally been procured. As Deanne Hanchant has observed of her time as the archival researcher on the National Skeletal Provenancing Project that was established in 1995, more than 1000 remains – about one fifth of the total then held by Australian museums and medical institutions – could not be provenanced (Hanchant 2002: 312). Having read my way through a number of museum archives in the United Kingdom and continental Europe, my sense was that the ratio of remains that left Australia between the late 1790s and 1930s with no documentation beyond vague geographical descriptors such as 'Australian', or 'From Central Queensland', was slightly higher.

Pickering and I also had impressions and stories to share about the debates within Australian museums, anthropological and archaeological circles that were provoked by Indigenous people's growing determination through the 1980s to end unconstrained investigation of their dead and to have remains that were resting in museums and medical collections unconditionally returned for burial.

Colin Pardoe has vividly described these demands for '... control, accountability and recognition of ... [Indigenous] ownership of the past' as having a cyclonic impact on the Australian archaeological profession, amongst whose members were researchers with the largest intellectual investment and most active interest in seeing work on remains continue (Pardoe 1991: 16). Certainly, as campaigning gathered momentum, there were angry exchanges, accusations and both scientific and Indigenous aspirations were misleadingly and divisively represented in national media. Key figures in Indigenous representative organisations, notably the Tasmanian Aboriginal Centre (TAC) and the Brisbane-based Foundation for Aboriginal and Island Research Action (FAIRA), unjustifiably accused archaeologists as being no different from racial scientists of the later nineteenth century whose plundering of the Aboriginal dead provided the raw intellectual material from which colonialist notions of Indigenous evolutionary inferiority were fashioned. Some in archaeological and museum circles responded with the equally false and misleading claims that repatriation activists were espousing a new and dangerous species of ethical relativism – a 'Black Creationism' with little or no connection with Aboriginal culture. Nevertheless militancy, especially on the part of TAC and FAIRA, was influential in generating public awareness and sympathy for the Indigenous case that in turn led some researchers and museum personnel to reevaluate the ethics of continuing to privilege their aspirations over the ancestral obligations of Indigenous people in respect of the dead.

However, it is vital not to overlook that the winds of change were stirring well before controversy spilled into the public domain.Since the early 1970s, there were many anthropologists and a number of archaeologists who had been questioning the ethics of exhuming burial places and retaining bones for study. The late Peter Ucko, for example, when principal of the Australian Institute of Aboriginal Studies in Canberra between 1972 and 1980, made no secret of his commitment to Indigenous self-determination in respect of remains and sacred cultural items. During his tenure, he negotiated the repatriation of remains at the request of several north Australian communities. By the early 1980s, the state museums of South Australia, Victoria and New South Wales were working in concert to transcend their colonial past by establishing new relationships with Aboriginal and Islander people that were likewise grounded in recognition of their rights to determine the uses of their cultural heritage that was held by museums. These new partnerships inescapably brought new obligations, as Des Griffin, director of Sydney's Australian Museum through the 1980s, aptly put it in the early 1990s. Indeed, what was going on within most Australian museums with little publicity was to create the essential preconditions for their accepting and supporting repatriation with what limited resources were at their disposal. Despite ongoing claims by FAIRA that museums continued to be opposed to repatriation, the reality by the mid 1990s was that failures to resolve the fate of remains were due to museums' lacking the resources to support the research and often lengthy periods of consultation the appropriate recipients of remains saw as necessary to ensure that they could be confident of fulfilling their obligations to the dead as demanded by ancestral law.

Moreover, in the case of the Australian Archaeological Association, it was concerned to refute publicly claims that some of its members were morally on a par with racial scientists of the Victorian period. It rightly expressed dismay at the 'negative and socially divisive' comments made by prominent Indigenous activists about John Mulvaney, Australia's most eminent archaeologist, and those of his colleagues who publicly declared that they could not condone the loss of remains to researchers through their reburial on the grounds that it would deny all humanity potentially important new insights into their shared deep past. Even so, by 1984, the association agreed that repatriation was justified in the case of known individuals, or when those with clear ancestral affinities to the dead wanted their remains reburied. Again, the preconditions were laid for accepting that the fate of all remains was ultimately the right of Indigenous Australians to determine. Today, the association is one of the most vocal advocates for the repatriation of remains that are still held by overseas museums and medico-scientific institutions.

When I visited the Museum in 2004, Pickering and I spoke at length about this shift in how repatriation has come to be understood within and beyond Australia's museum and research communities. We were struck by a number of things about this new landscape. Growing public support for repatriation since the mid 1990s had led the Australian federal and state governments to sponsor research to determine the provenance of remains before returning them to communities, and to provide support for elders and community leaders to negotiate the return of remains from overseas collections. In 2000, the Australian Government began enlisting the help of the British and other European Union governments to persuade institutions in their respective spheres of authority that held remains to agree to negotiate their repatriation. This had had various positive results with notably, in 2001, the British Government convening a parliamentary working group on the status of human remains in public collections.

As Elizabeth Bell explains in her chapter in this volume, the recommendations of this British working group were a major factor in persuading several British museums and scientific institutions, who had hitherto declared themselves ethically bound to deny repatriation claims, to see that entering into negotiations for the return of remains was inevitable, and best begun without further delay. Although, as Bell points out, what also weighed in this decision was the publicity surrounding the history of the illicit removal of hundreds of organs from dead children at Liverpool's Alder Hey Hospital. This helped generate British awareness and support for the return of Aboriginal remains. Moreover, in the case of the British Museum (Natural History), the decision to discuss repatriation was clearly undertaken in the hope that some reconciliation of scientific and Indigenous interests in their holdings might yet be achieved.

Even so, we were aware that repatriation continued to have its critics in Britain and continental Europe. As in Australia during the 1980s, these critics argued that returning remains to Indigenous ownership and probable reburial would deny all humanity the possible benefits accruing from various lines of medical or scientific research. They were clearly and genuinely disturbed by what they saw as the triumph of cultural relativism over science's universalist, humanitarian aspirations. Indeed, for some, this slide into cultural relativism seemed to stem from irrational and unnecessary guilt about the treatment Aboriginal and Islander people experienced in Australia's colonial past. Obviously, the meanings and values repatriation have accrued since the 1980s are entangled with and shaped by ongoing reappraisal of this colonial past. It has also had much to do with envisaging a future in which the aspirations of Indigenous Australians to reclaim and freely enjoy their cultural heritage are respected and supported. However, it seemed to Pickering and I that it would be useful to start a wider conversation in which scholars from a range of disciplinary perspectives could provide greater insight into the phenomenon of repatriation.

This was the background to the multidisciplinary conference that Pickering and I convened with Howard Morphy, a leading anthropologist of Aboriginal art and culture, in September 2005. The conference was generously supported by the Museum and the then Centre for Cross-cultural Research at the Australian National University. This book offers selected essays about various aspects of repatriation that in most cases have their origins in papers given at the conference. Following the conference, we invited the authors to revise their papers in the light of the discussions that went on during and several months following the event.

One further goal of the conference was to ensure that there was ample time for Elders and other Indigenous people involved in repatriation to speak freely about their experiences and concerns. For it was clear, from talking to both museum professionals and Indigenous people in the planning stages of the event, that repatriation continued to raise problems and issues that could be valuably considered in sessions during which Elders led discussions involving all participants. This was to be how the numerous Indigenous participants at the conference contributed to the conference. However, two discussants were kind enough to write about the issues they raised in discussion and helped us understand those issues with greater clarity. Their essays appear as the first two chapters in this volume. The first is by Henry Atkinson, a Wolithigia Elder and spokesperson for the Yorta Yorta Nation Aboriginal Corporation. Atkinson has been involved for over two decades in securing the repatriation of the remains of his people and the protection of burial places in their ancestral country which is located in the region of the junction of the Goulburn and Murray Rivers in present-day north-east Victoria. His essay underscores the profound obligations the Yorta Yorta have to the dead, while providing insights into how repatriation is entangled with memories of past colonial oppression and the continuing struggle to fully overcome its pernicious legacies.

The second essay is by Franchesca Cubillo, a Larrakia woman and museum professional who has worked in several Australian cultural heritage institutions over the past two decades. Cubillo reflects on the development of repatriation policies in Australian museums since she began working as a curator at the South Australian Museum in 1989. She points out that, even though the right of

Indigenous communities to determine the fate of ancestral remains is no longer at issue, their return to ancestral country continues in many instances to be a long journey that has not yet ended. Museum professionals continue to encounter difficulties, the most significant being the lack of funding that they have to support and assist communities satisfactorily to the point at which they are confident that they can give remains to the care of country as prescribed by ancestral law.

Cubillo also questions the adequacy of current Australian laws and policy frameworks in respect of repatriation, and draws attention to Indigenous dissatisfaction with the Australian Government's management of repatriating remains from overseas institutions since 2005. On this latter issue, the problem, she argues, has arisen since the demise of the Aboriginal and Torres Strait Islander Commission (ATSIC). A federal authority with an elected Indigenous leadership, ATSIC was designed to give Indigenous Australians an effective voice within the Australian Government. It had responded to its constituency by provided funding to enable Elders and their nominees to negotiate personally with overseas museums and scientific institutions on the return of remains and to then oversee their repatriation, ensuring appropriate ceremonies and other cultural obligations were observed. With the abolition of ATSIC in 2005, overseas repatriations came to be administered by the Office of Indigenous Policy Coordination (OIPC), initially established within the then federal Department of Immigration and Multicultural Affairs. Cubillo expresses concern that such arrangements do not provide for sufficient consultation with Indigenous communities, and that there needs to be a more co-ordinated approach that recognises that it is problematic for non-Indigenous staff of OIPC to assume roles in repatriation that ought rightly to be undertaken by Indigenous people only.

The next two chapters explore key aspects of the legal and policy dimensions of repatriation. Bell discusses the findings and recommendations of the working group on human remains that was established in 2001 by the United Kingdom's Department of Culture, Media and Sport, and then considers the implications of 2004's legislative reform that governs the uses of human tissue in the United Kingdom. Bell points out that, while guidelines enabling repatriation negotiations from British museums and medical schools now exist, they remain simply guidelines. Institutions still holding Indigenous Australian remains continue to have the power to decide their fate on the basis of advice from their own internally established expert committees.

Kathryn Whitby-Last's essay examines the legal impediments Indigenous people face, when seeking the return of items of cultural property of religious or other great cultural significance, in both international and national legal systems that originate in British common law. She begins by reminding us that Indigenous people continue to have little control over how their cultural heritage is defined for the purposes of deciding the relevant law by which such claims to objects are judged. For these legal definitions largely reflect other culturally engrained assumptions that seriously misconstrue the significance that objects have for Indigenous claimants. Whitby-Last goes on to explain the implications of repatriation claims being, legally speaking, not claims for restitution that can easily be judged by analysis of property rights. She explains that, in the domains of both public and private international law, repatriation claims for items from overseas institutions invariably become moral arguments in which recourse to legal precedents may play little part beyond possibly influencing the terms under which items might be returned to their community of origin. Indeed, Indigenous claims can be adversely affected by institutions relying on the state of relevant law to maintain what may generally be seen as morally dubious continued possession of human remains and religiously significant items.

In reflecting on the Australian experience of repatriation, several contributors to this volume draw attention to relevant North American law and policies, noting in particular the impact of the United States' Native American Graves Protection and Repatriation Act (NAGPRA), that was enacted in late 1990. However, as Virginia Myles' chapter on the Canadian experience of developing policies guiding the repatriation of human remains shows, developments north of the 49th parallel are equally of interest and relevance to nations where Indigenous peoples experienced large-scale loss of their cultural patrimony to museums and other scientific institutions. Myles reviews the work of Parks Canada and its responsibilities as a key federal agency in the development of policies and guidelines for the repatriation of Indigenous Canadian remains. Myles sketches the development of Canadian Government responses to Indigenous groups since the 1960s through several government commissions and task forces. In doing so, she highlights that much of the success that Parks Canada has had in managing repatriation claims has been due to its fostering of dialogue with Indigenous groups and its involvement in providing young Indigenous Canadians with practical experience in cultural resource management.

Repatriation not only has its legal complexities, but also raises theoretical and ethical questions about objects, their possession and their potential to have very differently enculturated meanings. Chapters 6, 7 and 8 are by researchers in the disciplines of anthropology and philosophy who seek to engage with these questions. Martin Skrydstrup is an anthropologist who has extensively researched the politics and ethics of material culture and repatriation in a variety of different contexts. In his chapter, he reflects on the complexities that are inherent in repatriation and similar transactions in cultural property, outlining a persuasive case for the development of a new conceptual vocabulary enabling the development of a broader and more just understanding of the meanings of cultural property after colonialism. Elizabeth Burns Coleman is a philosopher who has written with great insight on the ethics of appropriation and meanings of intellectual and cultural property. In this chapter, she considers how the concept of inalienable possession has been central to the justification of repatriating ancestral remains and other objects of sacred or profound cultural significance.

Burns Coleman is especially concerned to show that there are serious moral and political risks in advocates of repatriation assuming that patrimonial and sacred objects are things that cannot be alienated, and that this inalienability should be reflected in laws governing repatriation. For in doing so, she points out, there is real danger of construing Indigenous cultures much as they were in colonial times: frozen in time and unsusceptible to change. Indeed, Burns Coleman alerts us to the disturbing possibility that advocating the rights of Indigenous peoples to inalienable possession of objects may actually serve to diminish their rights to determine freely the fate of ancestral objects, including their alienation through gift or sale.

John Morton is an anthropologist well known for his studies of Aboriginal Australian land tenure, religion and the representation of Indigenous cultures in museums. In this volume, he reflects on how Indigenous Australian cultures have been construed within Australian public discourse and government circles in connection with repatriation. Morton argues that, in becoming a national issue in Australia, repatriation has been seen as simply a matter of promoting reconciliation between Indigenous and non-Indigenous Australians through returning human remains and religious objects that were often originally acquired by museums in morally dubious circumstances during earlier colonial times. He presents a compelling case for regarding repatriation as a phenomenon that in fact has much to do with the re-assignment of power to Indigenous Australians. Consequently it raises complex issues concerning the differentiation of Indigenous and other Australians within the Australian nation state, indeed how the future of the nation state is imagined.

The next two contributions to this volume are historically focused. As an historian who is interested in the uses of Indigenous human remains by scientific communities since the late eighteenth century, my chapter first considers the significance of the adoption of the Vermillion Accord on Human Remains by the World Archaeological Congress (WAC) in 1989 and looks at how the accord marked the beginnings of an important shift in how repatriation was understood within scientific circles. However, my main concern is to suggest that understanding how and why remains first found their way into museums and bio-medical institutions can serve two useful purposes. Firstly, it can assist repatriation in practice by providing Indigenous communities and museum professionals with knowledge of potential value in deciding the fate of remains. Secondly, it seems clear to me that efforts to resolve repatriation claims have not been helped by polemic and inaccurate claims of science's complicity in the colonial oppression of Aboriginal people, nor justifications of the worth of science grounded in older positivist histories of its achievements. Rather, I argue that what is needed is a historiography of scientific interest in the Indigenous body that highlights the cognitive distance of contemporary research on remains from the aspirations of earlier racial scientists, but simultaneously reminds us that science is a process that continues to be potentially susceptible to cultural and personal predispositions that might have unjust consequences. In short, in deciding the future of ancestral remains that became scientific specimens, there is a need to examine the historically engrained assumptions that all participants bring to the discussion.

In chapter 10, Claes Hallgren writes about the remarkable and disturbing recollections of Eric Mjöberg (1882–1938), a Swedish zoologist who secured Indigenous human remains during expeditions to the Kimberley region of Western Australia and coastal North Queensland between 1910 and 1913. Hallgren locates Mjöberg in the scientific landscape of his day while seeking to account for why lurid descriptions of his 'skeleton hunting' figure so prominently in his published accounts of his Australian travels. The answer, Hallgren suggests, lies in Mjöberg being a respected scientist and yet a man with literary aspirations who was fascinated by the capacity of fiction to depict repulsive or abhorrent behaviour so as to generate curiosity and horror in its readers. In recounting his Australian exploits, Indigenous people are portrayed as blindly addicted to cannibalism, with the effect that both his own mutilations of the dead and the brutal treatment meted out to the living by frontier authorities are justified. Mjöberg turned his hand in the mid 1930s to science fiction. In appraising this fiction, Hallgren is drawn to suggest that, in seeking to understand why it was that in Mjöberg's lifetime few moral doubts were raised by the process of plundering Indigenous burial places, we would do well to consider that his 'skeleton hunting' spoke to deep and barely articulated obsessions in the European imagination.

In chapters 11, 12, 13 and 14, prominent museum professionals and Indigenous community-based researchers reflect on their involvement in the return of human remains and sacred objects.

In the first of these chapters, Howard Morphy engages with a number of the issues that are explored by Skrydstrup, Burns Coleman and Morton; though he does so from the perspective of an experienced museum curator and visual anthropologist who has worked closely for over three decades with the Yolngu people of north-east Arnhem Land. Morphy points out that museum personnel cannot escape immersion within the complex political and cultural negotiations that claims for the repatriation of human remains invariably entail. Nor should they try; rather, they need to look to anthropological knowledge as offering valuable intellectual resources for appraising and trying to resolve the moral dilemmas caused by differences in cultural values that are thrown into sharp perspective by the process of repatriation.

To this end, Morphy pursues a careful analysis of the rights vested in human remains by museums and by the communities in which they have their origins. In doing so he draws attention to how repatriation has come to occur in a landscape that has greatly changed over the past three decades. The positivist assumptions that once informed much of earlier scientific work and museum practice have given way to recognition of what in many instances are different yet complementary aspirations in respect of research involving human remains and sacred objects. Indigenous peoples have established new partnerships with museums and are among the most active users of collections. There is now a multiplicity of Indigenous views concerning the preservation of remains and cultural objects by museums; and non-Indigenous researchers generally now take a more culturally informed and pragmatic approach in seeking to pursue research using these items. In short, Morphy suggests that the prime lesson of repatriation is to be found in analysing its cross-cultural complexities and the sometimes heated debates it has provoked. For, in doing so, there is the promise of our gaining a clearer appreciation of the hazards of regarding museum objects simply as traces of the past colonial domination of Indigenous peoples, and that resolving the moral legacies of that past requires ensuring that law and policy frameworks for repatriation recognise that these objects are things whose future can only be ethically decided through localised dialogues between Indigenous communities and museums.

Morphy's conclusions are shared by Pickering who, in his chapter, reflects on the experiences of the repatriation program of the National Museum of Australia since the early 1990s. He describes the policies and processes followed at the Museum and the main challenges encountered in assisting communities with repatriations. Even though the Museum has been successful in negotiating many of the difficulties it has encountered in helping return the remains of well over 1000 individuals over two decades (with over 600 in the last 7 years), Pickering argues that the practice of repatriation could be improved from being more informed by perspectives generated through dialogue with anthropologists, philosophers and scholars in other disciplines beyond archaeology and physical anthropology. Pickering is especially concerned that museum audiences still only vaguely understand why the repatriation of Indigenous human remains is occurring and that, in engaging with these audiences, museum professionals need to be able to explain, in depth and with clarity, the cultural and ethical considerations that have weight in the Museum's decision to be committed to returning unconditionally remains and sacred objects to their ancestral communities.

In the chapter that follows, Kim Akerman illustrates Morphy's point that Indigenous Australians hold markedly differing opinions about what should happen to human remains and sacred objects that remain in the custody of museums and medico-scientific institutions. Drawing on many years' experience of repatriation and working as a community-based anthropologist in the Kimberley and Pilbara regions of Western Australian, Akerman explains how factors such as shifting patterns of cultural exchange between peoples, migration to centres of European settlement and conversion to Christianity can variously complicate the process of repatriation. Within the Kimberly region alone, he points out, sacred objects have over the course of the past 100 years accrued quite different meanings for different cultural groups. This history has rendered the process of determining who can interpret whether an object is sacred or secret, and thus decide to whom it should be returned and under what conditions, a necessary if complex and time-consuming process.

Steve Hemming and Chris Wilson further underscore this point in reviewing the recent repatriation experiences of the Ngarrindjeri people of the lower Murray region of South Australia. From the late 1830s onwards, more Ngarrindjeri remains were procured for scientific ends by plundering ancestral burial places than any other Indigenous Australian people. This was in spite of the fact that their lawful ownership and rights to bury their dead in accordance with ancestral law was recognised by the British government in 1837. Indeed, at the turn of the twentieth century, Ngarrindjeri bodily remains were procured for medico-scientific researchers in contravention of laws governing the treatment of dead Indigenous and non-Indigenous bodies alike. Hemming and Wilson argue that such was the scale and devastating effects of this desecration and plunder that government and museums have a responsibility for compensating Ngarrindjeri, and a duty to ensure that they have the resources to support them through the lengthy and distressing process of caring for the many dead now making the journey home for reburial in accordance with ancestral law. However, as Hemming and Wilson show, the Ngarrindjeri have been severely hindered by lack of financial and other resources in fulfilling their obligations to the dead. They have also been frustrated by what the Ngarrindjeri see as new forms of colonialism in the form of government initiatives to manage the natural resources and promote tourism in their ancestral land. This has not stopped the Ngarrindjeri people successfully developing strategies for negotiating the burial of the dead; but, as Hemming and Wilson observe, Ngarrindjeri have yet to secure the resources to heal the profound spiritual and social damage that the theft of the dead has caused.

Many of the ideas and arguments offered in this volume continue to be the subject of conversations amongst the Indigenous Elders, museum professionals and scholars in various disciplines who participated in the conference that gave rise to this book. While what appears here reflects a consensus that Indigenous remains must be allowed to make the long journey home to the care of their ancestral communities, it will become clear to the reader that there are many aspects of repatriation that present practical problems and ethical uncertainties. Even so, what is also clear is that our contributors generally agree that the nature of these problems are such that their resolution is only to be achieved by fostering dialogue in which the concerns of all those who have legitimate and possibly conflicting interests are able to be expressed and understood as sincere appraisals of what is to be gained and also what could be lost through repatriation.

Bibliography

Hanchant, Deanne. 2002. 'Practicalities in the Return of Remains: The Importance of Provenance and the Question of Unprovenanced Remains', in C. Fforde, J. Hubert and P. Turnbull (eds), *The Dead and Their Possessions: Repatriation in Principle, Policy and Practice*. London: Routledge, pp. 312–16.

Mackenzie, Colin. 1935. Letter to George Murray Black, 4 September 1935, Murray Black Correspondence, National Museum of Australia, File 02/637.

Pardoe, Colin. 1991. 'The Eye of the Storm: The Study of Aboriginal Human Remains in Australia', *Journal of Indigenous Studies* 2: 16–23.

Part I

Ancestors, Not Specimens

1

The Meanings and Values of Repatriation

Henry Atkinson

On behalf of the people of the Yorta Yorta Nation, I want to begin by acknowledging the Ngunnawal people, the traditional owners of the land on which the conference which led me to write this chapter was held. I thank the Ngunnawal people for generously welcoming all of us who journeyed to their country. And I also want to pay my respects to the ancestral spirits and to the spirits of those who are not yet home in the land of their birth.

I feel we have a long way to go in the process of repatriation for there are many of our ancestral remains still in institutions and museums the world over, which we know about; and there are many more in countries yet to be located, identified and returned to country. It is hard to think of any words that adequately capture the meanings and values of repatriation to my people. The theft of ancestral remains and secret sacred ceremonial objects I can best describe as a form of genocide. And when we speak of the values of repatriation, I am moved to say what value can you put on your ancestors? There is no dollar value and no words that can really describe the value of our ancestors. For you, they have no emotional value – except in the immoral way in which Indigenous people were exploited. To me, my people and other Indigenous groups around the world, it is an entirely a different matter. These skeletal remains belong to me and I belong to them. Some of my people were given burials according to the custom of each clan group, but there were people who were not given the chance of a burial and now lie in an undignified manner all over the world.

It has been documented by the European scientific world that the Indigenous people of Australia have existed for about forty to sixty thousand years. However, I was taught that we have been here since time began and in that time we lived as one with the land and water, adapting parts of it to suit our people's needs and requirements. And still today, in this modern world, we continue to have our own beliefs and deep spiritual connections to our country. They are deep inside me, my children and grandchildren.

The present-day states of Victoria and of New South Wales are divided by the Murray River. However, the traditional country of the Yorta Yorta Nation lies on both sides of the river. Within a particular part of my country there are many sacred sites and areas where graves have been robbed of remains and the goods that were buried with the dead. The dead must not be disturbed again, not in the course of construction and certainly not for any kind of scientific research. Indeed, scientific use of the remains of my people must cease or dialogue between researchers and Indigenous people on the meanings and values of repatriation will be impossible.

Yorta Yorta country was once stocked with all manner of food sources for my people. The land provided all we needed and when she was taken away in the course of European settlement – an invasion that saw the decimation of our people – we came to be regarded as a threatened race in our own land, especially by men of science. Over the years numerous scientists – medical doctors, anthropologists, dentists, archaeologists, in Australia and other parts of the world – sought to procure Indigenous remains. Some wanted soft body tissue that had to be preserved in alcohol. Others wanted craniums, or entire skeletons. The remains of my people were collected like one collects stamps or swap cards. It was what I call the 'ivory trade' of my people, the first stolen generation. However, my people were not elephants. They were parents and children, all belonging to a family just like yours.

My people were hunted down, poisoned, shot or hacked to death. Where there were massacres, people were left behind to endure the pain of having seen their beloved family members battered or shot to death. Can you imagine just what this would have been like? To have been sitting under a gum tree, by the river, when out of nowhere comes the thunderous sound of horses and, before you have time even to think, the horde is upon you and if you are unlucky enough to survive you are left with the terrors of that moment forever. What you see is like a fast running movie with butts of guns flaying through the air, rifle shots piercing the quietness and sending the bird life into a screeching mass to join with the screams of pain inflicted upon the oldest, and the youngest, of your family. Honestly, I don't know how my people survived this. The pain of this history is deep within me, and continues to affect my children and grandchildren.

For those scientists who wanted to obtain whole bodies, these were put into barrels of spirits to preserve them on the long journey overseas, while others were reduced to skeletons. My people were wrapped in brown paper or put in a rough hessian bag and shipped overseas. There was no thought of this being a person, a living human. How can the spirits of one's ancestors rest when they have been subject to this type of inhumane treatment. How can they rest when, even to this day, they are still subject to the prying eyes and the jabbing tools of a so-called civilised society? My people's skeletal remains are in museums and other scientific institutions in many countries. We believe that there are over ten thousand skeletal remains in the United Kingdom awaiting repatriation. It is beyond me how Australia permitted the remains of so many people to be stolen and sent overseas for experimentation. What really makes it especially hard to comprehend is that this occurred in the 200 years and more since colonisation, and no government has made any conscientious and sustained effort to bring my people home.

A lot of people do not know that the remains of my people have aided the medical world in fields such as dentistry and bone structure, and that the results of experimentation on soft body tissue and bone has been the subject of academic theses and doctorates. However, is this justification for plundering of the remains of so many of my Indigenous brothers and sisters Australia wide? The gaining of doctorates and the like through the use of remains as a path to higher professional status has been at the expense of my ancestors. What benefit has this research had for Indigenous people? Our babies still die younger, our youth have less opportunity and our elders live approximately twenty years less than the non-Indigenous population. Despite all the money poured into research and the money made by some from this research, Indigenous people are still no better off. They have less of the basics of everything.

To add insult to injury, as if my people have not had enough experimentation performed on their remains, it has been suggested that they undergo DNA testing. One wonders, why? I am worried about the terms used by non-Indigenous for acknowledging one's Aboriginality? Will governments then be able to say that a person's DNA does not have enough of certain characteristics and that, therefore, they are not Indigenous?

We are looking forward to future negotiations with overseas museums in repatriating our people and those of their possessions that were taken from Australia without consent. While in England in 2003, I was part of a delegation that was able to bring home some people from the Royal College of Surgeons and we were grateful for the way in which the college repatriated my people. It was a moving experience and one which we hope to be able to repeat.

In April 2004, I went with a delegation to America to bring back some of my people whose remains had been offered for sale on the web. Their remains had been traded for plastic boomerangs and the purchaser sought to resell the remains, even though this is illegal in the United States. He was reluctant to turn over the remains until he had our assurance that he would not be prosecuted for illegally possessing the skeletal remains of an Indigenous Australian.

While visiting the University of Michigan, we were offered more remains of our people for repatriation. It seems incredible to me that some of the remains that we brought home from Michigan had only left Australia approximately fifteen years ago. They had apparently been received from a medical institution. I want to know how the remains of my people could have been sent overseas just fifteen years ago. The government is supposed to protect ancestral remains, artefacts and sacred objects and prevent them leaving the country. It leads me ask, does this still happen? Will it continue to happen?

While in America we also met with Indigenous people who welcomed us with traditional ceremonies and we were shocked to hear that, while the University of

Michigan had gladly returned our people, they resisted in returning the remains of their own Indigenous people to country. My view is that it is much the same here in Australia with the museums wanting to return Australian Indigenous remains but unwilling to return those of the Indigenous people of another country. You cannot show respect for the Indigenous people of Australia and not for the Indigenous people of all countries. We share similar histories and a common identity. All Indigenous remains, skeletal and otherwise, must be returned to their country of origin. It is important to the healing processes of Indigenous people, for the past holds much pain with not only the ancestors being taken by force and brutal means but also the tearing apart of the fabric of our lives. All remains need to be given ceremony which will ease the pain of the Indigenous community and restore some self respect and pride as their ancestral spirits are united.

One organisation, the Freemasons Lodge Society of Victoria, returned skeletal remains to the Indigenous community in 2001. I wonder why this body of people would want to use the skeletal remains of my people in their ceremonial practices. Further, there are many Freemasons' lodges not just in Victoria but throughout Australia and overseas. To my knowledge, at this point in time, none have come forward to return any skeletal remains they have of our people. However, it leaves me wondering whether there are other instances where our remains are the subjects of bizarre practices.

There is one thing that can never be stolen from our people and that is their spirit. They can box us up, stack us on shelves, experiment to no end, trade us and even swap us but our spirit will never be broken; while I am alive I will do all in my power to right the wrongs of history and force the keepers and collectors and the like to return my people home so their spirits can rest at last.

I remember being with my father in the bush as a young man. He would point out places of interest where there were many sacred and spiritual sites to further my knowledge. He would also show me many burial sites and tell me stories about how these sacred resting places of our ancestors were robbed and we could not do a thing about it. There was no protection as we were still classed as nothing more than decoration of this country and on the same level as the animals. I also remember being with my mother on one of those very rare visits to the city for a country boy. We went to the museum and one has to be in my shoes to appreciate the pain and tears on my mother's face when confronted with displays of her own people. There, for all to stare at, were her ancestors and artefacts with deep spiritual meaning on display. Some were things that only women should see; others were associated with men's business. As a young boy I did not understand her pain and my parents did not want to talk about it. Now, as a man with family and grandchildren of my own, I feel my parent's deep sorrow and wish I could have lifted some of the pain from their shoulders. Yet, all I can do is work as hard as I can to bring our people home and let their spirits roam free in their ancestral country.

On behalf of the Indigenous people of this country and particularly the Yorta Yorta Nation, I would like to acknowledge Mr Bob Weatherall and thank him for his foresight and endeavours in bringing so many of our people home. I would also like to thank Robyn Weatherall, Bob's wife, for all the support she has given him in securing the return of our people. Bob has spent most of his life in repatriating our people. He has made sure that those being returned home are treated in a dignified manner. This is something Bob has insisted upon, ensuring that everyone, from the transport carriers to the airline cargo handlers, understand the crucial importance of respecting the spirits of the dead. Unfortunately, the federal government has different views. It wants a 'government to government' approach to the repatriation of our people that largely excludes Indigenous people from the process and does not involve the observation of proper cultural protocols.

Prior to its disestablishment in March 2005, the Aboriginal and Torres Strait Islander Commission (ATSIC) supported research allowing us, in many instances, to identify the area of country from which remains had been taken, thus enabling us to return them to their rightful place in the land. Before further ancestral remains are brought home, this research must continue. ATSIC also supported the central involvement of Indigenous people in the repatriation of our ancestral remains, research and grave goods. Non-Indigenous people do not have the spiritual connection to the remains of our people and, therefore, there is a greater chance that they may act in an excessively bureaucratic or insensitive way, with the result that remains are simply shipped in a box and delivered to us with the expectation that we will inter them in any old way. This is not good enough. Our people, the living and the deceased, have profound obligations to ensure our ancestors are returned to their country and not just thrown in the ground anywhere.

I plead with men and women of the scientific world – anthropologists, archaeologists and the like – to pressure governments and institutions not to make it so difficult to bring our people home. The remains of our people must be allowed our customs and ceremony before they leave the prisons that have held them for so many years. Indigenous custodians who will give our people the respect they deserve must bring them home.

Indigenous people must be allowed to have this spiritual connection with their ancestors – beginning with the performance of ceremonies by Indigenous custodians when their remains are released from their obscene holding areas before they commence the long journey home, where they can be joined by the waiting Indigenous community before – after due traditional customs – they are returned to the earth of their beginning. This is the way Bob Weatherall commenced his days in repatriation, caring for all we hold in relation to our spiritual beings, and this standard must continue. I have laughed with this man and I have cried with him, when our physical and spiritual pain digs into our being as Indigenous men, for the great spirits of our ancestors from the beginning to our Dreamtime connects us.

2

Repatriating Our Ancestors: Who Will Speak for the Dead?

Franchesca Cubillo

This paper may contain information regarding Indigenous human remains that may cause distress to some people and I apologise for this.

Indigenous Australian communities today have a cultural and spiritual responsibility to ensure that our ancestors' remains are returned to their homelands. As a nation of people, we have had to fight for the rights of our ancestors because their remains are held in research institutions throughout the world. In the last twenty years, Indigenous people in Australia have discovered that the remains of at least 7,200 of their ancestors are held in museums in Australia, 5,500 whose provenance is known. It is estimated that another ten thousand are held in overseas institutions. Our ancestors, despite state policies, continue to be trapped within these facilities by historical constructs, political agendas and scientific debate and they are denied proper burial rights.

Museums in Australia have been actively involved in repatriation for the last twenty years, but what are the results, who is monitoring their efforts and who is advising them at a national level? Have these mechanisms been effective and what lessons have we learnt? This chapter will discuss the achievements and shortfalls of repatriation efforts in Australia to date. It will investigate the effectiveness of state and federal policies and government programs and consider what the future options are for the efficient and timely repatriation of the remains of our ancestors.

Today I would like to speak to you as both a museum professional and an Indigenous person. I have been fortunate to work in Indigenous cultural heritage institutions for the last fifteen years; twelve of these have been specifically within museums. My initial introduction to museums was through the Strehlow Collection, which in 1989 was held at the South Australian Museum (and is now housed in the Strehlow Research Centre in Alice Springs). I was intrigued by the political and ethical dilemmas surrounding this important collection of central Australian restricted objects and associated archival material.

I soon gained employment at the South Australian Museum and, fortunately, it was at a time when repatriation of restricted ceremonial objects and human remains was being discussed. It was an exciting time within museums as they were becoming more responsive to Indigenous concerns regarding access to collections, repatriation and providing employment and training opportunities for Indigenous people. The South Australian Museum was in the midst of the process of developing new and productive relationships with Indigenous people. One of the initial outcomes of this process was the establishment of policies governing the repatriation of Indigenous Human Remains and the repatriation of Restricted Secret/Sacred objects. These two separate documents provided best practice standards for engaging with Indigenous people in regard to these two sensitive collections.

A key factor that was negotiated and then included in the early repatriation policies during the late 1980s was that museums should be receptive and accommodating of requests from Indigenous communities regarding the repatriation of their ancestors' remains and that repatriation should be unconditional. Museums, however, were under no obligation to employ staff to work on repatriation full time, to conduct inventories or to engage with communities once the inventories were completed. Rather, they were obliged only to respond to requests by Indigenous groups to have their ancestors' remains returned to them.

Thus began the repatriation of Australian Indigenous human remains in Australia. It was an ad hoc, uncoordinated and reactionary process that was subsidised by the budgets of state museums. Obviously, the museums, including board members and staff, who embarked on this process did so with the best intentions; but it really was not the best approach to take, especially since other countries were setting better standards for best practice in this area at the same time.

In 1989, on the other side of the world, the American Indians were successful in encouraging the US Congress to pass the *National Museum of the American Indian Act*. This legislative act made reference to human remains and funerary objects. In particular, it stated that the Smithsonian Institution, in consultation with Indigenous nations, was required to conduct inventories of its collections of human remains and funerary objects. Once these inventories were completed, the Smithsonian was required to contact the communities concerned, notifying them of these collections and beginning negotiations for their repatriation.

In 1990, the United States also passed the *Native American Graves Protection and Repatriation Act* (NAGPRA), almost twelve months after the enactment of the *National Museum of the American Indian Act*. This legislation is quite detailed and complex. It does, however, mandate procedures and standards regarding the repatriation of human remains, funerary objects and objects of cultural patrimony and gives protection and ownership of materials unearthed on federal and tribal lands to the appropriate ancestral community.

By the early 1990s, all state museums within Australia had developed their own policies regarding the repatriation of Australian Indigenous human remains. In 1993, Museums Australia launched a national policy document titled, *Previous Possessions, New Obligations: Policies for Museums in Australia and Aboriginal and Torres Strait Islander Peoples*. This document also provided guidelines for the repatriation of human remains.

When we compare the American achievements regarding repatriation of Indigenous remains and consider what has taken place within Australia, I am embarrassed to say that we are lacking in our approach. Australian policies have come a long way towards recognizing Indigenous ownership of the ancestral dead. However, museums can change their institutional policies regarding repatriation at any stage.

In 1998 the Australian government, through the Cultural Ministers' Council, recognised the need to engage and assist in repatriating efforts and established the Return of Indigenous Cultural Property (RICP) Program. The program was funded for a three-year period from 2000 to 2003 with a budget of $A3 million, and has since been extended. The funding allocated is to cover the costs associated with the identification of the origins of restricted objects and human remains, the notification of communities regarding those collections and the facilitation of repatriation of collections in a culturally appropriate manner.

All RICP sponsored projects within museums were managed independently by the department. Museums were not encouraged to work together or coordinate their repatriation efforts. Indigenous communities were thus engaging with different museums at various times throughout the project. A national approach to repatriation, the National Skeletal Provenancing Project, was considered and implemented by DCITA in 1995. The project was managed by the South Australian Museum. It was envisaged as providing the federal and state governments with an accurate assessment of how extensive these collections were and the locations from which the remains were originally procured. The methodology employed during the project included physically examining every set of human remains held within Australian state museums and the National Museum of Australia, and consulting archival material associated with these collections. Yet, the information gathered through this process has not informed repatriation policies and practices in any systematic way.

Museums were informed that the RICP program would cease at the end of September 2005. However, we have been left wondering what were the outcomes of this project? What was learnt? How has it informed the thinking of the Cultural Ministers' Council? One would have hoped that the information has not simply been gathered for use by museums alone. Indigenous communities who have participated in repatriation and particular specialists (and non-Indigenous) should have been consulted as part of an evaluation of the effectiveness and potential benefits of the project.

International Repatriation

The Aboriginal and Torres Strait Islander Commission (ATSIC), Aboriginal organisations and Indigenous people have campaigned for many years for the repatriation of ancestral remains from overseas institutions. Until the Australian Government abolished ATSIC in March 2005, the commission was instrumental in supporting repatriation efforts. On 4 July 2000 the British and Australian governments agreed to increase and facilitate the repatriation process of remains from government-funded museums and universities within the United Kingdom. A direct initiative of this agreement was the establishment of a British working group that invited submissions from Australia and the United Kingdom regarding repatriation. A report was tabled in the British parliament recommending that the UK legislation be 'relaxed' so that repatriation could occur if the institution wishes.

The Office of Indigenous Policy Coordination (OIPC) was previously part of ATSIC. Since the disbanding of ATSIC in 2003, it has been located within the Department of Families, Housing Community Services and Indigenous Affairs. OIPC continues to be charged with facilitating the repatriation of remains from overseas institutions. However, we still do not know how many Australian Indigenous remains are held in overseas collections. A report produced by Carol Cooper in 1989 suggests there may be potentially hundreds awaiting return to their ancestral country. Former commissioner of ATSIC, Rodney Dillon, estimates that there are at least ten thousand. It is hard to quantify until comprehensive research is undertaken.

The largest collection repatriated to Australia was that held by the Anatomy Department of Edinburgh University in Scotland. Most of the collection was returned in 1991 with some additional remains that were subsequently identified being returned in 2000. It was estimated that the university had acquired approximately three hundred sets of remains since the early nineteenth century. After the collection was unpacked and individuals rearticulated, the remains of eighty-seven individuals were returned to the Larrakia community in Darwin and three hundred ancestors to the Ngarrindjeri community. It was estimated that forty per cent of the Edinburgh collection was repatriated through this process. Additional research and reunification of remains has identified that the collection contained the remains of 603 individuals – just over twice the initial estimate.

When collections of Indigenous human remains return to Australia they are protected under the *Aboriginal and Torres Strait Islander Heritage Protection Act 1984*. The federal minister responsible for administering the Act has the right to take receipt of remains until such time as the origin of the remains is determined. The National Museum of Australia is the sole authority designated with custody under the provisions of the Act. Hence all collections returned from international institutions go to the Museum until their provenance is determined.

The process of repatriation in Australia is informal in that while policies and legislation exist, they are not as detailed and specific as comparable American legislation. Therefore successful repatriation is often dependent on experience and goodwill between the participants, rather then legislative requirements. If we consider each of the state and national museums individually and examine their repatriation efforts since 2000 we can see that their experiences and results differ dramatically.

Repatriation is such an important priority for Indigenous Australians and I believe that, after twenty-five years of seeking the return of the ancestral dead to country, it should still be based on goodwill. Museums, state governments and the Commonwealth need to re-evaluate the strategies that they currently have in place. They need to consider the effectiveness of their policies and dedicate resources, both financial and personnel, to ensure a more effective and efficient repatriation process.

Museums

For example, the National Museum of Australia has a dedicated unit focused specifically on repatriation. Consultants are brought in on a short-term basis to assist in the process of writing community reports. Indigenous communities often request that a community report is produced as part of the repatriation process. Most state museums in Australia do not have dedicated staff employed to deal specifically with repatriation. Curators and collection managers are responsible for collection development, exhibitions, research, outreach programs and repatriation. This is a huge workload and one that does not help repatriation efforts. State museums with large collections should have a dedicated staff member working full time on the repatriation of collections until they decrease substantially. In fact it should be a requirement of funding agreements from state and federal agencies that museums match these funds to ensure that the project is successful and taken seriously by the institutions. Imagine if one of the requirements for RICP funding had been that museums had to match these funds; I suspect the results of repatriation would have been very different.

Museums also need to communicate and coordinate with each other and be strategic in their efforts regarding repatriation. This would be beneficial to both the Indigenous communities in that they would then have one repatriation process to deal with. Equally this process would prove cost effective for museums in that they would be able to share the financial costs associated with repatriation. Currently, Indigenous communities are approached intermittently by different institutions or museums at different times to take receipt of their ancestors' remains. The extra strain these varied approaches place on Indigenous communities is unnecessary. Equally, the communities are unaware of the full extent of ancestral remains that are held in all state museums across Australia and therefore cannot prepare themselves for the overall impact of the repatriation of their ancestors.

Another issues of concern is that the federal government has made major steps towards working with the British Government to ensure the repatriation of Indigenous remains from the United Kingdom. Once these collections begin to come back to Australia extra funds will be required to develop appropriate strategies covering the identification of remains and their provenance, consultation with Indigenous communities and repatriation of remains to those communities. We have already seen problems emerging from this process with the Ngarrindjeri community refusing to accept the repatriation of any of their ancestors remains until such a point when their cultural priorities are accommodated at handover ceremonies. Again, consideration and strategic planning needs to be in place regarding the repatriation of overseas collections. Communities should be notified in the first instance of the full extent of the collections held in the United Kingdom, they should be informed of institutions willingness, or lack of, to repatriate those collections; and then a coordinated and culturally appropriate repatriation effort should occur at the one time. Currently different institutions are returning items on an ad hoc basis. This is not cost effective and, most importantly, places undue pressure on individual communities who may have to go through repatriation negotiations at later dates with different institutions.

Long-term strategies need to be put in place. Equally, collections that are to be repatriated from overseas need to be in order and returned to Australia with all known associated archival information.

Indigenous Communities

Indigenous communities need to be provided with the resources to take receipt of and rebury their ancestors. An instance of repatriation in which I was involved typifies how urgent and real problems of unpreparedness to receive ancestors are in communities. The Ngarrindjeri community of the lower Murray region of South Australia have received, or are in the process of regaining, the remains of approximately 775 of their ancestors. At least three hundred of these remains were taken from twenty-seven different locations along the Coorong lakes in South Australia. The Ngarrindjeri understandably want to rebury their ancestors in the original locations from which they were disinterred. However, their rights in respect of these ancestral burial places are not secure and, if they are to be so, the community has to find the financial and political means to secure title to these places before they can even consider reburial. Also, there are the costs of reburial itself and associated ceremonies. In 2005 the Ngarrindjeri community was in receipt of fifty per cent of their ancestors' remains and were still waiting for one museum to participate in the repatriation process. They are strongly of the view that they cannot consider reburial until they have received all of their ancestors' remains.

Indigenous communities were not responsible for the problems associated with repatriation, and yet they have to carry the cultural, spiritual and financial burdens. Failure to provide communities with adequate resources to fulfil their obligations to rebury their ancestors' remains is an insulting denial of their human rights.

Conclusion

What has been learnt over the last twenty years regarding repatriation? Collections of provenanced and unprovenanced remains are huge; they number in the thousands. These collections are held in national and international institutions as diverse as museums, universities and private collections. We still do not know the full extent of these collections as no comprehensive investigative inventory has ever been undertaken.

Long-term, coordinated and cost-effective mechanisms need to be implemented at a national level to ensure that the process of repatriation is undertaken in a strategic manner. Legislation specifically related to Indigenous human remains needs to be developed and enacted to ensure that state and national facilities, including museums, continue to maintain repatriation as a priority. Currently, institutions may choose to adhere or not to the policy guidelines outlined by Museums Australia in *Continuous Cultures, Ongoing Responsibilities* (2005), particularly as they relate to Indigenous human remains. This is a real concern to Indigenous communities, especially in light of the demise of ATSIC in 2005 and the shift in the prioritisation and delivery of Indigenous affairs within Australia. What guarantees do Indigenous people have regarding the future repatriation of their ancestor's remains?

Indigenous communities need to be resourced to take receipt of ancestral remains, conduct ceremonies and to purchase and secure land and build facilities to house these large collections. They also need to be informed on an ongoing basis regarding destructive and nondestructive techniques associated with determining the provenance of Indigenous human remains. Meetings and workshop discussions need to be held with key Indigenous people and museum staff working in the area of repatriation to explore options for dealing with poorly provenanced remains held in collections in Australia and overseas.

Obviously, we still have a long way to go and many problems to resolve. However, repatriation should not be viewed negatively, whereby museums lose collections and research opportunities. Rather, repatriation should be seen as providing positive opportunities for museums to reestablish good working relationships with Indigenous communities within Australia.

Bibliography

Cooper, Carol. 1989. *Aboriginal and Torres Strait Islander Collections in Overseas Museums* Canberra: Aboriginal Studies Press.

Council of Australian Museum Associations. 1993. *Previous Possessions, New Obligations: Policies for Museums in Australia and Aboriginal and Torres Strait Islander Peoples.* Melbourne: The Council.

Museums Australia. 2005. *Continuous Cultures, Ongoing Responsibilities: Principles and Guidelines for Australian Museums working with Aboriginal and Torres Strait Islander Cultural Heritage.* Canberra: Museums Australia Incorporated.

Part II

Repatriation in Law and Policy

3

Museums, Ethics and Human Remains in England: Recent Developments and Implications for the Future

Liz Bell

English Museums hold between them tens of thousands of human remains (Weeks and Bott 2003: 3); many of which belong to cultures that have for years fought for the return of their ancestors from institutions both at home and abroad. Despite these numbers, England has managed to stay on the sidelines of the repatriation debate, failing in numerous instances to address satisfactorily the concerns of Indigenous groups. Mounting pressure from these Indigenous groups, from the Australian Federal Government, and a growing realisation that the concerns raised over the continued retention of human remains are valid has led to changes that will have a major impact upon museums. It is the aim of this paper to discuss these changes and their potential impact upon the repatriation debate in England.

Several English institutions have earned themselves something of a poor reputation due to the negative stance they have taken towards repatriation. There have been numerous successful requests for repatriation, but these have been overshadowed by the failed attempts. Some museums, the British Museum and Natural History Museum amongst them, have until recently been prohibited by law to even consider repatriation due to the inalienable status of their collections. The Natural History Museum also refused Indigenous representatives access to archives pertaining to human remains, stating that collections would remain available only to 'bona fide research scientists undertaking research on human evolution and human variation' (Heywood 2000).

Understandably, such incidents continue to cause enmity between Indigenous groups and the institutions concerned. Attitudes as to what is ethical and respectful when it comes to the treatment of human remains vary considerably amongst museum professionals, as indeed does opinion as to whether scientific value should outweigh ethical considerations. For this reason, there has never been any uniformity in the handling of, or responses to, repatriation requests. In recent years however, these varied responses and attitudes appear to have given way to a gradual acceptance by the majority of museums that requests for repatriation cannot and should not be ignored. The Royal College of Surgeons, for example, refused requests for the return of Australian Aboriginal remains in 1997. However, in 2002 it changed its policy to allow for their release (Heywood 2002). It is the growing realisation that the concerns of Indigenous groups are justified, as well as continuing pressure, that has led to the issuing of legislation and guidance that are aimed at placating the concerns of Indigenous groups worldwide.

The *Human Tissue Act 2004* was passed in the wake of a number of organ retention scandals. The most notable of these occurred between 1988 and 1996 at the Alder Hey Hospital in Liverpool, where thousands of organs and tissue samples were removed from children without any form of consent being given.[1] This legislation applies to England, Wales and Northern Ireland, with only a few sections applicable to Scotland. It governs the removal, storage and use of human organs and tissue as well as any activities involving human tissue. Existing holdings and human remains older than one hundred years old fall outside the scope of the Act. This means that the majority of the Act has no direct relevance to museums, as few museums hold human remains under one hundred years old. However, section 47 of the Act gives nine national museums in the United Kingdom the legal right to deaccession human remains and other items with which human remains may be mixed up or bound.[2] Even so, the Act does not allow for the release of all human remains. Only those dating to less than one thousand years old from the date on which the Act came into force may be released, but only if the museum in question agrees to do so.

In order to understand the potential impact of this legislation one has only to consider the actual number of human remains held by some of the nine affected museums. A working group on human remains, established by the UK Government's Department of Culture, Media and Sport (DCMS), sponsored a survey (Weeks and Bott 2003) to identify the scope of human remains held in English museum collections. A number of the museums affected by section 47 of the Act were included in this survey. Overseas human remains held by the London-based national museums appear to be the most numerous and therefore the most likely to become the target of the majority of repatriation requests. The Natural History Museum reported in excess of fifty thousand human remains to the survey, although a press statement released by the museum on 3 October 2005 states the actual number to be approximately 19,950 with the majority originating from the United Kingdom. However, a further report indicates that overseas human remains held by the Natural History Museum total forty-six per cent of their overall collection. If this figure is correct it would put their overseas holdings at somewhere in the region of 9,500.[3] The British Museum did not disclose its exact holdings but did confirm it held over 500 UK archaeological human remains and somewhere between 10 and 49 items of African origin, between 100 and 249 American specimens, 10 and 49 from Asia, 1 and 9 from New Zealand, and somewhere between 50 and 99 from the Pacific region. Since this time - and with the *Human Tissue Act* and the Department of Culture, Media and Sport's Working Group on Human Remains document *Guidance for the Care of Human Remains in Museums* in mind – the British Museum has adopted its own human remains policy. My current research (Bell forthcoming) confirms that the museum holds remains from the bodies of just over five thousand individuals.

The *Human Tissue Act* potentially allows for large numbers of repatriation requests to be considered, however, it is important to note that this legislation simply removes the legal impediment that up until now has not allowed requests for return to be considered. The Act only makes possible the successful repatriation of human remains whereas in the past failure was a certainty due to their legal status. Any request for repatriation will still need to be justified in the eyes of the holding institution.

The decision-making process at holding institutions should be eased by the work of the DCMS's Working Group on Human Remains. The group was set up in May 2001 following the issuing of a Joint Declaration by the UK and Australian prime ministers to increase efforts in repatriating human remains to the Indigenous peoples of Australia.[4] Its aim was to look at issues relating to the treatment of human remains in museums and to address ethical concerns relating to overseas human remains. It took until November 2003 before the group produced a report, and it was not until 2004 that a consultation document on the care of human remains, summarising the report of the working group and inviting comments and recommendations, was produced. A draft *Code of Practice for the Care of Human Remains in Museums* was published late in May 2005, just under a year after the consultation document was released. After a further period of consultation the final document, the *Guidance for the Care of Human Remains in Museums*, appeared in October 2005; some four years after the original working group was established.

Although the remit of the working group was to look specifically at human remains in England, the *Guidance* was drafted with a view to its application in England, Wales and Northern Ireland. It does not apply to Scotland, which has set up its own working group. The development of separate guidelines for the handling of human remains and changes to *The Anatomy Act*, the law governing the usage of human remains in Scotland, is also currently under consideration.[5] It should be remembered that the procedures outlined in the *Guidance* do not represent statutory requirements; rather they are aimed at encouraging what the panel charged with their development envisaged as 'good practice' that museums should develop and adapt to suit their own needs.

The *Guidance* suggests that when museums and other institutions are developing their own policies they should be guided by procedural responsibilities (rigour, honesty and integrity, sensitivity and cultural understanding, respect for persons and communities, responsible communication, and fairness) and ethical principles (non-maleficence, respect for diversity of belief, respect for the value of science, solidarity, and beneficence). These procedural responsibilities and ethical principles should then in turn be seen as a starting point for institutions developing their own policies and be used as a basis for decision making.

The *Guidance* emphasises that claims for repatriation should be considered on a case-by-case basis and that each case should be judged on its own merits. It is suggested that any claim should be considered using the following criteria:

- the status of those making the request and continuity with remains,
- the cultural and religious significance of the remains,
- the age of remains,
- how the remains were originally acquired,
- the status of the remains within the museum and the legal status of institution,
- the scientific, educational and historic value of the remains to the museum and the public, and
- how the remains have been used in the past.

There is no inference that museums should repatriate all Indigenous human remains. Indeed, museums affected by the *Human Tissue Act* may by law repatriate only human remains that are less than one thousand years old from the date that the Act came into force. Rather, the *Guidance* recommends that the status and relationship of the remains with the claimants, with the museum or scientific institution holding them and with the public should be assessed before a final decision is made. The *Guidance* also makes it clear that requests for the repatriation of older human remains are unlikely to be successful due to problems in establishing genealogical, cultural or ethnic continuity. Claims for the return of human remains over three hundred years old are therefore unlikely to be successful and claims for human remains over five hundred years old are unlikely to even be considered, unless very close geographical, religious and cultural links can be demonstrated.

The handling of requests for repatriation is not the sole concern of the *Guidance*. It looks much more generally at the handling and care of all human remains held in museum and other institution collections and suggests that all museums should develop their own human remains policies, which should include advice on acquisition, loans, deaccessioning, claims for return, storage, conservation and collections management, display, access and educational use, and research. The recommendation made in relation to display will be an extremely interesting issue to watch unfold in English museums. The *Guidance* suggests that 'as a general principle, human remains should be displayed in such a way as to avoid people coming across them unawares', in other words to warn visitors in case they do not wish to see human remains on display. This is something completely different for the majority of museums that display human remains. The English public show little concern over the display of human remains, hence, many museums display them in a very open way. However, even at this time, there is no unanimity from museum professionals as to whether human remains should continue to be displayed (Museums Journal 2005), so it will be interesting to see how individual institutions approach an issue that, for the majority of their visitors, is not a cause of concern.

Implications for the Future

The passing of the *Human Tissue Act* has opened a door that was once firmly shut. The two English museums that appear to hold the greatest number of overseas human remains have been given the means to put an end to years of poor relations between themselves and Indigenous groups after being given the legal right to allow at least some human remains to be released from their collections. Although the *Guidance* does ask all museums to adhere to a minimum set of standards, one does have to question whether museums will be willing or able to make such provision. It is also questionable as to whether an internal panel of decision makers is capable of making an objective decision about the human remains contained within its own museum collection. It is unlikely that all repatriation requests will be straightforward, and it may be that in some instances such decisions should be taken with advice from an independent panel of experts to avoid unnecessary confrontation. However, if each museum is transparent in its decision making then it will become increasingly difficult in the current climate to justify retention without a valid reason.

Only time is likely to tell whether the *Guidance* goes far enough both in assisting museums through the repatriation process and helping to address the concerns of Indigenous groups. Indeed, the purpose of my own research is to elucidate further on both of these points. Considering the past failure of some English museums to come to terms with the values and beliefs of Indigenous peoples, and their failure to deal satisfactorily with the return of ancestors, one cannot deny that an important step forward has been taken. Legislation and guidance have created the potential for a more positive dialogue to commence between museums and Indigenous groups; a potential that must not be ignored.

Notes

1.   Retrieved 26 November 2006 from http://news.bbc.co.uk/1/hi/health/1136723.stm
2.   These museums are: the Armouries, the British Museum, the Imperial War Museum, the Museum of London, the National Maritime Museum, National Museums and Galleries on Merseyside, the Natural History Museum, the Science Museum and the Victoria and Albert Museum.
3.   Retrieved 26 November 2006 from http://www.24hourmuseum.org.uk/
4.   Retrieved 26 November 2006 from http://www.24hourmuseum.org.uk/nwh_gfx_en/ART30860.html

5.   Retrieved 26 November 2006 from http://www.museumsgalleriesscotland.org.uk
     /information_services/publications/hr_pr.asp

Bibliography

Bell, E. (Forthcoming). 'Giving up the Dead: Museums, Ethics and Human Remains in
     England', PhD dissertation. Newcastle: Newcastle University.
Department of Culture, Media and Sport (DCMS). 2003. *The Report Of The Working Group
     On Human Remains.* London: DCMS.
———. 2004. *Care of Historic Human Remains: a Consultation on the Report of the Working
     Group on Human Remains.* London: DCMS.
———. 2005. *A Code of Practice for the Care of Human Remains in Museums,* consultation
     draft. London: DCMS.
———. 2005. *Guidance for the Care of Human Remains in Museums.* London: DCMS.
Heywood, F. 2000. 'Natural History Museum Agrees Better Access to Human Remains',
     Museums Journal 6: 1.
———. 2002. 'Royal College of Surgeons returns Tasmanian Aboriginal remains', *Museums
     Journal* 7: 8.
Museums Journal. 2005. 'Should Museums be Braver about Displaying Their Human
     Remains?', *Museums Journal* 10: 15.
Weeks, J. and V. Bott. 2003. *Scoping Survey of Historic Human Remains in English Museums
     Undertaken on Behalf of the Ministerial Working Group on Human Remains.* London:
     Department of Culture, Media and Sport.

4

Legal Impediments to the Repatriation of Cultural Objects to Indigenous Peoples

Kathryn Whitby-Last

In this chapter I will be drawing on both international and domestic law to highlight the problems faced by Indigenous peoples in making claims for the repatriation of cultural heritage. Before turning to the substantive legal issues, I will look at two preliminary issues: firstly, the definition of cultural heritage and, secondly, the distinction between restitution and repatriation. This will highlight some of the issues that must be considered when assessing the substantive law.

The Definition of Cultural Heritage

The first preliminary issue that deserves mention is the definition of 'cultural heritage'. There is not space in this paper to address all aspects of this issue,[1] however, I would like to highlight one particular aspect that is pertinent to claims by Indigenous peoples: control of the process of definition. This has implications for claims for return, in terms of establishing whether the relevant law encompasses the object in question.

The control of the process of definition is particularly important when one considers the heritage of Indigenous peoples. It raises the question of whose definitional voice is, or should be, determinative when there is a discrepancy between the value attached to objects by those who currently possess them and their claimants. Furthermore, where it is necessary to rely on the actions of the state to assist the recovery, the willingness of the state to bring an action may depend upon the values attributed to that object by members of the dominant culture.

For example, under the UNESCO Convention on the Means of Prohibiting and Preventing the Illicit Import, Export and Transfer of Ownership of Cultural Property 1970, it is state parties that are responsible for defining the objects to which the convention will apply. This gives scope for national approaches that reflect the values attributed to objects in that particular state. However, in multinational states where one culture is dominant, there is a risk that the heritage of minority cultures will be excluded. There is no recognition of the principle enshrined in recommendation 1 of the 1993 Mataatua Declaration on Cultural and Intellectual Property Rights of Indigenous Peoples, which states that Indigenous peoples should 'define for themselves their own … cultural property'.

Even if the heritage of minority cultures is included in state definitions, its inclusion may be premised upon different values. This was evident in the controversy over the Bighorn Medicine Wheel, located in the Bighorn Mountains in north central Wyoming, where the US Forest Service was concerned only with its archaeological value rather than its continuing use as a sacred site (Chapman 1999: 5–10).

Definition is often a political as well as a legal issue. One of the inherent problems with legal definitions of cultural heritage is that they reflect the culturally specific values of those framing the legislation, because categories of material culture are socially constructed (Mclaughlin 1999: 770). An example of this is the US *Native American Graves Protection and Repatriation Act 1990*, which distinguishes secular and religious objects, yet this distinction does not exist in some native cultures (Chapman 1999: 6). Therefore, when considering claims for the return of heritage it must be recognised that the definition of heritage is not objective.

Restitution or Repatriation?

At this point it is important to distinguish between restitution and repatriation.[2] Restitution is the return of an object to its owner, based on an analysis of property rights.[3] The nature of the object as an item of cultural heritage is generally irrelevant in such considerations.

Repatriation, in contrast, is premised upon the culturally specific value of the object. Even though Kowalski argues that repatriation is 'a return to *patria*, which means fatherland understood as a state' (Kowalski 2001a: 163), it also applies to objects returned to sub-state groups, such as Indigenous peoples, and is often applied where the claim is perceived as being moral rather than legal. Isar gives the example of:

> objects which have left their countries of origin as a result of colonial situations or an imbalance of power between nations and where, quite obviously, no one would claim for their return on legal grounds of any kind. This claim is quite different. It is a moral claim (Isar 1981: 21).

As we shall see, because of the difficulties that attend actions of restitution, many claims by Indigenous peoples are claims for repatriation, phrased in terms of moral obligation, rather than claims for restitution based on an assertion of property rights. However, even claims for repatriation face legal obstacles and are generally only pursued against institutions rather than individuals.

The Substantive Law: the Difficulties that Attend Restitution Claims in Private International Law

The issue to which I will now turn is how Indigenous peoples can be excluded from legal mechanisms for restitution of their cultural heritage when the object is located in a state other than that within which the group is located. The rules of private international law present a number of problems for claimants, but the particular difficulties will depend on the circumstances surrounding the object's removal.

Probably the easiest claim to resolve, and one that is rarely litigated, is a title dispute between the original owner of an object of cultural heritage and the person who stole it. The legal position is generally straightforward because a thief does not acquire title to the property. For example, in England and Wales, section 4 of the *Sale of Goods Act 1980* provides that the limitation period does not apply to an action against the thief of the object. However, in addition to theft, claims have also arisen as a consequence of transfers of title that are disputed.[4] Within this category, the most complex claims are those involving transfers of title based on *prima facie* valid contracts. These claims raise different issues from cases of outright theft and, as Palmer notes, 'claims based on surviving title are probably more difficult to pursue where the deprivation was not, at the time of its occurrence, locally unlawful' (Palmer 2000: 4).

Limitation of Actions

One must consider the possibility that an original owner's right of action, or even their title, has been extinguished through lapse of time if the dispute concerns property that is now in the hands of a third party, however it was removed. The lengths of these limitation periods and the date at which they start to run vary widely, however, claims by Indigenous peoples often relate to objects that have been appropriated some time ago and actions for restitution will often be time-barred because many of these limitation periods are relatively short.[5]

For example, in England, the limitation period is six years from the date of purchase by a bona fide purchaser,[6] whereas in Scotland, the period is twenty years from the theft.[7] In contrast, in the United States, some states have rules that favour the original owner and enable actions to recover the object after a considerable period of time through the adoption of a 'discovery rule'. An example of this is the decision in *Autocephalus Greek-Orthodox Church of Cyprus v Goldberg and Feldman Fine Arts, Inc.*[8] The case concerned Byzantine mosaics removed from the Kanakaria Church in Northern Cyprus and purchased by Peg Goldberg, an Indiana art dealer, in the 'free port' area of Geneva airport. The court held that the action was not out of time because, under Indiana law, which it judged to be the correct jurisdiction, the period did not start to run until Cyprus discovered that the mosaics were in Goldberg's possession.[9] A similar effect is achieved in states that have a demand and refusal rule. This can be seen *in Kunstsammlungen zu Weimar v Elicofon*.[10] Here, the Second Circuit of the Federal District Court held that a cause of action against a bona fide purchaser did not accrue until the purchaser refused to comply with a demand for the return of the paintings.

Article 3(3) of the UNIDROIT Convention on Stolen or Illegally Exported Cultural Objects 1995 provides a fifty-year limitation period for claims, but by virtue of article 10, the convention is not retrospective in its effect and few states have ratified.[11]

Forum

Civil law and common law jurisdictions take very different approaches to the issue of acquisition of title by a bona fide purchaser. Most civilian systems allow a purchaser of stolen property to acquire title if the acquisition is in good faith, whereas common law systems often rely on the maxim *nemo dat quod non habet* (no one can give a better title than he has) to maintain the rights of the original owner.[12] As a consequence, a common scenario will involve issues arising from the object in question having been moved between among states to take advantage of differences in the prevailing law. The *lex situs* rule means that the appropriate jurisdiction for determining the validity of transfers of property is the country in which the transfer took place. A strict application of this rule is evident in the decision in *Winkworth v Christie Manson and Woods Ltd*[13] where a collection of netsuke were stolen in England, purchased in Italy then returned to England for sale. The original owner was unable to secure the return of his property because Italian law was applicable and the purchaser had acquired good title to the objects (i.e. the objects were now legally owned and free from any encumbrance, lien, claim or other legal claim on them).[14]

However, the issue of forum is subject to varying interpretations by different states. In *Autocephalous Greek-Orthodox Church of Cyprus v Goldberg*[15] Goldberg argued that Swiss legal forum had jurisdiction under the *lex situs* rule.[16] However, the Indiana court held that Indiana law applied because of the residence of the defendants, the origin of the purchase money and the current location of the object. Thus it may be unclear which legal system's rules will apply to any claim for return.

Group-specific Problems

The issues of the limitation of actions and forum present problems for all claims for restitution of cultural heritage. However, there are also a number of issues that present particular problems for claims by Indigenous peoples: legal personality and property rights. Both are related to the restitution paradigm of private international law, which is concerned only with restitution not repatriation.

Claims for restitution are usually made by an individual 'owner' or by a state that has proprietary rights in the object. However, the claimant must be recognised as a juristic entity in the courts of the forum. The recognition of Indigenous peoples can face similar problems to unrecognised nation states, as in the case of *Federal Republic of Germany v Elicofon* [17] where the court held that an agency of the East German government could not assert a claim to works of art in an American court because East Germany was not recognised at the time.

Some jurisdictions are flexible in interpreting the requirements of legal personality, and a good example of this is the case of *Bumper Development Corp v Commissioner of Police of the Metropolis* [18] where the English Court of Appeal held that an Indian temple, from which a statue had been stolen, was entitled to sue for recovery of the statue in England because the temple was accorded legal personality in Indian law. However, with many Indigenous peoples, ascertaining the appropriate community authority to represent the group may be difficult. As Bell and Paterson note, 'It may not necessarily be the band council or other political body. For example, in the case of sacred property it could be the elders or religious societies within the community' (Bell and Paterson 1999: 208).

The second issue for Indigenous peoples making claims for restitution is the need to establish a property right. In the case of *Attorney General of New Zealand v Ortiz*, [19] New Zealand brought an action in respect of a series of five Maori carved totaro panels, which were removed from New Zealand without an export licence. Under New Zealand's *Historic Articles Act 1962*, this gave rise to forfeiture of the property and the attorney-general's claim was therefore based on a right of ownership. The English House of Lords held that since seizure of the property had not taken place, the Crown was not its owner. The interesting point about *Ortiz* is that the claim had been brought by the state because it was considered difficult for the Maori group from whom the panels had been taken to establish their claim to ownership. [20]

Establishing original property rights can be particularly difficult in the case of communal property. The difficulty relates to the fact that many legal systems focus on Western assumptions of property and individualism and often fail to recognise communal property.

As Elizabeth Coleman points out in her chapter in this volume, the problem is exacerbated where the object has been transferred by a member of a group rather than stolen; bringing the transfer within the category of appropriation that is *prima facie* lawful. For example, a person appointed as the caretaker of an object may have sold it even though he did not have the authority to transfer it

(Woodford 2002). This was the situation with the wampum belts of the Onondaga Nation.[21] which were sold by the tribe's designated wampum-keeper to a US Government official in 1891 (Sullivan 1992: 286). In such situations, when the argument for return is based on tribal custom and law that the original transferring party did not have the authority or right to transfer title to the object in the first place, it may be difficult to establish that a purchaser has not acquired good title to the object (Boyd 1990: 912).

Hurtado (1993: 67) has argued that US courts would not recognise the validity of a sale by an individual Native American of property that belonged to a Native American tribe or nation as a whole. However, the invalidity of such sales may not be recognised by the courts of the forum, particularly if the sale has taken place in a jurisdiction that allows bona fide purchasers to acquire title.[22]

In addition, for some Indigenous peoples, proof of ownership can occasionally be established only through oral testimony. Bell and Paterson note that in Canada, 'judges are reluctant to give weight to oral histories that consist of out-of-court statements passed through successive generations of Aboriginal peoples' (Bell and Paterson 1999: 176). In this respect, the decision in *Delgamuukw v British Columbia* [23] regarding the admissibility of oral evidence will assist those attempting to make a claim, but again this approach may not be taken in other jurisdictions.[24]

A Solution in Public International Law?

The difficulties in bringing an action for restitution resulted in the UNESCO Convention on the Means of Prohibiting and Preventing the Illicit Import, Export and Transfer of Ownership of Cultural Property 1970. Article 7(b) of the convention requires state parties to take appropriate steps to return cultural property stolen from a museum or secular public monument that is located in another state that is party to the convention, provided that such property is documented as appertaining to the inventory of that institution.

However, being an instrument of international law, the UNESCO convention concerns states. Indigenous peoples therefore face problems accessing the system. The return of cultural property under the convention is dependent upon the state from which the object was removed making a claim. A group cannot utilise the convention unless the state is prepared to act on the group's behalf.

Furthermore, the UNESCO convention applies only to those objects designated cultural property by the signatory state and stolen from a museum or public monument. I mentioned earlier the risk that the state may not include the cultural objects of minority cultures in this regime and many items that are the subject of repatriation claims by Indigenous peoples have not been removed from museums or public monuments. Thus the usefulness of the UNESCO convention for claims by Indigenous peoples is limited.

Repatriation

Because of the difficulties that attend claims for restitution, many Indigenous peoples are seeking alternative modes of dispute resolution.[25] This is reflected in the fact that there is a general absence of litigated claims and in most countries the majority of claims are the subject of private negotiations (Paterson 1999: 207). As mentioned earlier, these claims for repatriation are often viewed as moral rather than legal claims but legal rights continue to play a role, albeit as part of the negotiation process, defining the parameters of potential agreements (Bell and Paterson 1999: 169).

Claims for repatriation can, however, be less attractive to Indigenous peoples because, unlike an order for restitution of property, conditions are often imposed in the agreement for return and, if the object is currently held in a museum, there is often a presumption of return being to an alternative museum rather than to the group making the claim for continuing use. A classic example is the Ghost Dance Shirt that was returned to the Lakota Sioux by Glasgow Museum. Glasgow Museum imposed a number of conditions in the agreement to return the shirt;[26] these included an obligation to preserve the Ghost Dance Shirt in perpetuity and to ensure that it be displayed at all times in an appropriate place accessible to members of the public. The agreement also contained an obligation to loan the shirt for public display in Glasgow.

In this context, the return of the ceremonial head-dress to the Blood tribe of Canada by Aberdeen's Marischal Museum is unusual. The Museum agreed that the head-dress should be returned to its traditional role and no conditions were imposed. Furthermore, the Museum agreed not to ask for a replica or to publish photographs of the head-dress as that would run counter to the acceptance of the spiritual importance of the head-dress ('Tribal Headdress Returned to Canada', Associated Press 7 July 2003).

If a group is required to house an item in a museum this may negate the effect of its return to the group, its value within that group and thus its nature as cultural heritage. This is particularly problematic where the group wants possession of an artefact that they perhaps intend to destroy. Different concepts of stewardship can impede claims for repatriation because those representing museums often give priority to the conservation and security of objects and to their continuing accessibility for scientific purposes. Indeed Lewis has argued that, 'unless there is adequate technical support to maintain them in good condition, the return of certain items must be seriously questioned' (Lewis 1981: 6). Yet this reflects a culturally specific view of the value of these items.[27]

The first stage in making a claim for repatriation is to establish the relationship between the object and the group, often referred to as 'cultural affiliation'.[28] Although there is not a requirement to prove continuing title, the question of this relationship is fundamental to any claim for repatriation because the basis of such claims is the cultural significance of the object. The issue of cultural affiliation can be seen in the criteria established by the Glasgow City Council Repatriation Working Group, founded in 1998 to consider the Ghost Dance Shirt claimed by the Lakota Sioux.[29] These criteria include: (1) the right of those making the request to represent the community to which the artefact originally belonged, (2) the continuity between the community which created the object and the current community on whose behalf the request is being made and (3) the cultural and religious significance of the object to the community (Glasgow City Council: 1998). The working group concluded that the shirt should be returned even though there was no legal obligation to return it ('Ghost Shirt Dances Back', BBC News 2 August 1999).[30]

However, some approaches to repatriation have been criticised because 'the determination of what is "culturally significant" has sometimes been unilaterally made by the museum or institution in possession of the relevant object, with very little input from Indigenous peoples themselves' (Gii-dahl-guud-sliiaay 1995: 183). A further problem with relying on cultural significance as a justification for return is that claims for repatriation are sometimes met with the argument that the object now forms part of the culture of another society.[31] Tolhurst argues that such claims lack authority when they concern Indigenous artefacts (1998: 21) yet he concedes that they have greater force where the artefact has been attached to or become incorporated within some other object (Tolhurst 1998: 25).[32]

Claims for repatriation also raise the issue of who is the claimant. The group still needs a representative or institutional structure in order to make a claim and for title to the object to be transferred to it. It is here that the constitutional status associated with self-government plays a role. If power is devolved, the associated institutional structure enables claims to be made.

There is often a reluctance to return items where there is no legal duty to do so for the fear of a flood of claims that would denude museums of their collections. This reluctance is reflected in the Declaration on the Importance and Value of Universal Museums, which refers to the 'threat to the integrity of universal collections posed by demands for the restitution of objects to their countries of origin'.[33] Furthermore, museums may be concerned about potential liability to claimants who might come forward in the future if the item has already been repatriated to some other person or group.

With respect to claims for items held in the United Kingdom, the recent decision in *Attorney General v Trustees of the British Museum*[34] highlights the impediments to repatriation where museums and galleries are concerned. Section 3(4) of the *British Museum Act 1963* restricts the ability of the British Museum to deaccession objects. The case concerned four 'Old Master' drawings acquired by the museum between 1946 and 1949, that had been stolen by the Gestapo in 1939. Despite recognising the moral claim of the heirs of the original owner, the English High Court held that the museum could not return the paintings in the absence of a successful claim for restitution. A number of other museums and galleries in Britain are subject to similar restrictions on deaccessioning in their statutes. This is a serious obstacle to claims for repatriation.

A formal claim could be made through the Intergovernmental Committee for Promoting the Return of Cultural Property to its Countries of Origin or its

Restitution in Case of Illicit Appropriation, whose mandate would include a claim by Indigenous peoples. However, as Kagan (2005: 1–43) notes, any claim must be pursued by the state rather than the group and the committee acts only in an advisory capacity.

Conclusion

In conclusion, I hope that I have demonstrated that a number of difficulties attend claims by Indigenous peoples for the return of their cultural heritage, whether through claims for restitution or repatriation. Many of these difficulties stem from issues surrounding the recognition of these groups and the prevailing concepts of ownership in many market nations.

Notes

1. For a fuller discussion of the issue see: Last (2004: 53–84) and Blake (2000: 61–85).
2. Merryman criticises the use of the term repatriation as a form of 'romantic nationalism', however, this is due to his avowedly internationalist stance. See Merryman (1990: 521).
3. For a discussion of the concept of restitution see: Kowalski (2001b: 9–244) and Gerstenblith (2001: 197–246).
4. Sometimes it is difficult to distinguish such cases from claims of theft. Probably the most famous example of this is the request by Greece for restitution of the Parthenon sculptures based on the fact that Lord Elgin did not legally acquire them. See Greenfield (1996: 56).
5. This is highlighted by the refusal of the government of New Zealand to return the carved meeting house of Mataatua to the people of Ngati Awa because of the passing of the limitation period: Mead (1995: 74).
6. *Limitation Act 1980*, section 5.
7. *Prescription and Limitation (Scotland) Act 1973*, section 8.
8. *Autocephalus Greek-Orthodox Church of Cyprus v Goldberg and Feldman Fine Arts, Inc.* 917 F.2d 278 (7th Cir. 1990).
9. For a full discussion of the case see: Farrell (1992: 790–800). A similar result regarding limitation can be seen in *O'Keefe v Snyder* 83 NJ 478, 416 A2d 862 (1980).
10. *Kunstsammlungen zu Weimar v Elicofon* 536 F Supp 829 (EDNY 1981), aff'd 678 F.2d 1150 (2d Cir 1982). In this case, a German art gallery sued an American art collector for the return of paintings that had disappeared after the Second World War.
11. There are currently only twenty-six states in which the UNIDROIT convention is in force. See www.unidroit.org/english/conventions/1995culturalproperty/main.htm Retrieved 23 October 2005.
12. This is the principle that no one can give that which he has not, for example, no one can give a better title than he has.
13. *Winkworth v Christie Manson and Woods Ltd* [1980] 2 WLR 937.
14. Winkworth had tried to argue that English law, which would have given him a right to return of the collection on the principle of *nemo dat quod non habet*, should apply because of the close relationship with England but the court rejected this argument.

15. *Autocephalous Greek-Orthodox Church of Cyprus v Goldberg and Feldman Fine Arts, Inc.* 717 F Supp 1374 (SD Ind 1989).
16. Switzerland has generous rules regarding the acquisition of title by purchasers and it has been suggested that the reason for the transaction occurring in Switzerland was to benefit from this.
17. *Federal Republic of Germany v Elicofon* 478 F.2d 231 (2d Cir. 1973).
18. *Bumper Development Corp v Commissioner of Police of the Metropolis* [1991] 1 WLR 1362.
19. *Attorney General of New Zealand v Ortiz* [1984] AC 1.
20. Failing in their claim of title to the carving, the Crown had only a claim for violation of its export law, which was unenforceable as foreign penal law.
21. This was acting as wampum-keeper for all of the six nations comprising the Iroquois Confederacy: the Mohawk, the Oneida, the Onondaga, the Cayuga, the Seneca and the Tuscarora nations.
22. Bell and Paterson argue that in Canada 'Aboriginal perspectives on the rights of individuals to transfer such property will be considered along with common-law principles of property and contract law to establish the tests for legitimate acquisition and transfer of title. In situations where an individual has removed, sold, or donated collective property without consent of the appropriate community authority, the combination of Aboriginal perspectives with principles of property law may operate to invalidate title that assumes the object is capable of individual ownership.' Bell and Paterson (1999: 180).
23. *Delgamuukw v British Columbia* [1998] 1 CNLR 14.
24. 'In *Delgamuukw* the Chief Justice reiterated that the unique nature of Aboriginal rights demands that courts must not reject evidence of oral history outright but must identify specific features of the evidence in question that justify treating it with suspicion.' Paterson (1999: 206).
25. Such an approach is justified because 'unlike the purchase of other property, cultural property is a unique category, requiring different consideration from normal recovery laws' Kastenberg (1995: 39).
26. (1) To preserve in perpetuity the Ghost Dance Shirt; (2) ensure that the Ghost Dance Shirt is displayed at all reasonable times in an appropriate place where the shirt and details of its historical and cultural significance is accessible to members of the public; (3) acknowledge, in any public display of the Ghost Dance Shirt, the role of the people of Glasgow in its history and preservation; (4) agree to loan the Ghost Dance Shirt, which would be accompanied by representative(s) of the Wounded Knee Survivors Association, for public display in Glasgow for such periods as may be agreed between Glasgow City Council and the Association (Glasgow City Council Working Group on the Repatriation of Artefacts: 1998).
27. For example, with the Zuni war gods, 'physical preservation of the objects is diametrically opposed to their cultural function' Mastalir (1993: 1046).
28. This is to be distinguished from approaches that rely on a territorial link. The problem with focusing on territory is in establishing the appropriate territory, often referred to as the 'country of origin.' Lewis (1981: 6) highlights the issues raised by such terminology: 'does the phrase signify the country of manufacture; the nationality of the maker; the last country to hold the object before its removal; or … the site of its discovery?' Even if the site of discovery is adopted as the criterion there are still difficulties. For example, the Lydian hoard has been claimed by Turkey from the Metropolitan Museum of Fine Art. However, since the fall of Lydia, Asia Minor has been occupied by the Assyrian, Bronze

Age Greek, Roman, Byzantine and Turkish civilizations. See *Republic of Turkey v Metropolitan Museum of Fine Art* 762 F.Supp. 44 (SDNY 1990).

29. The shirt had been purchased by Kelvingrove Museum, thirteen months after the massacre at Wounded Knee, from the Lakota interpreter for Buffalo Bill Cody's travelling Wild West Show.

30. Although the lord provost of Glasgow had argued against its return, claiming the shirt to have greater cultural value in Glasgow ('Scots Return Wounded Knee Shirt', *South Dakota Telegraph*, 20 November 1998).

31. For example, Vittorio Sgarbi, an official from the Italian Culture Ministry claimed that the Obelisk of Axum, removed from Ethiopia, had become Italian through a process of 'naturalisation' ('Italy to Keep Ethiopian Monument', BBC News 20 July 2001). Similarly, the director of the British Museum has claimed that the Parthenon sculptures are part of the heritage of mankind rather than simply the cultural heritage of Greece ('Elgin Marbles to Stay in UK', BBC News, 15 January 2002). Indeed, the leading article in *The Times* claimed that the sculptures are 'uniquely the common property of Western Civilisation' ('Europe's Marbles', 22 June 1998).

32. The example given by Tolhurst is the Koh-i-Noor diamond, which is attached to one of the crowns in the British Crown Jewels. The diamond is claimed by Pakistan, Iran, India and Afghanistan ('Indian MPs Demand Kohinoor's Return', BBC News, 26 April, 2000; and 'Taleban Demand Gem from UK', BBC News, 7 November 2000).

33. Declaration on the Importance and Value of Universal Museums (2003) Retrieved 10 November 2008 from http://www.tomflynn.co.uk/UniversalMuseum.html

34. *Attorney General v Trustees of the British Museum* [2005] EWHC 1089 (ch).

Bibliography

Bell, C. and R. Paterson. 1999. 'Aboriginal Rights to Cultural Property in Canada', *International Journal of Cultural Property* 8: 167–211.

Blake, J. 2000. 'On Defining the Cultural Heritage', *International and Comparative Law Quarterly* 49: 61–85.

Boyd, T. 1990. 'Disputes Regarding the Possession of Native American Religious and Cultural Objects and Human Remains: a Discussion of the Applicable Law and Proposed Legislation', *Missouri Law Review* 55: 883–936.

Chapman, F. 1999. 'The Bighorn Medicine Wheel 1988–1999', *Cultural Resource Management* 3: 5–10.

Farrell, P. 1992. 'Foreign Relations – Unrecognized Foreign States – Title to Church Mosaics Unimpaired by Confiscatory Decrees of Unrecognized State, Autocephalous Greek-Orthodox Church of Cyprus v Goldberg and Feldman Fine Arts, Inc.' *Suffolk Transnational Law Journal* 15: 790–800.

Gerstenblith, P. 2001. 'The Public Interest in the Restitution of Cultural Objects', *Connecticut Journal of International Law* 16: 197– 246.

Gii-dahl-guud-sliiaay. 1995. 'Cultural Perpetuation: Repatriation of First Nations Cultural Heritage', *University of British Columbia Law Review*, special issue – *Material Culture in Flux: Law and Policy of Repatriation of Cultural Property*: 183–202.

Glasgow City Council. 1998. 'Glasgow City Council to Return Ghost Dance Shirt', *News Flash Archives* 9 December 1998.

Glasgow City Council Working Group on the Repatriation of Artefacts. 1998. *Report to Arts and Culture Committee: Lakota Ghost Dance Shirt*. Glasgow City Council.

Greenfield, J. 1996. *The Return of Cultural Treasures*, 2nd ed. Cambridge: Cambridge University Press.

Hurtado, D. 1993. 'Native American Graves Protection and Repatriation Act: Does it Subject Museums to an Unconstitutional "Taking"?', *Hofstra Property Law Journal* 6: 1–83.

Isar, Y. 1981. *Appropriate Technologies in the Conservation of Cultural Property: Technical Handbooks for Museums and Monuments 7*. Paris: The Unesco Press 1981.

Kagan, T. 2005. 'Recovering Aboriginal Cultural Property at Common Law', *University of Toronto Faculty of Law Review* 63: 1–43.

Kastenberg, J. 1995. 'Assessing the Evolution and Available Actions for Recovery in Cultural Property Cases' *DePaul-LCA Journal of Art and Entertainment Law* 6: 39–60.

Kowalski, W. 2001a. 'Repatriation of Cultural Property Following a Cession of Territory or Dissolution of Multinational States', 6 *Art, Antiquity and Law*: 139–66.

———. 2001b. 'Restitution of Works of Art Pursuant to Private and Public International Law', *Recueil des Cours* 288: 9–244.

Last, K. 2004. 'The Resolution of Cultural Property Disputes: Some Issues of Definition' in Permanent Court of Arbitration (ed.), *Resolution of Cultural Property Disputes*. The Hague: Kluwer Law International, pp. 53–84.

Lewis, G. 1981. 'Lost Heritage – Some Historical and Professional Considerations' in I. Staunton and M. McCartney (eds.) *Lost Heritage: The Question of the Return of Cultural Property: Report on the Symposium Held in London 1981*. Commonwealth Arts Association and the Africa Centre, p.4.

Mclaughlin, R. 1996. 'The Native American Graves Protection and Repatriation Act: Unresolved Issues Between Material Culture and Legal Definitions', *University of Chicago Law School Roundtable* 3: 767–90.

Mastalir, R. 1993. 'A Proposal for Protecting the "Cultural" and "Property" Aspects of Cultural Property Under International Law', *Fordham International Law Journal* 16: 1033–93.

Mead, H. 1995. 'The Mataatua Declaration and the Case of the Carved Meeting House Mataatua', *University of British Columbia Law Review*, special issue – *Material Culture in Flux: Law and Policy of Repatriation of Cultural Property*: 69–75.

Merryman, J.H. 1990. '"Protection" of the Cultural "Heritage"?', *American Journal of Comparative Law* 38 Supp: 513–22.

Palmer, N. 2000. *Museums and the Holocaust*. Leicester: Institute of Art and Law.

Paterson, R. 1999. 'Cultural Issues in Canadian Law: A Summary of Recent Developments', *Media and Arts Law Review* 4: 205–8.

Sullivan, M. 1992. 'A Museum Perspective on Repatriation: Issues and Opportunities', *Arizona State Law Journal* 24: 283–91.

The British Museum. Retrieved 23 October 2005 from http://www.thebritishmuseum.ac.uk/newsroom/current2003/universalmuseums.html

Tolhurst, G. 1998. 'A Comment on the Return of Indigenous Artefacts', *Art, Antiquity and Law* 3: 15–26.

Woodford, R. 2002. 'Repatriation Conference Helps Clans Learn About Bringing Their Past Home', *The Juneau Empire*, 9 December.

Legal Authorities

Attorney General of New Zealand v Ortiz [1984] AC 1.

Autocephalous Greek-Orthodox Church of Cyprus v Goldberg and Feldman Fine Arts, Inc. 717 F Supp 1374 (SD Ind 1989).

Autocephalus Greek-Orthodox Church of Cyprus v Goldberg and Feldman Fine Arts, Inc. 917 F.2d 278 (7th Cir. 1990).

Bumper Development Corp v Commissioner of Police of the Metropolis [1991] 1 WLR 1362.

Delgamuukw v British Columbia [1998] 1 CNLR 14.

Federal Republic of Germany v Elicofon 478 F.2d 231 (2d Cir. 1973).

Kunstsammlungen zu Weimar v Elicofon 536 F Supp 829 (EDNY 1981), aff'd 678 F.2d 1150 (2d Cir 1982).

O'Keefe v Snyder 83 NJ 478, 416 A2d 862 (1980).

Republic of Turkey v Metropolitan Museum of Fine Art 762 F Supp 44 (SDNY 1990).

Winkworth v Christie Manson and Woods Ltd [1980] 2 WLR 937.

5

Parks Canada's Policies that Guide the Repatriation of Human Remains and Objects

Virginia Myles

Introduction and Background

Parks Canada is a federal government agency that manages national historic sites, national parks and national marine conservation areas or reserves. It administers forty-two national parks, five national marine conservation areas or reserves and 158 national historic sites. In addition, there are 778 sites in the family of national historic sites that, although not administered by Parks Canada, often follow the agency's policies. Through Parks Canada's programs, the country's natural and cultural areas for which the agency is responsible are protected and presented for present and future generations.

This chapter describes the evolving policy framework informing how Parks Canada deals with the repatriation of human remains and objects claimed by Aboriginal people, that is, those within Canada who identify as Indian, Inuit or Métis. Background information is also included on the Canadian context for repatriations.

Located within the National Historic Sites Directorate of Parks Canada is the Policy and Government Relations Branch and within it the Archaeological Resource Management Section. This section develops and reviews policies and guidelines concerning archaeological resources, such as the directive and guidelines regarding the repatriation of human remains and objects. It also provides advice on the management of archaeological resources to Parks Canada staff as well as to other federal departments and reviews provisions related to culture and heritage in comprehensive land claim agreements, self-government agreements and implementation plans.

Parks Canada manages a variety of archaeological sites and related collections that vary greatly, for example, from precontact to military and shipwreck sites. Collections result from archaeological surveys and excavations on Parks Canada's lands and lands under water. In general, human remains and archaeological objects are discovered through planned archaeological work but they may also be discovered through site or park maintenance projects. Most of the recovered archaeological objects and associated records are stored in Parks Canada repositories located in service centres across the country, or are stored or displayed on site in interpretation centres. In some cases, such as human remains and associated funerary objects, material may be left *in situ* or reburied.

As well as archaeological objects, Parks Canada has acquired, mainly through purchase or donation, historical objects and reproductions that are aimed at supporting heritage presentation and public education programs. Archaeological objects comprise over thirty million, and historical and reproduction objects are in excess of eight hundred thousand. Only a small portion of this collection is comprised of objects of Aboriginal affiliation and based on inventories, only a small portion of these objects might be considered for repatriation, i.e., they may be funerary or sacred objects or claimed for legal and/or ethical reasons. Beginning in the late 1980s, most of the known human remains were reburied on Parks Canada's lands or transferred to communities. These include human remains of non-Aboriginal ancestry.

Most requests for repatriations to date have come from Aboriginal communities or individuals. The number of requests for human remains or objects to be repatriated has been low and most have been requests for human remains. Parks Canada staff open communication with interest groups when human remains or funerary objects are found in existing collections or during fieldwork. Land claims and treaties often contain wording regarding human remains and objects with respect to their return, cooperative management arrangements and future custodial responsibility. However, few land claims to date have initiated repatriations within Parks Canada and most of our repatriations have taken place outside of the land claim context.

Parks Canada's approaches to repatriation have been influenced by international conventions, standards and guidelines, such as the World Archaeological Congress's 1989 Vermillion Accord on Human Remains, and the UNIDROIT Convention on Stolen or Illegally Exported Cultural Objects (1995); and by other countries' approaches, such as that of the United States, which passed the *Native American Graves Protection and Repatriation Act* (NAGPRA) in 1997. Canadian reports have also been influential, notably the *Task Force Report on Museums and First Peoples, Turning the Page: Forging New Partnerships Between Museums and First Peoples* (Assembly of First Nations, Canadian Museums Association 1992) and *The Report of the Royal Commission on Aboriginal Peoples* (Royal Commission on Aboriginal Peoples 1996).

Canada does not have comprehensive federal heritage legislation that protects archaeological sites on federal lands or federal lands under water, although Parks Canada is working on proposed federal archaeological legislation and heritage wreck regulations under the 2001 *Canadian Shipping Act*. Nor does Canada have general legislation that deals with repatriations or the treatment and use of human remains or funerary objects. Despite this, Parks Canada is able to protect its cultural resources through a variety of existing legislative instruments and policies. Provincial and territorial governments do provide some protection in their jurisdictions for human remains and cultural material through their heritage legislation and related policies (Denhez 1999). However, only the province of Alberta has repatriation legislation and it applies specifically to the Blackfoot First Nation.[1] The Government of Canada's *Cultural Property Export and Import Act 1985* provides some protection from the export of cultural property and the return of objects slated for sale and export, but it is limited in its application to Aboriginal repatriation requests for material that is presently in Canadian repositories. For this reason, it has been important for Parks Canada and other cultural institutions to develop policies that provide direction concerning repatriation.

Since the 1960s, there has been an active movement and pressure from Aboriginal groups in Canada to be involved in the interpretation and presentation of their cultural history and for the return of Aboriginal human remains, funerary and sacred objects. Support for this movement and repatriation grew across Canada and concerns were expressed regarding the appropriateness of disturbing burials and of retaining human remains, funerary and sacred objects for study and display. As a result of this movement many federal departments or agencies, provinces and territories and cultural institutions developed policies to help manage the treatment and use of human remains and objects and to deal with repatriation requests. While many policies are different, they share a sense of custodial responsibility and a principle of respect for any human remains or objects and when dealing with Aboriginal collections (Dunlop and Leduc 2004).

Many Canadian repatriation policies, including Parks Canada's, are based on the recommendations of the 1992 *Task Force Report on Museums and First Peoples*. This was an important step in enabling repatriations. The task force was formed as a result of controversy that arose over the display of a sacred, false facemask in an exhibition at the Glenbow Museum during the 1988 Winter Olympics Arts Festival in Calgary, Alberta. Comprised of representatives of the Assembly of First Nations (AFN) and the Canadian Museums Association (CMA), the task force examined the relationship between Aboriginal peoples and the museums that hold human remains and material culture of Aboriginal affiliation and made recommendations based upon a series of national consultations. Three major recommendations in its report were that Aboriginal peoples: be actively involved in the interpretation of their culture and history; gain improved access to museum collections; and be able to secure the return of human remains and funerary objects, sacred objects and objects of cultural patrimony (AFN, CMA 1992).

Another fundamental guiding document on Aboriginal issues for Parks Canada is the *Report of the Royal Commission on Aboriginal Peoples* (1996). The commission spent four years consulting and examining a wide range of long-standing issues in the relationship between Aboriginal peoples in Canada and the Canadian Government and Canadian society. Amongst its many recommendations, the commission urged adoption of ethical guidelines for collecting and treating objects related to Aboriginal culture; the creation of inventories of Aboriginal objects in collections; and the repatriation of human remains and sacred objects to Aboriginal communities upon their request. Many Aboriginal communities and organizations have pressed for action on its recommendations. As well, both the Canadian Archaeological Association's (CAA) *Statement of Principles for Ethical Conduct Pertaining to Aboriginal People* (2000) and the CMA's *Ethical Guidelines* (1999) provide a sound basis for the development of Parks Canada's principles relating to Aboriginal people.

For further information on repatriation in Canada, Catherine Bell from the University of Alberta has developed a website to communicate on her 'Project for the Protection and Repatriation of First Nation Cultural Heritage'. Her team is conducting a national survey of recent issues and initiatives and exploring the potential for legislation on repatriation in Canada. As well, in 2004 and 2005, Aboriginal people in Canada organised two First Nation international repatriation symposia.

In 1990, responding to the emerging international importance of archaeological ethics and the treatment of the dead, Parks Canada reviewed an earlier management directive concerning the treatment of human remains. This was revised and formed the basis for Parks Canada's 2000 Management Directive 2.3.1: Human Remains, Cemeteries and Burial Grounds. In the same year, Management Directive 2.3.4: Repatriation of Moveable Cultural Resources of Aboriginal Affiliation was developed. Both directives are currently being revised. Management Directive 2.3.4 will be replaced with a directive that will have general application and apply to all legal and/or ethical claims. As well, in 2008 'Guidelines for the Repatriation of Human Remains and Objects to Aboriginal People' and Management Directive in respect of the Acquisition and Disposal of Historical and Archaeological Objects and Reproductions were drafted. Several other policies and collections management directives guide the treatment and use of collections. These have evolved as we have gained more experience and knowledge through carrying out repatriations and from Aboriginal advice. What follows is a summary of the key approved principles and directives for repatriation followed by practices that are incorporated in the latest drafts.[2]

Approved Principles and Directives

- All human remains and funerary objects should be treated with respect and dignity.
- As each situation is unique, decisions regarding disposition of human remains and objects are made on a case-by-case basis and in cooperation with the next of kin or culturally affiliated community if known.
- In cases where there may be valid competing claims, the relevant parties are asked to resolve the competing claim(s) between themselves.

- Agreements are negotiated and approved by both the Parks Canada authority and the Aboriginal community authority; and for human remains a protocol may be developed in advance with the community so that procedures are understood prior to any discoveries.

Practices Pending Approval

- Access to relevant collections is provided to requesting communities and individuals.
- Aboriginal communities are asked to submit written requests for repatriations identifying what they are claiming and providing any supporting background information for the claim.
- Expert advice may be required and research conducted to ascertain the next of kin, culturally affiliated group or integrity of information in inventories and other documentation.
- Preservation practices are carried out according to Parks Canada's standards and in ways that maintain the physical and cultural integrity of the objects while respecting and incorporating, where practicable and reasonable, the handling protocols requested by communities or individuals.
- Communication on repatriations is carried out effectively and appropriately, with Aboriginal communities consulted on whom to contact in a community.

Managing Repatriation

Management Directive 2.3.4: Repatriation of Moveable Cultural Resources of Aboriginal Affiliation gives direction on how to carry out a repatriation, what can be repatriated, to whom objects can be returned, who has authority to negotiate or make decisions regarding repatriations in Parks Canada and specifies that at the request of an Aboriginal group, cooperative management may be considered.

Following the report from the task force and the leads of other Canadian institutions, Parks Canada will consider repatriating objects for legal or ethical reasons or because they are sacred or funerary. Some general criteria are applied in helping determine what can be repatriated; but most requests are looked at on a case-by-case basis. Overriding definitions would be difficult, for example, no single definition of sacred would be acceptable to all Aboriginal peoples and also acceptable to Parks Canada.

The repatriation directive addresses requests from Aboriginal people within Canada for objects that are in Parks Canada's permanent collection and applies to requests from both within and outside the land claim and treaty process. The directive does not apply to repatriation requests from communities or individuals outside Canada, nor does it deal with requests from Aboriginal people for Parks Canada's help with international repatriations.

The directive is currently being revised and will have general application to requests from all ethnocultural communities and individuals. The new directive will clarify that Parks Canada will consider returning objects for legal and/or ethical reasons; consider requests from individuals as well as communities; and identify who may be a recipient. The updated directive will contain guidance on the return of associated records and address copyright issues. As well, the directive will emphasize the importance of identifying and consulting all people with an interest in a specific repatriation.

Management Directive 2.3.1 Human Remains, Cemeteries and Burial Grounds provides direction on managing cemeteries, burial grounds, human remains, funerary objects and grave markers found on Parks Canada's lands and lands under water regardless of ethnic, cultural or religious background. It also applies to human remains and associated funerary objects now in Parks Canada's collections. However, it does not apply to cemeteries covered in the *National Parks Cemetery Regulations*,[3] where people are still being buried, or to human remains of forensic interest.

The directive requires that human remains and funerary objects should, if possible, be left undisturbed. In the case of accidental discovery, the next of kin or culturally affiliated group(s) have to be consulted on how to proceed and a local protocol established and disposition agreement developed with them. In principle, Parks Canada will not display human remains to the public; however, display of reproductions or images may occur, but only if consent is given by the next of kin or culturally affiliated group (Dunlop and Leduc 2004).

Any activity related to burials or human remains must be undertaken in consultation and cooperation with the next of kin or culturally affiliated group(s), when known. The directive states that the scientific community should have an opportunity to express its interests in scientific research on human remains to the next of kin or culturally affiliated group.

Repatriation Guidelines

The Guidelines for the Repatriation of Human Remains and Objects to Aboriginal People have been developed in response to questions from Parks Canada staff and Aboriginal people raised during the implementation of repatriations. They offer pragmatic advice formulated by a multidisciplinary working group of Parks Canada staff that was drawn from across the country on the basis of their experience and understanding of specific cases. The guidelines, which apply to human remains, funerary objects and to historical and archaeological objects, cover key issues, such as

• Effective communication and the importance of seeking Aboriginal advice, accurately identifying Aboriginal contacts within communities and establishing advisory groups when appropriate.

- Developing financial strategies and coping with resource issues, both human and financial.
- How to negotiate, gain approval and carry out a repatriation.
- Determining ownership and the identification of cultural affiliation or next of kin.
- The importance of good information and records management.
- The importance of research and inventory accuracy.
- Access to information and copyright issues.
- Parks Canada's practices in respect of preservation and access to original documentation relating to items subject to repatriation requests.
- The care and handling of human remains and objects.

Repatriation Issues

Key issues are being examined as part of the review of the repatriation and human remains directives and the development of the repatriation guidelines that have surfaced through the review of repatriation case studies. Parks Canada policy acknowledges the uniqueness of each repatriation situation. Staff are learning that there needs to be a balance between consistency and case-by-case approaches.

Definitions are being reviewed in light of Aboriginal, national and international meanings, such as Parks Canada's definition of cultural affiliation. As well, the definition of the term repatriation to mean the return of human remains or objects to the father or native land does not apply to most of our transfers to Aboriginal people or reburials to date. Parks Canada is looking at the contexts and conditions of repatriations and realising that often transfer (gratuitous), restitution, return or reburial might be more appropriate terms to be used according to the circumstances of the case. In the 2002 national pilot workshop, Treatment and Use of Aboriginal Objects, we learned from an Ojibway Cultural Foundation member that they prefer the term 'cultural recovery' instead of repatriation and a member of a matrilineal Mowhawk community felt that the use of 'rematriation' would be a more meaningful term for them.

Communication and partnership building are important. Parks Canada must find a balance between the wishes of Aboriginal communities and its obligations to them, and its fiduciary obligations as a federal agency responsible for managing its resources for the benefit of all Canadians. Communication strategies must be in place to ensure that the proper people within communities, such as the Elders, chief or band council are identified and consulted. We are also aware that we must ensure that all interested communities are contacted and that all competing claims are resolved by the claimants prior to repatriation. (Note that as a convention, we usually capitalize Elder, as we do for Aboriginal.)

Funding for repatriations can be an issue for both Parks Canada and for Aboriginal communities or individuals. Parks Canada provides for collection maintenance while material is in its custody, packing and shipping and the ongoing maintenance of burials on lands it administers. However, it usually does not cover the costs of Aboriginal trips to view collections or fund the care and maintenance of human remains or objects once they have been transferred to Aboriginal repositories. Matters such as the nature and costs of ceremonies or the extent of packing are negotiated on a case-by-case basis.

Future Direction

Parks Canada will soon complete its review of the directives and creation of the guidelines relating to repatriation. Many of the issues mentioned above will be addressed by their completion. A strategy will be developed for repatriation that will include training related to repatriation. Training plans will be based on the national pilot workshop Treatment and Use of Aboriginal Objects and will involve Parks Canada staff, Aboriginal partners and professionals from outside institutions. Information from this national workshop as well as regional training initiatives have contributed greatly to approaches to repatriations, the directives and guidelines and to our treatment and use of Aboriginal collections in our custody. For example, staff in the Western and Northern Service Centre have set up their own Aboriginal awareness training as well as consulting with elders regarding the care and handling of sacred pipes in their custody. Quebec Service Centre has conducted a Cultural Resource Management workshop with Aboriginal partners. The Ontario Service Centre is collaborating with the Canadian Museum of Civilization in their Aboriginal Training Program. This program's goal is to offer Aboriginal participants professional and technical training in museum practices. Students who choose to come to Parks Canada for their placement are given cultural resource management experience in the Parks Canada setting. Last year a student from the program helped us develop a web site mock-up on repatriation for the Parks Canada web site. When in place it will help direct those interested in contacting Parks Canada regarding our collections and making requests for repatriation.

Parks Canada and Aboriginal people have both gained through face-to-face meetings. Access to collections in the custody of the agency and its expertise benefits the community; and advice from elders and other community members helps agency staff to understand and manage the collection better. Aboriginal elders and community members have visited and will continue to be welcome at Parks Canada's service centres and field units across the country where they can view relevant collections, discuss with staff the potential for repatriations and participate in the implementation of agreed to repatriations.

Notes

1. *First Nations Sacred Ceremonial Objects Repatriation Act.* Province of Alberta. RSA 2000, c F-14; *Blackfoot First Nations Sacred Ceremonial Objects Repatriation Regulation.* AR 96/2004.
2. The following policies, directives and guidelines have been prepared by Parks Canada in relation to the management of historic objects and remains: Management Directive 2.1.23: Collection Management System: Archaeological Research Services, 1986; Management Directive 2.1.21: Collection Management System: Management of Historic Objects and Reproductions, 1990; Cultural Resource Management Policy: Guiding Principles and Operational Policies, Part III, 1994; Management Directive 2.3.1: Human Remains, Cemeteries and Burial Grounds, 2000; Management Directive 2.3.4: Repatriation of Moveable Cultural Resources of Aboriginal Affiliation, 2000; Guidelines for the Management of Archaeological Resources, 2005; Management Directive in respect of the Acquisition and Disposal of Historical and Archaeological Objects and Reproductions, 2008 draft; Management Directive 2.3.4: Legal and Ethical Claims for the Return of Objects and Reproductions, 2008 draft (will replace MD 2.3.4. 2000); Guidelines for the Repatriation of Human Remains and Objects to Aboriginal Peoples, 2008 draft.
3. 'National Parks Cemetery Regulations', *Canada National Parks Act.* SOR/83–677, 1992

Bibliography

Assembly of First Nations (AFN) and The Canadian Museums Association (CMA). 1992. *Task Force Report on Museums and First Peoples, Turning the Page: Forging New Partnerships Between Museums and First Peoples.* Ottawa: Task Force on Museums and First Peoples.

Canadian Archaeological Association (CAA). 2000. *Statement of the Principles for Ethical Conduct Pertaining to Aboriginal Peoples* and *Principles of Ethical Conduct.*

Canadian Museums Association (CMA). 1999. *Ethical Guidelines.* Ottawa: CMA.

Denhez, M. 1999. *Unearthing the Law: Archaeological Legislation on Lands in Canada.* Archaeological Service Branch, Parks Canada.

Dunlop, H. and S. Leduc. 2004. 'Ownership and Treatment of Archaeological Human Remains in Canada', unpublished paper presented to the Theoretical Archaeology Group Conference, Glasgow, 17–19th December, 2004.

Royal Commission on Aboriginal Peoples (RCAP). 1996. *Report of the Royal Commission on Aboriginal Peoples* (RCAP). Department of Indian Affairs and Northern Development (DIAND).

University of Alberta. *Project for the Protection and Repatriation of First Nation Cultural Heritage in Canada.* Retrieved 18 May 2005 from www.law.ualberta.ca/research/aboriginalculturalheritage/index.htm

World Archaeology Congress (WAC). 1989. The Vermillion Accord on Human Remains, adopted at WAC Inter Congress, South Dakota, United States.

Part III

The Ethics and
Cultural Implications of Repatriation

6

What Might an Anthropology of Cultural Property Look Like?

Martin Skrydstrup

> *In December 1930, Franz Boas watched a potlatch feast at Fort Rupert, British Columbia. The host chief, Boas wrote, made a speech while the meat was distributed, saying 'This bowl in the shape of a bear is for you,' and you, and so on; for each group a bowl.' The speech was the same one that he had heard often before, 'But the bowls are no longer there. They are in the museums in New York and Berlin!'.*
> (Franz Boas in a letter to children, 14 December 1930; here after (Douglas Cole 1995)

> *In earlier days, people were sometimes taken by raiding parties. When they returned to their homes, either through payment of ransom or by retaliatory raid, they were said to have 'u'mista'. The return of our treasures from distant museums is a form of u'mista.*
> (U'mista Cultural Society, Alert Bay, B.C. Canada, 2006)

In the spring of 2004, the Museum of Victoria in Australia opened an exhibition of Aboriginal bark etchings on loan from the British Museum and the Royal Botanical Gardens in Kew (United Kingdom). The collection had been assembled around 1854 and the provenance of the bark etchings could be traced to the Dja Dja Warrung Aboriginal community in Central Victoria (Prott 2006). Like most other museums in Australia in the post-Mabo era, the Museum of Victoria was known to have taken a progressive stand towards engaging Aboriginal voices, knowledge and sensitivities in their exhibition work through extensive consulting with relevant Aboriginal organizations. The exhibition in question entitled *Etched on Bark 1854: Kulin Barks from Northern Victoria* was no exception to this praxis (Willis 2008). However, before the exhibition was closed, a senior representative of the Dja Dja Warrung community called for the Australian Prime Minister to ask the British Museum to let the bark etchings remain in Australia permanently.

Generally, the Aboriginal claim rested on the inalienability of the bark etchings with the source community, as the embodiment of their cultural patrimony. The claim caused a stir within the museum community in Australia and received a significant amount of publicity worldwide. Arguments were raised that if the Aboriginal claim were to prevail the implication would be that none of the museums with encyclopaedic collections – such as the British Museum and other so-called 'universal museums' – would even consider lending their collections for travelling exhibitions. Ultimately, this would lead to a halt in the international exchange of material culture. Grave concerns were articulated internationally that future opportunities to learn from and appreciate the rich cultural and artistic diversity of the world, enhancing cross-cultural tolerance and understanding, could be lost.

In Australia, the Dja Dja Warrung community requested that an inspector from the Aboriginal and Torres Strait Islander Heritage Protection Act (1984) imposed a series of emergency declarations preventing the Museum of Victoria to fulfil its loan agreement with the British Museum (Prott 2006). After several months of negotiations between the Dja Dja Warrung community and the Museum of Victoria, the Museum took the case to court. Here, the legality of the imposed emergency declarations was challenged successfully and the Museum was able to meet its loan obligation and return the etchings to the United Kingdom. However, the Dja Dja Warrung community continue to claim ownership over the etchings based on loss, dispossession, customary title rights and cultural and intellectual property rights.

This chapter is concerned with the general question of how the discipline of anthropology is to make sense of events like this. Thus, what follows is a theoretical exposition of ways in which to think trough what is at stake in public controversies regarding "cultural property" such as the one in Victoria, Australia. The piece represents an attempt to get behind and beyond press and broadcast treatments of the event, where arguments seem embedded in institutional frameworks and normative horizons: Should the museum return the material in question, or not? What is right and what is wrong? The aim of this chapter is to show how such predicaments open up a set of larger theoretical questions about *objects, property* and *recognition*.

I shall briefly map some important thematic contributions on repatriation, before sketching my own analytical approach, pointing to its methodological and theoretical implications. I am not arguing that the sort of background conceptual work I am advocating does not have normative implications. Rather, I am arguing that the thematic literature on repatriation has yet to grapple with these broader theoretical questions.[1] Further, a caveat is required: what follows is a prospectus for a bold theoretical move, rather than the results of a research project already conducted. I wish to open up a new vocabulary and show potential avenues for an anthropology of cultural property.

The Three R's Axis: Restitutions, Restrictions, Rights

How have scholars come to understand transactions in cultural properties? In one of the most cited and influential volumes on the topic *The Ethics of Collecting Cultural Property: Whose Culture? Whose Property?* (Messenger 1999 [1989]), the feminist philosopher Karen J. Warren has provided a framework for understanding and assessing the variety of claims and perspectives in the debate over cultural properties (Warren 1999). She defines cultural property 'in the widest sense to include both physical remains of the past and perceptions of the past itself' (Warren 1999). She proceeds to organise the debate into what she calls the three R's: Restitution of an object to its place of origin, Restriction in the movement of cultural properties and Rights of ownership, access and inheritance. She then identifies six arguments con and three arguments pro claims made to the three R's by 'countries of origin' (Warren 1999).

One of the more obvious problems with this representation of the debate is that the three R's axis is inherently contradictive. Whereas arguments in favour of the first two R's (Restitution and Restriction) most often run in tandem, arguments for the last R (Rights to ownership, access and inheritance) are asserted across the entire spectrum of the debate. However, the last R is internally inconsistent. For example, in the paradigmatic case about the human remains discovered at Kennewick, direct conflicting arguments about rights are asserted to 'access' and 'inheritance'. Warren's chart seems primarily to account for the main arguments deployed in the debate on the proper place of archaeological antiquities between nation-states. With regard to repatriation within a nation-state, her three R's model seems less persuasive. I would argue that this has to do with the fact that Warren subsumes repatriation and return under Restitution, instead of distinguishing between these three concepts. I have argued elsewhere for the need to make exactly this distinction (Skrydstrup 2004). Let me proceed to show what the current debate on cultural property would look like if we were to make this distinction.

A New Three R's Model: Restitution, Return and Repatriation

A more adequate representation of the debate on cultural property would need to understand the terms restitution, return and repatriation within specific historical genealogies tied to different legal regimes of value:

Restitution

The legal concept of restitution emerged out of complex negotiations within UNESCO in the late 1960s on how to grapple with the rampant illicit trafficking in antiquities. The evidence of this phenomenon were reports of pillaging, archaeological site destructions, plain theft from museums and illicit export of artefacts from South America, Africa and South-east Asia (Coggins 2005 [1972]; Meyer 1973; Schmidt and McIntosh 1993b). This occurred in conjunction with a rise in the demand for antiquities in North America, Western Europe, the Gulf States and Japan. This global commoditisation of the tangible fragments of past civilisations divided the world into the pull of 'market nations' and the push of 'source nations', resulting in a serious threat to the archaeological record *in situ*, as well as the safeguarding of cultural heritage in 'source nations'.

In an attempt to govern this problem, UNESCO adopted the Convention on the Means of Prohibiting and Preventing the Illicit Import, Export and Transfer of Ownership of Cultural Property in 1970. This legal instrument provided a mechanism for restitution in so far as it defined the export of cultural property from a state party's territory without a certificate as illicit (Article 6). The UNESCO convention also stipulated that the acquisition or import of documented stolen cultural property from the territory of a state party to the convention was illicit (Article 7). As of May 2008, 115 states were party to the convention.[2] Source nations like Mexico, Cambodia and Egypt became parties to the convention in the early 1970s, whereas market nations have ratified much more recently: United States in 1983, France in 1997, United Kingdom and Japan in 2002 and Switzerland in 2004. What is important about these ratification years is that the 1970 convention cannot be applied retroactively. This means that material imported illicitly to any state territory prior to the ratification of the convention by that particular state falls outside its jurisdiction.

The debate on restitution is essentially a debate about theft, illegality and stolen property. It revolves around two main questions. Firstly, there is the question of the vices and virtues of different legal instruments to hamper and govern the contemporary illicit trafficking in antiquities. More specifically, the question is whether illegally exported material, according to the laws of a source nation, should have any salience in the courts of the importing market nation (Brilliant 2001). Secondly, there is the question of what laws, mediation or arbitration mechanisms should be applicable in transnational cultural property disputes, e.g., disputes arising from takings by the Nazi regime before and during the Second World War (Simpson 1997). A case in point is the Metropolitan Museum of Art's decision in February 2006 to return to Italy one of the centrepieces of its collection, the Euphronios krater. This act was justified by new evidence of 'machinations, lies and clandestine night digging' (Solomon 2006). It is noteworthy that none of the three arguments listed by Warren in support of the three R's (Warren 1999) was advanced by Italy in their restitution claim. The argument was not that the object constituted the 'cultural heritage' of Italy, nor was it that the object was 'owned by the property's country of origin' (the Euphronios krater is Greek in origin) and nor was the 'scholarly and aesthetic integrity argument' deployed by the claimant. The restitution claim rested on the argument that the object had left Italy illegally, thus the museum had acquired stolen property.

Return

The concept of return emerged partly in response to the lack of retroactivity of the UNESCO 1970 convention. A number of new sovereign nation states argued for their right to be able to display at least part of their own cultural heritage, which had been removed during colonial times. In other words, we have a confluence of emerging political sovereignties coupled with a postcolonial inheritance of loss. In 1976, partly in response to this type of postcolonial claim, a committee of experts met under the auspices of UNESCO to grapple with the problem of colonial appropriations prior to the entry into force of the 1970 UNESCO convention. Out of this work came the Intergovernmental Committee for Promoting the Return of Cultural Property to its Countries of Origin or its Restitution in case of Illicit Appropriation established in 1978. The mandate of the committee supplements the legal repertoire of the UNESCO 1970 convention. The committee accommodates requests regarding cultural property[3] which have '... a fundamental significance from the point of view of the spiritual values and cultural heritage of the people of a member state' (1978). This means that the *ratione temporis* of the committee is not limited to misappropriations having occurred before 1978. The committee is responsible for 'seeking ways and means of facilitating bilateral negotiations' (1978), which implies that claims from nonstate actors, cannot be recognised by the committee. The mandate of the committee is advisory and its recommendations are not legally binding. Its founding spirit is perhaps best embodied in the appeal by the UNESCO director-general at its launch:

> One of the most noble incarnations of a people's genius is its cultural heritage ... the vicissitudes of history have nevertheless robbed many peoples of a priceless portion of this inheritance ... These men and women therefore ask for the return of at least the art treasures which best represent their culture, which they feel are the most vital and whose absence causes them the greatest anguish. (M'Bow 1979)

Contrary to the debate on restitution, which draws its register from legalities, the debate about return is essentially situated outside the law. Return is not a debate about reparation in a judicial sense, but about goodwill, ethics and what is at times referred to as 'natural justice' (Greenfield 1996). Claims are made in the name of the arguments listed by Warren in favour of the three R's: 'cultural heritage', 'country of origin' and 'scholarly and aesthetic integrity' (Warren 1999). When I participated as an external observer at the committee's meeting in Paris in March 2003, Greece's case for the Parthenon sculptures was reviewed alongside that of Turkey's for the return of the Hittite Sphinx from the archaeological site of Boguskoy. Both cases were brought before the committee in the mid 1980s and both are still pending. A similar American case is the possibility of a Peruvian claim (first mooted in early 2006) for artefacts removed during archaeological excavations by Yale University in the Machu Pichu area in 1912 to 1915. The material being debated in these return cases was not dug up by looters in recent decades or Nazi-era misappropriated property, but objects which were removed earlier, often with appropriate permits and with much more complex histories. Such cases are typically resolved through behind-the-scenes talk and bilateral diplomatic negotiations.

Repatriation

In the 1980s and 1990s, the term repatriation began to emerge within national frameworks in what is often referred to as 'settler colonial nation states': Canada, United States, Australia and New Zealand. In the United States, the term designates federally mandated transfer of human remains and specific categories of objects to the contemporary descendants of the cultures from which the material was originally removed. This federal mandate is codified as *Native American Graves Protection and Repatriation Act* (NAGPRA), which was signed into law in 1990. This law was preceded by the *National Museum of the American Indian Act* (NMAIA: 1989), which was the outcome of an agreement between the Smithsonian Institution and Native American constituencies. The NMAI Act's repatriation provisions were aimed at redressing 'some of the injustices done to Indian people over the years' and held the promise that 'one day their ancestors will finally be given the resting place that they so deserve' (Trope and Walter 2001 [1992]).

The moral genealogy of these two domestic legal regimes are to be found in the 'one-way transfer of Indian property to non-Indian ownership' (Trope and Walter 2001 [1992]), the failure of common law to protect native burial sites *en pair* with Christian cemeteries and an emerging public consciousness of the fact that many museums were in fact 'closets of Indian skeletons' (Preston 1989). Responding to this confluence of factors, a number of bills were introduced in the US Congress between 1986 and 1990 that grappled with how to redress these issues. The first proposal was a type of alternative dispute resolution mechanism, which was vigorously opposed by *inter alia*, the Smithsonian Institution, the American Association of Museums and the Society for American Archaeology. Instead, a *sui generis* judicially enforceable regime was adopted (NAGPRA), which protected native burial sites and directly required federally funded museums to conduct exhaustive inventories and notify tribes about their holdings. If claims were made for human remains, funerary objects, sacred objects and objects of cultural patrimony that meet the statutory definitions of the law, and 'cultural affiliation' could be established between the material in question and the claiming group, repatriation was mandatory.

With regard to the concept of repatriation as defined here, Warren's three arguments in support of the three Rs sit awkwardly. The 'cultural heritage' argument is somewhat congruent with the justification to repatriate objects of 'cultural patrimony', but the 'country of origin' argument understood in its territorial sense and the 'scholarly and aesthetic integrity' argument does not underpin any justificatory theories of NAGPRA. Most Native American tribes do not reside in the same territories as they did when the material was appropriated, hence the irrelevance of the 'country of origin' argument. Moreover, the NAGPRA repatriation mandate is conceived as putting the 'sacred' and 'ceremonial' values of objects *en pair* with any scholarly, aesthetic and scientific perspectives of the same material as 'artefacts', 'art objects' or 'specimens'.

What kind of law is NAGPRA? Some consider NAGPRA to be the most important piece of cultural policy legislation in the history of the United States (Tweedie 2002). The law has been designated as 'federal Indian law', 'cultural property law' and 'remedial civil rights legislation', but first and foremost as 'human rights legislation' (Hutt 1998), conceived to 'address the flagrant violation of the civil rights of America's first citizens' (Trope and Walter 2001 [1992]). In a recent evaluation of the law it was characterised by two of its leading practitioners as 'in the smaller scope of conscience perhaps the biggest thing we have ever done' (McKeown and Hutt 2003).

NAGPRA has had direct implications for archaeological and museum practice in the United States. The scholarly debate on repatriation has predominantly centred on whether archaeology's claim to human remains and artefacts as scientific evidence outweigh Native claims to repatriation based on ancestry (Garza and Powell 2001). This issue has often been perceived as one of access or control, where repatriation and reburial implies loss of access, control and consequently information, whereas retention of material means continued access and control over the embedded scientific information in the material (Baker, Varney, Wilkinson, Anderson, and Liston 2001). It was feared that archaeological research only had something to lose from NAGPRA, but the number of published articles on Native American archaeology has actually increased after the adoption of NAGPRA (Killion and Molloy 1998). At the institutional and disciplinary level, the debate has focused on critiques of more conventional archaeological knowledge production (Lilley 2000a; Lilley 2000b; Spector 2001; Swidler 1997; Watkins 2000; Zimmerman 2001), new types of ethics based on shared knowledge, inclusiveness, multiple voices and pasts, stewardship, consultation and collaborative approaches to understanding the past (Wylie 2002; Zimmerman, Vitelli, and Hollowell-Zimmer 2003). In the words of one influential volume on the subject *The Future of the Past* (Bray 2001b), 'The archaeology of the academy needs to be replaced by an archaeology of the community. Museum studies must address the needs and concerns of the Native communities whose material pasts they have so long held in trust' (Loring 2001). In other words, today it is almost inconceivable to do archaeology and exhibit Native American culture in the United States without the participation of Native American communities. Beyond the direct practical implications at the disciplinary level of archaeology and museum studies, the debate has centred on 'identity politics', cultural survival, revitalisation processes and the political sovereignty of descent communities (Barkan and Bush 2002; Fine-Dare 2002; Johnson 1999).

To sum up, we might distinguish the three R's in the following way: (1) Restitution concerns the problem of contemporary illicit trafficking in antiquities between source nations and market nations and hinges on the provenance (i.e., the ownership history) of the object. Restitution is most often mandated by a strict legal interpretation of 'cultural property'; (2) Return concerns the problem of international claims for historically removed material objects and turns on the inalienability of the object from its original context, that is, the *provenience* of the object. Return is most often based on voluntary action and goodwill underwritten by ethical considerations of what rightfully constitutes a nation's cultural patrimony; (3) Repatriation concerns the problem of Indigenous claims for human remains and cultural objects within the nation-state. Repatriation seems to pivot on the necessity of the object for a minority group's ceremonial practices, contemporary identity and 'cultural survival' within larger processes of national narratives and reconciliation within settler-colonial nation-states.

Following on from this initial characterisation of restitution, return and repatriation, I would like to shift gear and ask how an anthropologist might study them as imbrications of a larger phenomenon referred to as 'cultural property'.

The Three R's as a Site of Anthropological Inquiry

What then has 'cultural property' come to mean in the beginning of the twenty-first century? If we wanted to explore this question by looking at practice, as anthropologists often do, we would have to look at restitution, return and repatriation as different praxis forms of exchange and transaction. In building an appropriate methodology of such transactions would the conventional project of anthropology understood as the long-term study of small-scale societies in unfamiliar settings be of any use?

Anthropologists do fieldwork in existing living societies; they observe local practices and listen to explanations and people trying to make sense of local events. In the classical sense, ethnographic fieldwork entails concrete observation, inquiry and interpretation, carried out at a particular site. The objective is to try to figure out what is going on, what it means to the actors involved and how it relates to the collectives in which specific agents are embedded. In reflexive ethnography, one's own experience is central – i.e., what is being studied is not so much the social life of an alien community, but the situation provoked by the anthropologist being there. If we were to deploy such an ethnographic approach to the study of cultural property the immediate question would be where to venture and what kind of reactions the presence of an anthropologist would provoke. The empirical options are daunting: a Jewish family in California making a claim for a family heirloom that was misappropriated in Austria in the Nazi era, the ministry of culture in Ecuador making a claim for archaeological pieces in a museum in Italy, a Native Hawaiian organisation making a claim for a carved wooden figure in a museum on the east coast of the United States or an

Australian Aboriginal native title group claiming bark etchings from a museum in England. The choice of examples could be greatly extended.

Restitution, return and repatriation claims are large-scale phenomena. In their very nature they transcend local settings and national frameworks and seem to be all about networks and relations. As such, the phenomenon challenges more conventional anthropological notions of embedded practice and ethnographic fieldwork as holism, taking place within a relatively closed socio-cultural microcosm. Thus, it comes as no surprise that current anthropological approaches stress that repatriation should be understood as deeply embedded in relations of ongoing contact histories (Clifford 1988), occurring within a new kind of 'intercultural space' (Bray 2001a). Of course, the methodology and analytical toolkit we choose to deploy in the study of cultural property depends upon our theoretical interests. Here, I would like to sketch three theoretical *topoi*, which could frame an anthropological approach to cultural property.

A Matter of Materiality?

Few would disagree with the proposition that claims for restitution, return and repatriation have to do with the meanings of material objects. There seems to be a foundational relationship between the stance various stakeholders of the debate adopt toward the three R's and their stance toward the material record. Different notions of the same physical object as a 'nonrenewable resource', an 'artefact', an 'antiquity' or a piece of 'cultural patrimony' are coupled with distinctive arguments pro or con the three R's in the debate. Why be surprised? We all know how a photograph, a belt buckle or a champagne cork can seem ordinary to some people, but extraordinary to others. Objects can take on very strange meanings intimately tied to personhood, memories, social relations and inalienability.

However, things get a little more complicated if we talk about Native American medicine bundles, Zuni *Ahayu:ta* (war gods or twin gods), Iroquois wampum belts and Australian Aboriginal *tjuringa* (sacred stones), just to mention a set of widely different material objects which have been – in one way or the other – involved in cultural property claims. What they have in common is that they have all travelled as a congruent feature of imperialism, colonialism, capitalism and scientific expeditions. Contemporary repatriation efforts reverse such trajectories, which does not make the travelogues of these objects less colourful and dramatic. What biographies have such objects accumulated? What complex stories could they tell if they could speak? They seem to be a good deal more than their substances: wood, skin, stones, pearls, paint, metal pieces, etc. They come across more like persons than things. They seem almost imbued with a certain agency of their own.

This inference of intentionality to objects often transpires in narratives about repatriation. A case in point is the history of the potlatch collection from the Kwakwaka'wakw of British Columbia in Canada, well known from the writings of Franz Boas who referred to them as the 'Kwakiutl Indians'. In 1884, the federal government of Canada outlawed the potlatch, an institution of lavish feast giving, exchange and destruction of property. From the perspective of a protestant ethic and the spirit of capitalism in Ottawa the potlatch was wasteful, immoral and a heathen practice. A large collection of potlatch paraphernalia was 'confiscated' in 1921 through legal action. The federal law was dropped in 1951 and sustained attempts to repatriate the collection began in the 1960s. These efforts culminated with a compromise struck in the early 1970s, where repatriation was made conditional on the establishment of museum facilities to properly curate the collection. For that purpose the U'mista Cultural Society was incorporated in 1974. The society defines its name in the following way:

> In earlier days, people were sometimes taken by raiding parties. When they returned to their homes, either through payment of ransom or by retaliatory raid, they were said to have 'u'mista'. The return of our treasures from distant museums is a form of u'mista (U'mista 2006).

As Ira Jacknis remarks, *u'mista* is 'a perfect Native gloss for repatriation' (Jacknis 2000). Theoretically, this example speaks to the centrality of a notion of agentive objects. The U'mista Cultural Society infers that repatriated objects contain embedded human agency.

Edmund Ladd, a member of the Coyote Clan on the Zuni Pueblo also referred to the *Ahayu: ta* (war gods) as 'being held captive in different museums around the world' (Ladd 2001). He went on to remark the following about their properties:

> It is through the process of disintegration that these gods realize their protective powers. It is therefore imperative that they not be removed, collected, or preserved; such acts are both dangerous and insensitive. They are dangerous because these gods are mischievous and can play havoc with nature if removed from their shrines ... They are not art objects but 'Spirit Beings.' (Ladd 2001)

It seems that Zuni *Ahayu: ta*, Iroquois wampum belts (Richard W. Hill 2001) and Native American medicine bundles (Cash 2001) could be said to be neither objects nor subjects, but spiritual entities. Such objects not only 'play subtle tricks upon human understanding' (Taussig 2004), such 'things' or perhaps rather 'captives' open up a range of questions at the fore of an intensified concern with 'materiality' in anthropology.

Daniel Miller has recently set the intellectual agenda for such an endeavour. In his introduction to the volume entitled *Materiality* (Miller 2005), he tacks between high-altitude philosophy concerning the resolution (Hegel's *Aufhebung*) of the antithesis between subjects and objects and the more mundane level of ethnography where people think cars commit treason, because they will not start. Or vice versa, that people kill people – guns do not. Miller delineates what I understand to be three current attempts to theorise materiality: 1) a theory of object agency, where he locates Bruno Latour's (1999) and Alfred Gell's (1998) influential work, but with intellectual roots back to Durkheim and Mauss; 2) a more dialectical approach, revolving around the subtle relations between objectification, alienation, power and materiality; 3) the legacy of phenomenology, which would focus on the 'thing-ness' of things. The idea here is that some things (and people) are more material than others; in other words, what I understand to be the immanent and sensuous properties of objects. According to Miller: 'All of these will make claims to have finally and fully transcended the dualism of subjects and objects' (Miller 2005).

Since the material objects are most often the protagonists in cultural property disputes, I would argue that all three strands of thought could find fertile ground and rich ethnographical detail in the three R's. My proposition here is that repatriation speaks directly to the key questions in the analysis of material culture:

- How do people attribute value to objects and how do objects give value to social or international relations?
- What happens when things migrate across different spheres of values and framings of significance?
- How do discursive regimes define the reality of things, i.e., their taxonomy as human remains, funerary objects, sacred objects, objects of cultural patrimony, antiquities, art, artefacts, relics, specimens, etc?
- Do antiquities create markets, or do markets create antiquities?
- How do things take on meanings as gifts or commodities in different types of transactions?
- What makes things inalienable and what makes them alienable?
- How are objects owned, held in possession, cared for and put to different usages in relation to processes of identity formation, be that personhood or nationhood?

All of these questions could form part of an intellectual agenda in which: 'we need to show how the things that people make, make people' (Miller 2005).

How should we show how objects make subjects? The highly influential volume *The Social Life of Things* (Appadurai 1986) opened up a new methodological agenda by following a wide range of things through different 'tournaments of value'. Crucial here was the movement of things and their changing value attributions over time and space. A question that informed several of the contributions to the volume was the underlying social relations propelling different forms of exchange, circulation and trade. As a whole the volume softened the absolute dichotomy between gift and commodity exchange, which became a matter of degree. This takes me to consider the possibility of repositioning the Maussian notion of the gift with reference to repatriation.

In May 2002, I witnessed a NAGPRA dispute over eight ceremonial masks held by the Denver Art Museum in Colorado and claimed by the Western Apache Group in Arizona. In their own investigation of the case, the museum had determined that the objects were not subject to the law. Instead, the institution offered to return them on a voluntary basis to the tribe as a gift. However, the Western Apache did not want to receive the ceremonial masks as a gift, since they thought they had been wrongfully taken from them in the first place. The representatives of the Apache in the dispute hearing wanted the objects repatriated with recourse to the law. In this case, repatriation seems to be all about the nature of the transaction: a gift is carried by generosity and goodwill. Moreover, Mauss teaches us that it establishes a human bond of reciprocity and ultimately solidarity. However, the Western Apache did not want to receive the objects in question as gifts, but as judicial reparation for a misappropriation. Three R's cases such as this accentuate Mauss' fundamental questions about sliding scales of obligation and compulsion in exchange relations. It also reopens Jacques Derrida's rereading of Mauss and the Derridian question about the possibility of the gift (Derrida 1991). If the museum is conscious that it is 'gifting' instead of being compelled by the force of law, is the object still a 'gift'? And what happens with the status of the eight wooden ceremonial masks as property when they enter the Western Apache community to be used in religious ceremonies? Clearly, the lives of objects in cultural property disputes offer pathways to key theoretical questions centring on materiality, which could prove to be illuminating for theoretical contributions to anthropology.

A Matter of Property?

Some of the thematic contributions to the debate on cultural property have argued for abandoning the conceptual framework of 'cultural property' and adopting the concept of 'cultural heritage' instead (Prott and O'Keefe 1992; Schmidt and McIntosh 1993a; Warren 1999). Aside from the fact that there are important distinctions to be made between cultural property and cultural heritage, I would argue that the recent revival of interest in property among anthropologists (Hann 1998; Pottage and Mundy 2004; Strathern and Hirsch 2004; Verdery and Humphrey 2004b) opens new opportunities to push much harder on the conceptualisation of cultural property as property.

How then have anthropologists understood the concept of property? Surveying the history of anthropology, Verdery and Humphrey argue that the property concept has been understood as: 1) things; 2) as relations of persons to things; 3) as person–person relations mediated through things; 4) as a bundle of abstract rights (Verdery and Humphrey 2004a). I have largely addressed (1) and (2) under the rubrics of materiality, objectification, inalienability and the interface between objects and personhood. The prevalent understanding of property in anthropology is figured as (3), i.e., as a sanctioned social relationship between persons with respect to tangibles and intangibles seen as having value. This would take us away from the notion of cultural property as a matter of the relations between persons and things, or subjecthood and materiality, and towards exploring cultural property as a relation between persons, here understood as intra or interstate relations, mediated by tangible objects. One of the central questions of such an endeavour would be the links, if any, between indigenous claims and metropolitan property regimes. In other words, how do codified cultural property regimes enable or disenable the emergence and articulation of claims to the three R's in particular settings? In this vein, Ann Tweedie has recently explored the efforts by the Makah Indians of Washington State to make claims with recourse to a law, which presumes certain concepts of communal ownership foreign to Makah forms of personal ownership (Tweedie 2002). This type of community-state relations mediated through objects does not become less complex if we transcend the ordinary jurisdictional range of the nation-state, hereby accentuating a plurality of normative loci. The key here is to understand that locales and levels are interactive.

However, in tackling these issues it would seem that we have moved from a relational understanding of property to the notion of property as a 'bundle of rights'. Who makes these rights? What redefines them? What justificatory theories underwrite them? Inquiries about the ways in which norms are generated in different contexts has been a long-standing preoccupation of legal anthropology, as has the notion of property (Moore 2001). The 'bundle of rights' understanding (4) takes us into codified entitlements, court cases and legal bodies of knowledge. Annelise Riles has recently considered legal theory making about property as an ethnographic subject in its own right (Riles 2004). The premise here is that cultural property is the brainchild of legal theory, and hence must be understood ethnographically in the idioms of lawyers' particular methods of reasoning. Thus, the informants here are judges, lawyers, law professors and bureaucrats. The anthropological field method consists of the standard ethnographic repertoires and techniques for gathering data about knowledge practices. The key here is what these ethnographic subjects refer to as 'legal doctrine' (Riles 2004). Doctrine emerges from case rulings, where doctrine is defined as 'the artefact of the accumulation of individual cases' (Riles 2004). The ethnographic puzzle is to identify the judicial decisions, which makes visible the existing doctrine of a given property regime. Ethnographic contextualisation implies relating any given ruling or case in such a property regime to the existing doctrine. Such an endeavour resonates partly with the 'chain of means and ends' that Riles suggests as the object of ethnographic inquiry, or the actor-network theory of science studies deployed in Latour's recent ethnography of the judicial body *Conseil d'Etat* in France (Latour 2004).

The principal sites of legal-knowledge production on cultural property[4] are what I refer to as a 'metropolitan property regime', here understood as a 'textual polity' (Messick 1996 [1993]), which entails a number of interrelated dimensions: 1) high doctrine, i.e., the established legal doctrine; 2) intermediate level of institutions of judgment, i.e., courts where cases are adjudicated and rulings made; 3) ground level, i.e., museums and archival repositories, which make findings, recommendations and execute transactions. These dimensions correspond roughly to the distinctions Brinkley Messick has drawn between three levels of written legal texts in the *Sharia* property regime (Islamic law): high doctrine, court judgments and common instruments (Messick 2003). Part of the ethnographic puzzle in an anthropology of cultural property is to figure out how these various levels interrelate. For example, what changes at the level of high doctrine and intermediate level makes repatriation at the institutional level into common-sense and routine 'slowly taking on the trappings of normality within the museum', as the former director of the Repatriation Office at the Smithsonian National Museum of Natural History coins it (Killion 2001).

The task of identifying the ascendance of new forms of property as a product of complex interconnections over time within a regime reminds us of the limits of the presentist perspective of ethnography. As the celebrated Canadian political philosopher, Macpherson reminded us a few decades ago: 'The meaning of property is not constant. The actual institution, and the way people see it, and hence the meaning they give to the word, all change over time' (Macpherson 1978). The history of recorded debates about property go back at least to the writings of Plato and Aristotle who, among other things, discussed whether a slave could or should own the attire he was wearing. In the Renaissance, philosophers discussed whether the oceans could constitute property. Today, legal scholars debate whether the human genome could constitute property. With regard to cultural property, the historian Jordanna Bailkin has shown that 'it is anachronistic to describe objects as cultural property before the mid-twentieth century' (Bailkin 2004). Cultural property as a legal concept, which is what we are interested in here, emerged with the Hague Convention in 1954, although it has roots back to debates in the Enlightenment about the proper place of the classical art of Rome (Furet 1996; Héritier 2003; Merryman 2000; Merryman and Elsen 2002; Quatremère de Quincy 1836; Savoy 2003). However, the definition of cultural property in the 1954 Hague Convention differs significantly from the one given in the 1970 UNESCO convention (Merryman 1986). With reference to the legislative history of NAGPRA, Jack Trope and Walter Echo-Hawk have shown that in the *Antiquities Act 1906*, Indian human remains figured as an 'archaeological resource', which contrary to long standing common-law principles were converted into 'federal property' (Trope and Walter 2001 [1992]). The Act allowed such human remains to be excavated 'for the permanent preservation in public museums'. With the presidential signing of NAGPRA into US federal law in 1990, a new property concept that had been underway since the 1960s was elevated to high doctrine. To map how significant shifts on the international plain from the Hague Convention to the UNESCO convention interrelate with different national contexts of ratification and domestic legal histories, is a larger project, but one which is also about chains of legal connections. Anna Tsing has provided a portfolio of methods for the study of global interconnections, which could be useful to such an ethnography of global legal links (Tsing 2005).

I have suggested some different modes of approach, based on different conceptualisations of property: as a set of social relations and as a bundle of rights constituting legal knowledge as an ethnographic object in its own right. I have suggested elucidating the institutional architecture of what I call a 'metropolitan property regime' focusing on its legal doctrines, justificatory theories and interrelations between its different dimensions. Finally, I have stressed the historical contingency of the legal category of cultural property. Anthropologists may respond that what remains to be explored are the effects of the Western 'native category' of cultural property in the world at large. How does this legal category impact upon non-Western or Indigenous forms of life and sociability? How do the legal technologies of recognition inherent in the concept (Murphy 2004) silence the worlds of the claimants? Or force Aboriginal peoples to perform cultural difference in ways prescribed by common law in the guise of liberal forms of recognition, but alien to them (Povinelli 2002)? Or enable Indigenous agency to 'heal the wounds of imperialism and colonialism', and we might add, the conscience of the postcolonial state? I will now turn to consider some of these larger questions.

A Matter of Recognition?

Reflecting back on the field notes and the photographs which eventually made up the *Tristes Tropiques* (Lévi-Strauss 1992), Claude Lévi-Strauss evokes two cataclysms which dispossessed the Indians of central Brazil. In 1541, raiding parties of Spanish conquistadores journeyed up an unknown river, later named the Amazon, in search of food. When the Spaniards returned a century later their mission was to eliminate all the Indians. Thus, as Lévi-Strauss argues, the ethnographic observations made in the nineteenth and twentieth century, including his own 1935 observations and photographs of the Bororo people, do not reflect 'archaic conditions' (Lévi-Strauss 1995). Today, writes Lévi-Strauss, a second cataclysm is depriving the Indigenous people of central Brazil, the effects of which we typically gloss under the discontents of modernity:

> The Bororo, whose good health and robustness I had admired in 1935, are today being consumed by alcoholism and disease and are progressively losing their language. It is in missionary schools that Bororo youths are being taught about their myths and their ceremonies. But, for fear that they might damage the feather diadems, masterpieces of traditional art, the missionaries are keeping these objects locked up, entrusting the Indians with them only on strictly necessary occasions. (Lévi-Strauss 1995)

Obviously, this example raises the question of the difference between repatriation of the intangible and the tangible. However, it also highlights a paternalistic or conditional form of repatriation: the feather diadems are so 'precious' and 'rare' (a nonrenewable resource) that their custody, cannot be entrusted the Indians. What type of cultural recognition is at play in the property relation between missionaries and the Bororo community with regard to the feather diadems?

Instead of rushing to an answer, let us consider the other case Lévi-Strauss relates:

> Far away, in Canada, a contrasting yet strikingly parallel phenomenon is taking place. The Pacific Coast Indians, whom I visited in 1974, are placing in museums – in this case of their own creation – the masks and other ritual objects that were confiscated more than half a century ago and have now been returned to them at last. These objects are brought out and used during ceremonies the Indians are beginning to celebrate again. In this new climate they have lost a good deal of their ancient grandeur. The potlatch, formerly a solemn occasion at once political, juridical, economic, and religious, on which rested the whole social order, has been rethought by acculturated Indians imbued with the Protestant ethic and is degenerating into a periodic exchange of little gifts to consolidate harmony within the group and to maintain friendship. (Lévi-Strauss 1995)

Lévi-Strauss' observations offer an initial template for discriminating between two approaches to repatriation, which I shall characterise as 'paternalistic' and 'multicultural'. In the first example, we have a paternalistic approach to repatriation, in so far as the continued preservation of the object overrides its value as contemporary ceremonial object for the Bororo community. We are here in the realm of the International Council of Museums' (ICOM) professional ethics regarding return and restitution claims: 'For those in charge of cultural heritage, the *raison d'être* for their professional ethics is to ensure its conservation' (Ganslmayr, Landais, Lewis, Makambila, Perrot, et al. 1983). Thus, any questions about the property status of the object are overridden by preservationist concerns, which justify the retention – or precisely the occasional loan – of the feather diadems in the possession of the missionaries. In this case *indigeneity* seems to justify retention, since natives from the perspective of the missionaries do not have proper storage facilities for 'nonrenewable resources' such as feather diadems. We might ask the simple question of why the Bororo community is not in a position to exercise any property rights vis-à-vis the missionaries? The answer here does not seem to be about citizenship, but rather because the Bororo community does not have any standing as sovereign vis-à-vis the missionaries.

In the second case, we have a multicultural approach, where the value of ongoing ceremonial activities, i.e., the perpetuation of cultural particularism within the nation-state, seems to override any preservationist concerns the relinquishing museum might harbour.[5] This approach is spelled out in NAGPRA, where 'sacred objects ... mean specific ceremonial objects which are needed by traditional Native American religious leaders for the practice of traditional Native American religions by their present day adherents' (NAGPRA 1990: SEC. 2; Article 3C). Contrary to the first case, *indigeneity* here seems to justify repatriation, which completely overrides the issue about the continued preservation of the object. Moreover, why are Native American religious leaders in a position to exercise property rights vis-à-vis holding institutions? Again, the answer here does not turn on citizenship, but rather sovereignty vis-à-vis the federal government. Thus, a native community can act as a claimant exercising property rights in *parens patriae* (Trope and Walter 2001 [1992]), or as a dependent domestic nations (First Nations in Canada), vis-à-vis any holding institution within the borders of the nation state (Williams 1990).

What I am trying to show by these two contrasting case approaches is that the property status of an object, i.e., property relations, only has salience within regimes of recognition. In the two case studies Lévi-Strauss mentions we have seen how property rights are defined by complex acts of recognition of indigeneity and sovereignty. This opens up a number of complex theoretical questions: On what grounds does a metropolitan property regime recognise a claimant? For example in the second case, what if the U'mista Cultural Society wanted to exercise their property rights vis-à-vis a museum abroad with reference to the confiscated potlatch collection, instead of the federal government in Ottawa? The property status of the potlatch collection would change as a result of a realigned property relation, subject to a different regime of recognition of indigeneity and sovereignty. In other words, a non-Canadian museum presented with a repatriation claim from the U'mista Cultural Society could legitimately dismiss the claim and relate that such a claim would only have salience if forwarded through diplomatic protocol, i.e., by a sovereign state actor. In this property relation the question of indigeneity is foreclosed by a politics of recognition that only allow state sovereigns to make claims.

Thus, if we look at property relations from the vantage point of cultural recognition, we have intra and interstate claims, which turn on the relations between indigeneity and sovereignty. Here we are reminded of Charles Taylor's influential work on the politics of recognition (Taylor 1994). Taylor argued that contemporary debates about the survival of minority cultures turn on the Herderian idea that each culture has its own 'measure' and 'worth'. However, to figure out what is going on in these different property relations, I think we have to theorise the whole question of indigeneity in relation to sovereignty: are Indigenous property rights defined by states with recourse to restorative justice or distributive justice (Fraser and Honneth 2003)? This might lead us to very complicated and differential notions of postcoloniality, where the existing typologies of settler colonialism, imperial colonialism, internal colonialism, etc., seem inadequate. An ethnography of the politics of cultural recognition could explore how different forms of recognition (and denial) of property claims pan out differently on the ground, as Eva Mackey has done with reference to liberal multiculturalism in Canada (Mackey 1999) and Elizabeth Povinelli in Australia (Povinelli 2002). Framing such ethnographies within a historical framework would enable us to say something about the ascendance of different types of metropolitan property regimes.

Postcolonial Potlatching

The meanings and values of repatriation is a still unfolding process. We have scores of cases and elaborate debates about the proper place of cultural objects going back to the eighteenth century (Quatremère de Quincy 1796). However, the principal argument of this piece is that we have yet to establish a methodology for a broader understanding of the meaning of cultural property in the beginning of the twenty-first century. Departing from the three theoretical *topoi* of objects, property and recognition, I have attempted to sketch what such a methodology could look like. Its viability would depend upon its ability to produce analytic results and, in turn, set the agenda for a genuine transnational debate on the phenomenon.

I would like to close by returning to the two epigraphs at the outset. They represent the trajectory of an institution of singular importance in the history of anthropology, namely the potlatch, and the associated postcolonial story about the return of parts of its collection to the U'mista Cultural Centre in British Columbia, Canada. In closing, I intend to evoke a parallel between the potlatch and the institution of cultural property. When Marcel Mauss posed the double problem of what type of 'rule or legality compels the gift that has been received to be obligatorily reciprocated' and 'what power resides in the object given that causes its recipient to pay it back', he examined an overwhelming body of examples of ceremonial exchange in which the potlatch took on a special significance (Mauss 1990 [1924–25]) . Mauss characterised this institution as: 'at the same time juridical, economic, religious, and even aesthetic and morphological, etc.', adding 'political and domestic at the same time' (Mauss 1990 [1924–25]). In short, it was what he famously phrased as 'a total social fact'. I have tried to illuminate that the institution of cultural property tap some of the same conceptual sources as the potlatch and alas could be conceived as 'a total social fact'. As such, cultural property could be explored with Mauss' own comparative scope with reference to a range of transactions and events – such as the one in Victoria in 2004 – on sliding scales of obligation and reciprocity. Such an endeavour might lead to new answers to classic anthropological problems.

Notes

* I am indebted to the president of the World Archaeological Conference, Claire Smith, who initially encouraged me to contribute and organise a panel, entitled, 'Claiming Cultural Property across International Borders' at the 'Meanings and Values of Repatriation' conference at the Australian National University in Canberra, July 2005. I would also like to thank the panellists Richard West Jr., Deidre Brown, Lyndon Ormond Parker and the audience for a most stimulating discussion. I also wish to express my gratitude to the Department of Anthropology, Columbia University and the World Archaeological Congress for supporting my participation with travel grants. Among the many individuals who have helped me to shape my ideas and bring them to paper, I want to mention my teachers at Columbia, Elizabeth Povinelli,

Mahmood Mamdani and, especially, Brinkley Messick. Of course, none of these individuals is responsible for any of the remaining deficiencies.

1. Most academic treatments of repatriation do not explicitly pursue any theoretical interests and tend to gravitate towards normative implications at the institutional and academic disciplinary level (Bray 2001b; Bray and Killion 1994; Fforde, Hubert, and Turnbull 2002; Gibbon 2005; Jaarsma 2002; Messenger 1999 [1989]; Mihesuah 2000; Thomas 2000).
2. A list of signatories to the 1970 UNESCO Convention on the Means of Prohibiting and Preventing the Illicit Import, Export and Transfer of Ownership of Cultural Property is available at http://portal.unesco.org/la/convention.asp?KO=13039&language=E
3. The term 'cultural property' denotes historical and ethnographic objects and documents including manuscripts, works of the plastic and decorative arts, paleontological and archaeological objects and zoological, botanical and mineralogical specimens.
4. Legal scholars have been divided with regard to the question of whether 'cultural property' can be regarded simply as a branch of property law – along the lines of real property, personal property and intellectual property – or whether it requires its own legal regime. The argument in favour of a *sui generis* regime is that some objects are regarded as 'inalienable' by an entire community (be that a professional body of archaeologists, museum curators or an indigenous group) and therefore beyond any market value. Such objects are often vested with 'public interest': a form of collective responsibility to which duties rather than rights is attached (Merryman 1989). be exchanged for capital ((Radin 1993).
5. Jacknis (2000: 266–81) and Clifford (1997: 107–45) both state that the repatriation of the confiscated potlatch collection was conditional upon the material being professionally curated in a museum facility.

Bibliography

Appadurai, A. 1986. *The Social Life of Things: Commodities in Cultural Perspective*. Cambridge; New York: Cambridge University Press.

Bailkin, J. 2004. *The Culture of Property: the Crisis of Liberalism in Modern Britain*. Chicago: University of Chicago Press.

Baker, B.J., et al. 2001. 'Repatriation and the Study of Human Remains', in T.L. Bray (ed.), *The Future of the Past: Archaeologists, Native Americans, and Repatriation*. New York: Garland, pp. 69–89.

Barkan, E. and R. Bush. 2002. *Claiming the Stones/ Naming the Bones: Cultural Property and the Negotiation of National and Ethnic Identity, Issues and Debates*. Los Angeles: Getty Research Institute.

Bray, T.L. 2001. 'American Archaeologists and Native Americans', in T.L. Bray (ed.), *The Future of the Past: Archaeologists, Native Americans, and Repatriation*. New York: Garland, pp. 1–8.

——— and T.W. Killion. 1994. *Reckoning with the Dead: the Larsen Bay Repatriation and the Smithsonian Institution*. Washington: Smithsonian Institution Press.

Brilliant, R., M. Janeway and A. Szántó. 2001 (eds.). *Who Owns Culture?: Cultural Property and Patrimony Disputes in an Age Without Borders*. New York: National Arts Journalism Program.

Cash, P. 2001. 'Medicine Bundles: an Indigenous Approach to Curation', in T.L. Bray (ed.), *The Future of the Past: Archaeologists, Native Americans, and Repatriation*. New York: Garland, pp. 139–45.

Clifford, J. 1988. *The Predicament of Culture: Twentieth-Century Ethnography, Literature, and Art*. Cambridge, Mass.: Harvard University Press.

———. 1997. 'Four Northwest Coast Museums: Travel Reflections', in J. Clifford (ed.), *Routes: Travel and Translation in the Late Twentieth Century*. Cambridge, Mass.: Harvard University Press, pp. 107–145.

Coggins, C. 2005. 'Archaeology and the Art Market', in K. FitzGibbon (ed.), *Who Owns the Past?: Cultural Policy, Cultural Property, and the Law*. New Brunswick, N.J.: Rutgers University Press: The American Council for Cultural Policy, pp. 221–9.

Cole, D. 1995. *Captured Heritage: the Scramble for Northwest Coast Artifacts*. Norman: University of Oklahoma Press.

Coleman, E.B. 2005. *Aboriginal Art, Identity, and Appropriation, Anthropology and Cultural History in Asia and the Indo-Pacific*. Aldershot: Ashgate.

Derrida, J. 1991. *Donner le temps, La philosophie en effet*. Paris: Galilée.

Fforde, C., J. Hubert and P. Turnbull (eds). 2002. *The Dead and Their Possessions: Repatriation in Principle, Policy and Practice*. London: Routledge.

Fine-Dare, K.S. 2002. *Grave Injustice: the American Indian Repatriation Movement and NAGPRA*. Lincoln: University of Nebraska Press.

FitzGibbon, K. 2005. *Who Owns the Past?: Cultural Policy, Cultural Property, and the Law*. New Brunswick, N.J.: Rutgers University Press: The American Council for Cultural Policy.

Fraser, N. and H. Axel. 2003. *Redistribution or Recognition?: a Political-Philosophical Exchange*. London; New York: Verso.

Garza, C. and S. Powell. 2001. 'Ethics and the Past: Reburial and Repatriation in American Archaeology', in T.L. Bray (ed.), *The Future of the Past: Archaeologists, Native Americans, and Repatriation*. New York: Garland, pp. 37–56.

Greenfield, J. 1996. *The Return of Cultural Treasures*, 2nd ed. Cambridge: Cambridge University Press.

Hann, C.M. 1998. *Property Relations: Renewing the Anthropological Tradition*. New York: Cambridge University Press.

Heritier, A. 2003. *Genèse de la notion juridique de patrimoine culturel, 1750–1816*. Paris: L'Harmattan.

Hill, R.W. 2001. 'Regenerating Identity: Repatriation and the Indian Frame of Mind', in T.L. Bray (ed.), *The Future of the Past: Archaeologists, Native Americans, and Repatriation*. New York: Garland, pp. 81–96.

Hutt, S. 1998. 'Native American Cultural Property Law – Human Rights Legislation', *Arizona Attorney* 34: 18–21.

Jaarsma, S.R. 2002. *Handle with Care: Ownership and Control of Ethnographic Materials*. Pittsburgh: University of Pittsburgh Press.

Jacknis, I. 2000. 'Repatriation as Social Drama: The Kwakiutl Indians of British Columbia, 1922–1980', in D.A. Mihesuah (ed.), *Repatriation Reader: Who Owns American Indian Remains?*. Lincoln: University of Nebraska Press, pp. 266–81.

Johnson, T.R. 1999. *Contemporary Native American Political Issues, Contemporary Native American Communities*, vol 2. California: AltaMira Press.

Killion, T.W. 2001. 'On the Course of Repatriation: Process, Practice, and Progress at the National Museum of Natural History', in T.L. Bray (ed.), *The Future of the Past: Archaeologists, Native Americans, and Repatriation*. New York: Garland, pp. 149–68.

———— and P. Molloy. 1998. 'Repatriation's Silver Lining', in K.E. Dongoske, M. Aldenderfer and K. Doehner (eds.) Working Together: Native Americans and Archaeologists. Washington DC: Society for American Archaeology , pp. 111–17.

Ladd, E.J. 2001. 'A Zuni Perspective on Repatriation', in T.L. Bray (ed.), *The Future of the Past : Archaeologists, Native Americans, and Repatriation.* New York: Garland, pp. 107–15.

Latour, B. 2004. 'Scientific Objects and Legal Objectivity', in A. Pottage and M. Mundy (eds.), *Law, Anthropology, and the Constitution of the Social: Making Persons and Things.* New York: Cambridge University Press, pp. 73–114.

Levi -Strauss, C. 1992. *Tristes Tropiques.* New York: Penguin Books.

————. 1995. *Saudades Do Brasil.* Washington: University of Washington Press.

Lilley, I. 2000a. 'Native Title and the Transformation of Archaeology in the Postcolonial World', in I. Lilley (ed.), *Native Title and the Transformation of Archaeology in the Postcolonial World.* Sydney: University of Sydney.

————. 2000b. 'Professional Attitudes to Indigenous Interests in the Native Title Era: Settler Societies Compared', in I. Lilley (ed.), *Native Title and the Transformation of Archaeology in the Postcolonial World.* Sydney: University of Sydney, pp. 1–9.

Loring, S. 2001. 'Repatriation and Community Anthropology: The Smithsonian Institution's Arctic Studies Center, in T.L. Bray (ed.), The Future of the Past: Archaeologists, Native Americans, and Repatriation, New York: Garland Publishing, pp. 185–98.

McIntosh, R.J. and P.R. Schmidt. 1996. 'The African Past Endangered', in R.J. McIntosh and P.R. Schmidt (eds), *Plundering Africa's Past.* Bloomington: Indiana University Press, pp. 1–17.

————. 1996. *Plundering Africa's Past.* Bloomington: Indiana University Press.

McKeown, T. and S. Hutt. 2003. 'In the Smaller Scope of Conscience: The Native American Graves Protection and Repatriation Act Twelve Years After', UCLA Journal of Enviromental Law and Policy 21: 153–212

Mackey, E. 1999. *The House of Difference: Cultural Politics and National Identity in Canada, Sussex Studies in Culture and Communication.* New York: Routledge.

Macpherson, C.B. 1978. 'The Meaning of Property', in C.B. Macpherson (ed.), *Property, Mainstream and Critical Positions.* Toronto: University of Toronto Press, pp. 1–13.

Mauss, M. 1990. *The Gift: the Form and Reason for Exchange in Archaic Societies.* New York: W.W. Norton.

M'Bow, A. 1979. 'A Plea for the Return of an Irreplaceable Cultural Heritage to Those who Created It', *Museum* 31: 58.

Merryman, J.H. 1986. 'Two Ways of Thinking about Cultural Property', *American Journal of International Law* 80: 831–53.

————. 1989. 'The Public Interest in Cultural Property', *California Law Review* 77: 339.

————. 2000. *Thinking about the Elgin Marbles: Critical Essays on Cultural Property, Art, and Law.* The Hague: Kluwer Law International.

———— and A.E. Elsen. 2002. *Law, Ethics, and the Visual Arts,* 4th ed. The Hague: Kluwer Law International.

Messenger, P.M. 1999. *The Ethics of Collecting Cultural Property: Whose Culture?,* 2nd ed. Alburquerque: University of New Mexico Press.

Messick, B.M. 1993. *The Calligraphic State: Textual Domination and History in a Muslim Society. Comparative Studies on Muslim Societies 16.* Berkeley: University of California Press, pp. 1–50.

————. 2003. 'Property and the Private in a Sharia System', *Social Research* 70: 711.

Meyer, K.E. 1973. *The Plundered Past.* New York: Atheneum.

Mihesuah, D.A (ed.). 2000. *Repatriation Reader: Who Owns American Indian Remains?* University of Nebraska Press.

Miller, D. 2005. 'Materiality: an Introduction', in D. Miller (ed.), *Materiality*. Durham: Duke University Press.

Moore, S.F. 1978. *Law as Process: an Anthropological Approach*. London: Routledge and K. Paul.

———. 2001. 'Certainties Undone: Fifty Turbulent Years of Legal Anthropology, 1949–1999', *The Journal of the Royal Anthropological Institute* 7: 95–116.

Murphy, T. 2004. 'Legal Fabrications and the Case of "Cultural Property"', in A. Pottage and M. Mundy (eds), *Law, Anthropology, and the Constitution of the Social: Making Persons and Things*. Cambridge: Cambridge University Press, pp. 115–41.

Pottage, A. and M. Mundy (eds). 2004. *Law, Anthropology, and the Constitution of the Social: Making Persons and Things, Cambridge Studies in Law and Society*. Cambridge: Cambridge University Press.

Povinelli, E. 2002. *The Cunning of Recognition: Indigenous Alterities and the Making of Australian Multiculturalism, Politics, History, and Culture*. Durham: Duke University Press.

Prott, L. V. 'The Dja Dja Warrung Bark Etchings Case', International Journal of Cultural Property (2006) 13: 241–46.

——— and P.J. O'Keefe. 1992. 'Cultural Heritage' or "Cultural Property"?', *International Journal of Cultural Property* 1: 307–320.

Radin, M.J. 1993. *Reinterpreting Property*. Chicago: University of Chicago Press.

Riles, A. 2004. 'Property as Legal Knowledge: Means and Ends', *Journal of the Royal Anthropological Institute* 10: 775–95.

Savoy, B. 2003. *Patrimoine annexâe: Les biens culturels saisis par la France en Allemagne autour de 1800*. Paris: Maison des sciences de l'homme.

Skrydstrup, M. 2004. 'Should ICOM Adjudicate Cultural Property Disputes? A Review Essay from the Triennial in Seoul', *International Committee for Museums of Ethnography News* 39, http://museumsnett.no./icme2004/repatriation.html.

Solomon, D. 2006. 'Stolen Art? Questions for Philippe De Montebello', *The New York Times Magazine*, p. 30.

Spector, J. 2001. 'Reflections on Inyan Ceyaka Atonwan (Village at the Rapids) – a Nineteenth Century Wahpeton Dakota Summer Planting Village', in T.L. Bray (ed.), *The Future of the Past: Archaeologists, Native Americans, and Repatriation*. New York: Garland, pp. 201–213.

Strathern, M. and E. Hirsch. 2004. *Transactions and Creations: Property Debates and the Stimulus of Melanesia*. New York: Berghahn Books.

Swidler, N. 1997. *Native Americans and Archaeologists: Stepping Stones to Common Ground*. California: AltaMira Press.

Taussig, M. 2004. *My Cocaine Museum*. Chicago: University of Chicago Press.

Taylor, C. 1994. 'The Politics of Recognition', in A. Gutmann (ed.), *Multiculturalism*. Princeton, New Jersey: Princeton University Press, pp. 25–73.

Thomas, D.H. 2000. *Skull Wars: Kennewick Man, Archaeology, and the Battle for Native American Identity*. New York: Basic Books.

Trope, J.F. and W.R. Echo-Hawk. 2001. 'The Native American Graves Protection and Repatriation Act: Background and Legislative History', in T.L. Bray (ed.), *The Future of the Past : Archaeologists, Native Americans, and Repatriation*. New York: Garland, pp. 9–34.

Tsing, A.L. 2005. *Friction: an Ethnography of Global Connection*. Princeton, N.J.: Princeton University Press.

Tweedie, A.M. 2002. *Drawing Back Culture: the Makah Struggle for Repatriation*. Seattle: University of Washington Press.

U'mista Cultural Society. Retrieved 27 February 2006 from http://www.umista.org/

UNESCO. 1978. 'Statutes of the Intergovernmental Committee for Promoting the Return of Cultural Property to its Countries of Origin or its Restitution in case of Illicit Appropriation'. Paris: UNESCO.

Verdery, K. and C. Humphrey. 2004a. 'Introduction', in K. Verdery and C. Humphrey (eds), *Property in Question: Value Transformation in the Global Economy*. Oxford: Berg, pp. 1–25.

———. 2004b. *Property in Question: Value Transformation in the Global Economy*. Oxford: Berg.

Warren, K. 1999. 'A Philosophical Perspective on the Ethics and Resolution of Cultural Properties Issues', in P.M. Messenger (ed.), *The Ethics of Collecting Cultural Property: Whose Culture? Whose Property?* Alburquerque: University of New Mexico Press, pp. 1–25.

Watkins, J. 2000. *Indigenous Archaeology: American Indian Values and Scientific Practice*. California: AltaMira Press.

Williams, R.A. 1990. *The American Indian in Western Legal Thought: the Discourses of Conquest*. New York: Oxford University Press.

Willis, E. 2008. 'The Law, Politics and Historical Wounds: The Dja Dja Warrung Bark Etchings Case in Australia', *International Journal of Cultural Property* 15: 49–63.

Wylie, A. 2002. *Thinking from Things. Essays in the Philsophy of Anthropology*. Berkeley: University of California Press.

Zimmerman, L.J. 2001. 'Usurping Native American Voice', in T.L. Bray (ed.), *The Future of the Past: Archaeologists, Native Americans, and Repatriation*. New York: Garland, pp. 169–84.

———, K.D. Vitelli and J. Hollowell-Zimmer. 2003. *Ethical Issues in Archaeology*. California: Altamira Press.

7

Repatriation and the Concept of Inalienable Possession

Elizabeth Burns Coleman

The idea of an 'inalienable possession' is central to the justification of the repatriation of parts of museum collections, such as sacred objects, objects of patrimony, funerary objects and ancestral remains to the groups from which they were taken. The intuition that such objects are being rightfully returned does not rest on whether or not there is legal title to them, but on the special kinds of 'identity' relationships groups of people have with them. It is this identity relationship which defines an object as inalienable, as opposed something that is property, and alienable. For example, under the United States' 1997 *Native American Graves Protection and Repatriation Act* (NAGPRA), cultural patrimony is defined as an:

> object having ongoing historical, traditional, or cultural importance central to the Native American group or culture itself, rather than property owned by an individual Native American, and which, therefore, cannot be alienated, appropriated, or conveyed by any regardless of whether or not the individual is a member of the Indian tribe or Native Hawaiian organization and such object shall have been considered inalienable by such Native American group at the time the object was separated from such group. (Nason 1997: 241)

The implication here is that museums holding such objects do so wrongfully, on the basis that 'inalienable possession' creates or denotes an 'inalienable right'.

In this chapter, I will argue that the term 'inalienable possession' defines a kind of value, and a relationship between an object and a person or group's identity. This interpretation of the term is, I believe, uncontroversial. But it follows from this that objects of patrimony, and sacred objects, *can* be alienated. Repatriation laws should not be viewed as recognising an 'inalienable' right, or 'indigenous' (as opposed to western) values.[1] It should be thought of as the creation of a framework through which indigenous values can be expressed. Laws such as NAGPRA change the power relations between museums and indigenous groups in that they formally recognise that what indigenous people want for their cultural artefacts matters. However, if we do not recognise the potential for alienation in these, and in cultural rights, we risk 'freezing' the structures of indigenous societies, and, while seemingly giving them sovereignty in relation to objects of cultural patrimony, we deny them this sovereignty. These moral and political dimensions are at once uncovered and obscured by the term inalienable possession.

Inalienable Possession and Moral Rights

For nearly a century, linguists have been exploring the difference between alienable and inalienable possession. In 1914, Lévy-Bruhl noted that in Melanesian languages there were typically two classes of nouns, distinguished by a prefix that indicated different kinds of possession (Chappell and McGregor 1996: 3). One class of suffix-taking nouns designated parts of the body, kin, spatial relationships and objects closely related to a person, and all other nouns were represented by a free possessive morpheme. He described this difference as a difference between alienable and inalienable possession. Inalienable possession 'denotes an indissoluble connection between two entities – a permanent and inherent association between the possessor and the possessed' (Chappell and McGregor 1996: 4). As Lévy-Bruhl neatly encapsulated the concept, 'When I talk about my head, I do not intend to say that it belongs to *me,* but that it is *me*' (Chappell and McGregor 1996: 4). Since then, linguists have found many similar grammatical constructions in widely diverse languages.

For example, Susan Marsden says that, in contrast to a concept of property that implies something outside one's self, and can be taken from one, Gitksan and Tsimhian people (Canadian First Nations peoples) do not think of heritage and intellectual property as something external to them, but as a matter of identity: 'it is not so much "I own this" as "I *am* this" and "this *is* me", or perhaps more accurately, "we *are* this" and "this *is* us"' (Marsden, 2008: 159). Similarly, Fred Myers has pointed out that a distinction between alienable and inalienable property is made in Australian Pintupi constructions of property, which the Pintupi classify as either *walytja* or *yulytja*. The term *walytja* can refer to the objects associated with a person, a relative, to the possessive notion of 'one's own' such as 'my own camp' or 'my own father' or to reflexive concepts such as 'oneself', as in, 'I saw it myself'. The Pintupi concept of inalienable possession, which includes kin as well as experience, clearly connects the ideas of possession and identity.

We should not make the mistake of thinking that this contrast between alienable and inalienable possession is a conceptual difference distinguishing Western and non-Western societies. indigenous societies also recognise some objects as alienable. The Canadian First Nations, for example, initially grew wealthy from trade with settlers before being ravaged by smallpox and culturally suppressed within mission settlements. Small societies without a market economy may recognise and maintain the distinction in terms of the level of formality that surrounds objects with significance and objects that are defined by their utility (Keane 2001: 73). Moreover, Western societies also implicitly recognise this distinction, despite having no distinct term to designate it. According to Daniel Miller, inalienability may be created within a capitalist society through 'the power of consumption to extract items from the market and make them social or personal' (Miller 2001: 95). This is possible, Miller says, 'because it is the person who lies at the core of any local conceptualisation of the inalienable' (Miller 2001: 95). An example of this might be a woman's attachment to her wedding ring. Another ring of equal value or even one that is identical cannot replace such a ring. Its loss would involve the sense of losing part of her identity (Radin 1993: 37). This distinction is recognised at an institutional level, even if it is not categorised this way. Margaret Radin has pointed out that the strength of property claims in legal cases is perceived differently by jurors, and is determined differently by judges, when individuals credibly claim an attachment to property in some personal sense (Radin 1993: 2). Furthermore, the distinction is recognised in disputes over what should be viewed as property, or subject to commodification, in debates over whether blood or body parts such as kidneys should be available on the market, or whether we should allow women to carry pregnancies for financial gain.

This special, identity relationship in the concept of inalienable possession is the moral justification for repatriation, and presents the idea that there are people who should, rightfully, possess and control certain things because they are of special significance to them. But how strong a moral justification is it?

This might seem an unnecessary question, as the normative implications of possession and control appear to be built into the term. However, the idea that a right is inalienable has two interpretations. The first is that the right in question cannot be transferred, and the second is that it cannot be waived. An example of a right that cannot be transferred is a citizen's right to vote. This right cannot be transferred to another person. It is trivially true to say that some kinds of inalienable possession cannot be transferred. For example, my head is my head in a way that it cannot be your head. Similarly, my father was the man he was, and this relationship with me is not transferable to another person. Yet, other forms of inalienable possession can and must be transferable. For example, for paintings or carvings to be passed through generations as signs of identity, right to designs must be transferable. The very process of maintaining control of secret knowledge and, therefore, rights to land and sacred objects, and passing them on to the next generation, shows that they are conceived of as things that may be transferred, as well as potentially lost or alienated. The claim that they cannot be alienated, therefore, does not suggest that they cannot be transferred, but that the right person or group should control them.

To say that a moral right cannot be waived has a different implication. We might think that people have a right to freedom, and that right is inalienable, so that they cannot choose to become slaves. Similarly, we might think that if someone has a right to life, then it is always wrong for someone to take their life but, equally, if that right is 'inalienable', we may think that this is something that cannot be given up, so that a person cannot, morally, choose euthanasia, or to suicide. If the right to life is absolute, taking life is always wrong. If the right to life is inalienable, then the person whose life it is cannot choose to end it. So, if we thought inalienable possession implied an inalienable right to control objects, or to possess certain kinds of objects, we would be making a very strong claim indeed. We might think that this meant that museums could never be rightful proprietors of cultural heritage and that indigenous groups could not, morally, waive rights or alienate cultural property.

But a grammatical construction is not itself a moral justification – it is a categorisation. The grammatical construction reflects our view of the world and our values; it does not justify them. So while the term 'inalienable possession' may be useful in distinguishing between different constructions of possession grammatically, it is not as useful in moral reasoning. The reason for this is that any argument in which it is used will beg the question: the conclusion that dispossession is wrong, or impossible, will be already contained within the premise that something is 'inalienable'. This must be established, rather than assumed. To break out of this circularity, we need to find a way of discussing the relationship that is morally pertinent without conflating it with the conclusion that these rights cannot, or should not be waived.

In my discussion of the concept of inalienable rights in terms of transferability, I pointed out that the term inalienable possession suggests that the right person or group should control certain objects. This link has also been discussed by anthropologists. Myers comments that a similar foundation for the concept of inalienable property as *walytja* is suggested by the shared root of 'proper' and 'property' in the Latin word *proprius*, meaning 'private or peculiar to oneself' (Myers 1988: 54). A similar point is made by Stephen Pritchard, who has explored the concept of property and the concept of 'properness' in relation to the appropriation of Maori *ta moko* (tattooing) (Prichard 2001: 31). So, something may be private, or peculiar to oneself, and subject to proper and improper use or appropriation by others. A distinction may be drawn between the concept of 'inalienable possession' and the concept of 'property' in terms of the identity relationship contained within the concept, and the sense that an object properly belongs to someone. This is captured in the sense that something is 'properly one's own'.

From now on I wish to use the term 'ownership', in the sense of properly one's own, instead of 'inalienable possession'. If what is morally at issue is an identity relationship between people and things, then the way in which something relates to our identity, and is owned, determines the strength of our claims in relation to it.

'Constitutive' and 'Noncontingent' Ownership

I suggested above that the connection between identity and property in constructions of 'inalienable possession' is better referred to as 'ownership', in the sense of something properly one's own. The sense of ownership is possessive, but does not necessarily refer to 'property'. It also captures the sense of something being related to one's identity. Yet ownership involves at least two different relationships between possessors and possessed, which I will describe as 'constitutive', and 'noncontingent' possession.

A constitutive relationship concerns the rights that constitute something as the entity that it is. As Radin has pointed out, the word 'person' stems from the Latin word *persona*, meaning, in part, a theatrical role. In Roman law, *persona* came to mean 'an entity possessing rights and duties' (Radin 1993: 39). We can also see this in terms of a role an individual plays. For example, the rights and duties of a king are distinct from the rights and duties of a slave. The rights and duties one has may be considered as being constitutive of a role, and of having certain kinds of identity. An individual without rights did not have a persona. Thus, rights may be constitutive of being a person within a society. One might argue that this applies equally to rights in contemporary societies. For instance, for the Yolngu people described by Howard Morphy, rights in land and ceremonial objects are constitutive of being a person within those societies. In the Yolngu system of law, the foundation of all rights is clan ownership of *madayin* (which might be loosely described as the sacred law and the objects, paintings, music and ritual in which it is represented), and the land associated with the *madayin*. Rights in *madayin* and land are established through kinship or through a ceremonial relationship. So, a person who can establish rights in *madayin* has rights to speak for, and make decisions about, the land (Morphy 1991: 45–49). These rights are constitutive of the *persona*, as in the argument presented by Lévy-Bruhl: when we use the concept of possession in application to these rights, we do not say that we possess them in the way that we possess something that can be sold on a market. J.E. Penner has claimed that, 'one cannot conceive of them as separated from a person – they are constitutive of the rights [that] being a full person, a subject of the law, entails having' (Penner 1996: 804). Such rights constitute who we are as social beings; they are institutional facts.

A noncontingent relationship between possessor and possessed would include things like a person's body parts, friends and ancestors. These are historical facts. My history is something that is specific to me, even if I share a history, for example, having certain ancestors in common with other members of my family. Such facts are not a contingent feature of being the person I am. The Pintupi construction of *walytja* is a point of interest in this context, because it emphasises our individual, historical relationships with people and places. As such, it contains a concept of ownership that is not transferable and cannot be alienated. The concept of possession of an object, such as a wedding ring, as 'personal', that is, as an object that, for the person involved, has become part of their identity, is another example of a nontransferable relationship. While I might treasure my mother's wedding ring, it cannot mean to me what it means to her. My treasuring it as part of my family history creates it as part of my identity in a different way from the way it might be said to be part of her identity.

My treasuring my mother's wedding ring and keeping it from circulation as a commodity would also constitute it as an inalienable possession, yet this relationship is transferable. I could, for example, pass it on to my niece, and one would hope that she would treasure it. Myers has pointed out that, 'An object's value may shift through time as individuals or groups are forced or elect to enter treasures into the market place or as an ordinary commodity becomes revered by a collector or family members and takes on the value of an inalienable possession' (Myers 2001: 9). We should not consider inalienable possession to refer to a stable category of objects, but as a process of value creation (Kirshenblatt-Gimblett 1988: 291). This process involves investing an object with 'symbolic density', which it accrues over time, and a process of holding or keeping dear that restricts the object's circulation and exchange (Myers 2001: 9). Objects do not have a value in the way they have a colour or a weight or some other physical property; they are given values within social contexts and through social practices.

It is interesting that the Pintupi construction of *walytja* includes experiences. This highlights that some experiences, such as the Jewish experience of the Holocaust, or Londoners' experience of the Blitz, may also become dense with symbolic meaning and people may become 'possessive' of their experiences. Rituals and stories are created to pass these experiences on, and there are restrictions about how these experiences are represented. The creation of stories and rituals, and the symbolic density that may be associated with objects, is effectively the creation of 'a form' for transferability.

Strictly, one might say that both constitutive and noncontingent possession are contingent, historical facts. A contingent truth is something that is not necessarily true. All historical truth is contingently true, because things might have been different. Australia might have been colonised on 30 January 1788, rather than 28 January, had the winds been different. Similarly, it might be thought, if I had been born 100 years earlier, I would not have enjoyed voting rights. I might not have been born. But I was. And it is true that I was born in Australia, in 1961, and that my parents are the people that they are, and that I spent my childhood in Warrandyte, outside Melbourne, Victoria, and that I have a right to vote. While none of these are necessary truths from some 'objective' perspective, my history is necessary to being who I am as a person. However, I want to maintain a distinction between institutional facts and noncontingent facts, as the institutional facts about me, such as the fact that I am a citizen of Australia, and that I have voting rights, may be changed, suddenly. I could have my voting rights removed from me by law, just as suddenly as women alive at the creation of the Australian nation had them given to them. So, the idea of ownership as being 'inalienable' must rely heavily on what I am calling noncontingent ownership. Noncontingent ownership creates certain kinds of moral rights that we can easily recognise and identify with, while constitutive possession requires an independent justification. Let me elaborate on this difference by means of some examples.

Ownership, Property and Rights

I possess a table and chairs that I was given by my father. They are probably sixty or seventy years old. I remember sitting at the table with my sisters for family occasions, such as Christmas dinners, at my grandmother's house. I can remember where it was in the room, and the view out the window, and I can imagine my father's family sitting around it for Sunday lunches. This table is now my legal property. But, I do not possess it in the same way that I possess other legal property, such as my car.

If I were to go outside now and destroy my car with an axe, my action might be considered stupid, and I might be criticised for being wasteful, but in the end it is no-one else's business. If I take to the table with an axe, it is clearly the business of other people, and, potentially, a serious breach of my family relationships. I can sell my car, however, I feel I cannot sell my table without consulting my sisters. If I want to get a different table, I am, or at least I would feel, obliged to ask my sisters if they wanted it, and to offer to sell it to one of them, or to give it to one of them, before I sold it to someone outside the family. This limit to my property right is not a function of possessing joint property in the table with my sisters, or of some other kind of legal reason. My father gave my sisters other tables, and they possess other items from the family. This limit is a function of the value I place on the table as an object that is emblematic of my history. It now has symbolic density.

Part of what limits my potential actions in relation to my table is the fact that my sisters have the same identity relationship with the table as I do. We all stand in the same noncontingent relationship to it, firstly because we share the same father, and secondly because we all share those memories of my grandmother's house, and the family dinners. This relationship is quite independent of which of us holds property in it. In valuing the table as part of my identity, and recognising the same historical connection between the table and my sisters, I appear to acknowledge that my family has moral rights in relation to the table, and that I hold and possess it as a steward.

My table became symbolically dense through the process of valuing. First, the gift to me from my father has significance, particularly now he is dead. But then, the table came to be representative of more than my relationship with my father, but of the identity and the history of my family. It was able to become emblematic of this history because of its noncontingent relationship with it. It might be thought that the moral rights I recognise my sisters as having in my table, conceived of as a family heirloom of which I am a steward, are one of the structures through which the concept of the family is embodied. The rights that I acknowledge structure my relationship with my sisters in certain ways, and they also structure the distinction between who is and who is not 'family'. It also seems that these rights can grow or diminish for future generations, as the noncontingent relationship depends in part on traditions being maintained, and memories of those traditions.

Accordingly, we might say that although a proprietor has legal rights in what they possess, at the same time there might be moral rights determined by ownership relations that limit their actions. So legal property and ownership in the sense that I am using it, come apart. One can be said to own something one does not possess as property, and to possess as property something one does not own. This point is important in relation to whether possession more generally is necessary in relation to cultural patrimony and heritage, for there are some things that one might own that one does not, and cannot, possess.

Consider this. Though not everyone would agree, it might be argued that if there were a single site of significance for Australians, and the '*mana*' of Australian identity, it would be Gallipoli, in Turkey. Gallipoli is a small cove, a beach surrounded by high cliffs. On 25 April 1915, the Australian and New Zealand Army Corps (ANZAC) landed there as part of an attack on Turkey by the Allied forces. The Turkish forces had advance warning. The ANZAC soldiers landed, climbed up the cliff faces through a hail of bullets and dug themselves trenches, where they remained for eight months, until their retreat. Eight thousand young men died. This battle and defeat is considered by many people to be central to Australian identity. Through it we weave the myths of our egalitarianism and mateship. At that time, and since, the conflict at Gallipoli was considered the test of 'fire and blood' that made Australia, which had only become a commonwealth of states in 1901, a nation. ANZAC Day is a national public holiday, commemorated all over the country with services for the fallen. No other celebration of the nation, such as Australia Day, nor other public symbol, nor site such as Uluru (Ayers Rock) or the Sydney Opera House, can be said to be as important for our national identity. A Durkheimian theorist would describe the site of the ANZAC landing as sacred. It is a symbol of our national identity, and draws people together in acts of collective remembrance. On 25 April each year, thousands of Australians go to Gallipoli for a dawn memorial service. Here is a site of national significance for Australian identity, yet it is not Australian property, and it is not in our possession. There is nothing about a site of national significance, even one that is intrinsic to collective identity, that morally requires it to be property or to be possessed by its owners.

However, just because an object or place can become an intrinsic part of a person or group's identity, it does not necessarily follow that it will always be a part of this identity. Take the example of a wedding ring that a person considers to be part of their identity. Marriages fall apart. People get divorced. A ring, which once might have seemed so important, might be taken off and eventually misplaced. Similarly, cultural patrimony might no longer be considered important to the identity of cultural groups. Kim Akerman, for example, has spoken of being involved in negotiations for the repatriation of secret sacred objects to Aboriginal groups, and of being told, 'You keep it – we are Christians here' (see Akerman in this volume). Here, cultural values have changed, and the old religion repudiated. The sacred objects in question were no longer a part of this group's identity. They were no longer considered sacred and they were no longer considered an important part of their cultural patrimony and identity.

The example of my grandmother's table shows that property and ownership can come apart, and are logically distinct. The example of ANZAC Cove shows that one can own things one does not, never has and, in all probability, never will possess. While the sense of ownership may be a necessary condition for people to claim rights in relation to an object, it is not a sufficient reason for handing something over to them as their possession. The Turkish Government is under no obligation to hand over Gallipoli to the Australian Government.

It is often said that property is not so much a relationship between a person and a thing, but a relationship between people, mediated by a thing. On Wesley Hohfeld's widely accepted analysis, a right is correlated with a duty (Hohfeld 1919). For example, if a person has a property right in something, everyone else has a duty not to interfere with it. Repatriation recognises, and in some cases legally creates, a set of rights in terms of a specific class of objects, and redistributes power in relation to those objects. It recognises that people other than the property holder may also be rights holders, and that the property holder may have a duty to them. It does not follow that the owner must also be in possession of an object. The duty to the owner is a duty for consultation about the use of objects we possess. But there is more than 'mere' consultation involved. The recognition of rights in this context is also an institutional recognition that there are particular people who are 'the proper' people to determine what happens to something, and who may restrict its circulation and use. This does not privilege the possessor or proprietor of an object in relation to rights in an object, but may severely limit their rights.

Recognising that this is a process of value creation, rather than a stable situation, is important to understanding the broader moral and political implications of the recognition of rights that flow from this kind of relationship. My examples of the ring, and the sacred objects, show that changes in our values can lead to the repudiation of things we previously considered ours. The moral justification for repatriation, and for control over the use of an object, depends on a sense of ownership. Without this sense of ownership, there is no justification for something being repatriated, or for a group to claim to control an object's use. Accordingly, to say that a group, even after consultation, *cannot* alienate something is ridiculous. While promising sovereignty, the use of the term 'inalienable possession' may actually deny it by denying the group choices. The suggestion that something cannot be alienated does not respect indigenous people's ideas of what is or is not a part of their identity.

Let me turn now to the wider claims that can be made for cultural rights based on constitutive ownership. Conceptually, one can concede that one's identity may be tied up with legal rights, for example, the right to vote. I referred to this earlier in the paper in my discussion of Roman law and the concept of a persona, and I suggested that some cultural rights such as Yolngu rights in *madayin* might be considered rights that are constitutive of being a person within Yolngu law. Legal rights depend on the existence of particular social institutions and if these institutions do not exist, then neither do the rights. This point appears to have been at the heart of Justice Brennan's decision in Mabo v Queensland (No. 2), a landmark case in the Australian High Court that recognised a form of native title. Brennan was of the opinion that:

> Where a clan or group has continued to acknowledge the laws ... to observe the customs based on the traditions of that clan or group, whereby their traditional connection with the land has been substantially maintained, the traditional community title of that clan ... can be said to remain in existence. (Borrows 2004)

But even if the social institutions do remain in place, it does not follow that the associated rights should be frozen in time. We can change the rights we have within an institution, without destroying the institution itself. For example, until the Magna Carta it was widely held legally, and by custom, that the king ruled absolutely and without limitation. Yet people curtailed the rights and liberties of the king. Other countries, such as France, rid themselves of the monarchy entirely. (It would be a conceptual mistake, therefore, to think that the only rights indigenous people could have in relation to land are the traditional rights and customs observed at the time of colonisation. This is the reason that the High Court's decision that native title rights to resources in land were of a customary or traditional kind and did not include a right over minerals and petroleum in *Western Australia v Ward; Attorney-General (NT) v Ward; Nigarmara v Northern Territory* [2002] may have seemed so unsatisfactory to many people.)

While it is a social fact that rights are intrinsic to our identity, the idea that these rights cannot be alienated also constitutes a demand that the structure of a group itself remains frozen in time. This is not merely conceptually absurd, but it is morally unsupportable. Institutional and customary rights require independent moral justification; they do not justify themselves. If a husband were to claim, based on medieval law and custom, that he had a right to treat his wife as a chattel, and to rape her if he chose, and then tried to justify this on the basis that this right was 'inalienable' because it constituted his identity, we would not accept his 'identity' or sense of ownership to be sufficient as a moral justification of such a relationship. The rights we have cannot be justified in relation to our identity without introducing circularity to our argument, as our rights constitute our identities. Rights may be gained and they may be lost, even when an institution that supports them, such as the family or the monarchy, remains in place. This is not necessarily something to be lamented. To deny this is to deny indigenous groups the autonomy to reinterpret their institutions. The effect of legislation stating that there is a class of objects, places or things that cannot be alienated by indigenous groups is to freeze the structure of their societies.

Before concluding, I wish to raise, and answer, three objections to my argument. The first that I anticipate is some shock that I appear to have argued the impossible: that inalienable possessions are alienable and may be held as the property of other people. And it might be thought that my examples, which are largely based on my explanations of relationships with rights, tables and European history, are too culturally specific and fail to adequately address the significance of ancestral remains and sacred objects for indigenous peoples. But I think the objection misses the point of my argument. I have not attempted to justify the *status quo*. I am not suggesting that ancestral remains should not be returned to groups who think reburial is important, or who need ceremonial objects for the observance of ritual. The analysis of noncontingent identity in part explains why it might be important for remains to be in particular places, and the role of people who claim to speak for them. What I have attempted to justify is the choice of these groups to alienate certain things. It might be obvious to point out that different practices are acceptable within different cultural groups, but it is an obvious point worth making in this context. I have spoken to museum curators who hold objects in their collections, including human remains, that they feel they hold legitimately because the community from which those remains came consider this an acceptable practice. If these were inalienable, this would not be possible. To insist that human remains, sacred objects and cultural patrimony are inalienable does not respect cultural differences, and does not reflect all indigenous peoples' cultural values. It imposes a moral value.

A second conceivable objection is that my examples of tables and rings constitute an explanation of the values involved in inalienable possession, rather than a justification of them. I believe I have explained in a way that can be easily recognised by non-indigenous people some of the values involved in the concept of inalienable possession. But what justifies holding these values? It might be suggested that these values are inherently conservative, and support nationalistic jingoism and that therefore we should not adopt or support them. They are conservative. Moreover, it is true they support forms of nationalism and collective identity that can be extraordinarily destructive.

Radin's work on what she has called property for personhood, which I have termed noncontingent ownership, identifies the danger of fetishism about objects (Radin 1993: 43). Not all of our relationships with objects that form part of our identity can be considered 'healthy' or conducive to human flourishing. Serbia and Kosovo have fought wars for possession of an ancient battleground, with both sides claiming it as essential for their national identity. Such wars might be considered an example of this kind of fetishism and of the potential for 'inalienable possessions' to fuel nationalism. Yet this strikes me as a further reason for recognising that possession as property and absolute control over cultural patrimony are not necessary for the maintenance of identity relations between people and objects. If each group were to recognise, and to respect, the historical relationship of the other with the battleground, it would not matter which territory the site fell in any more than it matters that Gallipoli is not in Australia.

I think the best justification for the recognition of rights of ownership comes from understanding how ownership constitutes our relationships with others. Cultural patrimony or heritage is symbolically dense, that is, it is a symbol for community as well as creating a structure for that community. My recognition of a table as a family heirloom structures my relationships by connecting me with some people (family members) in terms of our similarities, and excluding others (non family members). Furthermore, the table as heritage mediates relationships between family members. But similarly, the recognition of these relationships is not coincidental to our relationships with other groups; it is the embodiment of our relationships with other groups. Turkey's recognition of Australia's (and New Zealand's) connection with Gallipoli is recognition of similarity: a shared experience of a war, and an expression of empathy for the loss of lives. This recognition and cooperation embodies the 'friendship' between the nations. The recognition of indigenous rights in relation to ancestral remains, sacred objects and objects of patrimony is similarly the creation, and embodiment, of a particular kind of relationship with them. This involves an acknowledgement of their histories and differences as distinct groups and it also creates a certain kind of ethical relationship with them. By acknowledging indigenous groups' ownership of cultural patrimony, ancestral remains and sacred objects we recognise their distinctive history and identity and we engage with those groups in a different fashion.

The Value of Inalienable Possession

The relationship between person and object that is generally termed 'inalienable possession', which I have called ownership, justifies a claim for consultation about, and a significant degree of control over, what happens to certain objects, without necessarily justifying their possession as property. It does not justify an inalienable right to those objects, or to cultural rights that constitute identity. This is a very modest conclusion and it is far from the levels of control and possession that many people might think desirable. But the power and moral certainty promised in the concept of inalienable possession rested on an error of reasoning. The concept of inalienable possession is a grammatical category that reflects values but does not justify them. While it may be used as a rhetorical tool in claims for cultural rights, and while it may sound impressive for the strong moral claim it seems to make, it presupposes an outcome that does not necessarily reflect the values it supposedly protects. Moreover, the term contains a sting in its tail: it freezes rights and the structures of society in a way that limits indigenous rights to those that were held in the past. By recognising that inalienable possession is a process of holding dear, of interpreting and creating a value, we limit the moral claim that seems to follow from the assertion that something is an inalienable possession but we also acknowledge and validate the processes by which social institutions change.

Debates about repatriation and inalienable possession do more than highlight the different ways in which we value things. They highlight the social structures we create in the recognition of those values. Repatriation is a formal recognition that there are different values for something that may be held as property and it redistributes rights in a way that provides a platform for these values to be expressed. In doing so, it formally recognises the ethical relationships of rights and duties held by owners and proprietors and changes the power relationships between indigenous people and museums. This outcome may be more modest than some may have hoped, but it is significant.

Notes

1.   In Australia, it is common to use the term 'Indigenous' capitalized as a proper noun when referring to Aboriginal and Torres Strait islander peoples. However, in this paper, the term 'indigenous' is used to refer to any indigenous people anywhere. I have carefully reserved capital letters for proper nouns, for example, Aboriginal (referring to Aboriginal Australians), Yolngu, Torres Strait Islanders.

Bibliography

Borrows, J. 2004. 'Living Traditions: the Resurgence of indigenous Law', *Australian Institute of Aboriginal and Torres Strait Islander Studies Seminar, 22 March 2004*. Canberra: AIATSIS.

Chappell, H. and W. McGregor. 1996. 'Prolegomena to a Theory of Inalienability', in H. Chappell and W. McGregor (eds), *The Grammar of Inalienability: a Typological Perspective on Body Part Terms and the Part-Whole Relation*. Berlin: Mouton de Gruyter, pp. 3–30.

Hohfeld, W.N. 1919. *Fundamental Legal Conceptions as Applied in Judicial Reasoning and Other Legal Essays*. New Haven: Yale University Press.

Keane, W. 2001. 'Money is No Object', in F.R. Myers (ed.), *The Empire of Things: Regimes of Value and Material Culture*. Sante Fe: School of American Research Press, pp. 65–90.

Kirshenblatt-Gimblett, B. 2001. 'Art and Material Culture: a Conversation with Annette Weiner', in F.R. Myers (ed.), *The Empire of Things: Regimes of Value and Material Culture*. Sante Fe: School of American Research Press, pp. 257–68.

Marsden, S. 2008. 'Northwest Coast *Adawx* Study', in C. Bell and V. Napoleon (eds), *First Nations' Cultural Heritage and Law*, vol. 1, *Case Studies, Voices, and Perspectives*. Vancouver: University of British Columbia Press, pp. 114–49.

Miller, D. 2001. 'Alienable Gifts and Inalienable Commodities', in F.R. Myers (ed.), *The Empire of Things: Regimes of Value and Material Culture*. Sante Fe: School of American Research Press, pp. 91–118.

Morphy, H. 1991. *Ancestral Connections: Art and an Aboriginal System of Knowledge*. Chicago: Chicago University Press.

Myers, F.R. 1988. 'Burning the Truck and Holding the Country: Property, Time, and the Negotiation Identity among Pintupi Aborigines', in T. Ingold, D. Riches and J. Woodburn (eds), *Hunters and Gatherers 2: Property Power and Ideology*. Oxford: Berg, pp. 35–51.

————. 2001. 'Introduction: the Empire of Things', in F.R. Myers (ed.), *The Empire of Things: Regimes of Value and Material Culture.* Sante Fe: School of American Research Press, pp. 3–61.

Nason, J.D. 1997. 'Native American Intellectual Property Rights', in B. Ziff and P.V. Rao (eds), *Borrowed Power: Essays on Cultural Appropriation.* New Brunswick: Rutgers University Press, pp. 237–54.

Penner, J.E. 1996. 'The "Bundle of Rights" Picture of Property', *UCLA Law Review* 43(3): 711–820.

Prichard, S. 2001. 'An Essential Marking: Maori Tattooing and the Properties of Identity', *Theory, Culture and Society* 18(4): 27–45.

Radin, M.J. 1993. *Reinterpreting Property.* Chicago: University of Chicago Press.

Legal Authorities

Western Australia v Ward; Attorney-General (NT) v Ward; Nigarmara v Northern Territory [2002] High Court of Australia, 8 August 2002.

8

Consigned to Oblivion:
People and Things Forgotten
in the Creation of Australia

John Morton

> The Australian Government recognises that the preservation, support and promotion of Indigenous culture, art and heritage is an essential component in addressing some of the disadvantages faced by Indigenous Australians. The Government also acknowledges that Australia's Indigenous culture, art and heritage are dynamic and powerful forces in contemporary Indigenous society and a unique aspect of Australian life.

These are the first words appearing on a web page devoted to 'Indigenous arts and culture' maintained by the Australian federal Department of Foreign Affairs and Trade. Later, on the same web page, the following paragraph appears:

> In September 2000 the Federal Government funded two support programs to assist with the return of Indigenous human remains and secret sacred objects from national, State and Territory museums within Australia. The Museums Support Program assists museums with identification and the Community Support Program assists Indigenous communities with the return of ancestral remains and secret sacred objects.

From these remarks, I initially register two straightforward (but not trivial) matters: that repatriation is a national issue and that this issue, while being particularly associated with museums and 'the return of ancestral remains and secret sacred objects', is part of a larger attempt to promote 'Indigenous art and culture'. In this chapter, I want to argue that repatriation should be understood as much more than the return of 'ancestral remains and secret sacred objects'. Rather, this 'national issue' is one of a more general reassignment of power to Indigenous Australians – although the very idea that this is a national issue calls into question the degree to which and how 'Indigenous Australians' and other kinds of Australians can be distinguished.

In this I take my cue from a number of writers who have commented on the ways in which official and public views of Aboriginality position Aboriginal people as what one might paradoxically call 'near strangers'. So, for example, Gelder and Jacobs have undertaken a discursive study of the way in which 'indigenous claims for sacred sites and sacred objects' in recent decades have been 'crucial in the recasting of Australia's sense of itself' (Gelder and Jacobs 1998: xi) – a matter of mirroring between 'black' and 'white' Australia that Maddock had earlier drawn attention to when he wrote about the idea of sacred sites spreading from anthropological discourse on Aborigines into common parlance about places of national significance in Australia and overseas, such as the Melbourne Cricket Ground and Gallipoli (Maddock 1991: 213–32). More specifically, Lattas (1990: 50–69: 1991: 307–24; 1992: 45–58) has convincingly demonstrated how the project through which the nation refounds itself through the appropriation of Aboriginality by Australians at large is essentially redemptive in character – a perspective that Batty has recently deployed to describe the repatriation of secret sacred objects as a 'white redemption ritual' (Batty 2005: 29–36). The position consistent in and common to these outlooks is that some sort of problematic 'hybridisation' is occurring in the encounter between Aborigines and other Australians – the implication being that repatriation in general stems from such 'cross fertilisation'.

'Cross fertilisation' is not a new phenomenon but, as this chapter argues, the idea of repatriation is a result of hybridity having undergone a number of transformations – transformations that are indeed ongoing. The notion of reassigning power presupposes that power has been distributed differently in the past, such that a particular kind of adjustment is required, a matter which places repatriation squarely in the domain of the national narrative and, more particularly, within the struggle for ideological high ground that is characteristic of the so called 'history wars' (Macintyre and Clark 2003). My view in that regard is that the history wars are not really about history at all, if by that term we mean that complex manner by which the future unfolds an outcome of the past. Rather, the history wars are about ideology, or what I prefer to call 'foundational mythology', in this case the founding in question being the creation of Australia by an act of settlement in 1788 – the date of the assumption of sovereignty. The very idea of Australia is fundamentally conditioned by that one act and, to the extent that Australia has persisted since that founding, the national narrative could only have continued so long as the act has been continually affirmed.

Australia, as we know from its birthday on 26 January, came into being in 1788. Before that, there was nothing, or better to say, 'nothing of the kind' (no other nation) – hence *terra nullius* or 'empty land'. On the other hand, for this creation story to continue, and hence for the nation to continue as a legitimate entity, the latter needs constant refounding and the former needs constant reaffirmation. This is the only way that the continuity of Australia can be instituted in the face of change – as we know, for example, in the 1992 Mabo judgement, when the High Court of Australia stated (though not quite in these terms) that it could not tamper with sovereignty without sawing off the branch on which it was sitting. Hence, as Wolfe has suggested, at the moment that the High Court denied *terra nullius*, it simultaneously affirmed it (1994: 93–152). It could not be otherwise. To the extent that native title can be taken as paradigmatic of the very idea of repatriation, I want to suggest that 'it could not be otherwise' in all registers of repatriation: of land, of human remains, of objects and of 'voice'.

A Typology of Repatriation

Taking my cue from Elazar Barkan and Ronald Bush (2002: 1–15), I want to suggest that repatriation is much more than the return of human remains and material objects of various kinds, because those things are part of a much larger concept of 'cultural property' that, in Barkan and Bush's terms, encompasses at least three different types of phenomena. As they say:

> … one might divide cultural property into three 'ideal types' according to the 'tangibility' of what is involved. One type is material and tangible property, which is unique and indivisible. In cases of disputes over such property, where the condition of sole possession obtains, there is always a potential demand for repatriation and restitution. Another type is intangible property, such as folktales, music, and folk remedies, where the primary issues concern not restitution but license and control, particularly in those cases where the group regards outside appropriation as either 'unfair' or 'sacrilegious'. The third type is still more intangible: trade in 'representations', especially those involved in the advancement of an insurgent identity whose embodiment has to do with new forms or discourses. (2002: 8)

However, it is perhaps too problematic to think of tangible property being more amenable to 'potential demand for repatriation and restitution', because demands for rights in so-called intangible property also often take this form. In each case, the right to possess and freely dispose of cultural property is claimed in terms of the restoration of some 'original' right that has been occluded, lost or appropriated. In the Australian Indigenous arena one need only think of demands for recognition of artistic copyright or for the right to 'self represent' in film or literature to see that they are part of a more general demand to recognise rights and interests in an otherwise colonised domain. The drive to transcend colonialism is naturally rooted in a precolonial past when Aboriginal peoples possessed their own forms of sovereignty. And it finds its expression in many diverse phenomena, most notably including land rights and native title, as well as the return of portable objects, the recognition of intellectual property rights, and the fostering of Indigenous agency in fields of representation. Even the demand for self-sufficiency in the economic sphere has been couched in these terms – that is, in terms of what I have called the reassignment of power.[1]

When we think in these terms, it is evident that repatriation as a whole finds its logic not simply in nationalism, but in the latter's late-modern or 'postcolonial' form. As the Department of Foreign Affairs and Trade's web site says, 'the preservation, support and promotion of Indigenous culture' becomes an issue not simply because 'Indigenous culture, art and heritage are dynamic and powerful forces in contemporary Indigenous society', but also because they are 'a unique aspect of Australian life'. Indeed, the logic of repatriation follows perfectly that of the simultaneous enhancement of localisation and globalisation characteristic of late capitalism (Friedman 1990: 311–28) in the sense that it is at once figured as a demand that things tangible or otherwise become more parochial, in being rightfully returned to their 'original' owners, and yet also a demand that this be achieved within the ideological structure of inalienable human rights guaranteed by international law. Hence, the global logic of repatriation mirrors the idea of a nation as a plural entity within a framework of multiculturalism and universal citizenship.

Of course, it is as citizens of Australia that Indigenous people make privileged claims upon those aspects of Australian heritage that can be said to be primarily, primordially or exclusively their own. Barkan points out that 'The modern concept of "cultural property" was coined by the Hague Convention of 1954 and is based on the belief that "damage to cultural property belonging to any people whatsoever means damage to the cultural heritage of all mankind since each people makes its contribution to the culture of the world"' (Barkan 2002: 21–2). Paraphrasing this to more adequately reflect the Australian situation, one might say that our ideas of cultural property are based on the belief that damage to the cultural property of Australia's Indigenous peoples means damage to the cultural heritage of Australia as a whole since Australia's identity arises out of the many contributions of its diverse peoples.

Yet Indigenous cultural property is uniquely positioned and is in certain respects quite unlike the cultural property of other groups occupying space under the national umbrella, including (perhaps especially) that of the Anglo–Celtic population. This is simply because its national lineage is deeper, thus reflecting the quite peculiar position that Indigenous groups have within the framework of Australian multiculturalism: they are now known as the original owners of the country. In the heritage stakes, Indigenous people therefore have what might be called a 'prior claim' – a claim on the nation that is discursively articulated by such phrases as 'We were here first' or the provocatively ambiguous 'White Australia has a black history'. When coming to terms with the general matter of repatriation, then, it is hardly surprising that the first major concrete legal instantiation of this phenomenon was in the area of land rights, with the passing of the *Aboriginal Land Rights (Northern Territory) Act 1976*. But this act was restricted in scope to cover so-called 'traditional ownership' in a remote area of Australia where Aboriginal traditions were – and are – popularly thought to be most 'alive', a trend that has been carried through to the operation of the *Native Title Act 1993* and the difficulties that Aboriginal people in so-called 'settled'

Australia have consequently had in establishing recognition of continuity in their systems of 'laws and customs' – as in the Yorta Yorta native title case, where the ultimate decision in December 2002 denying native title hinged partly on consideration of the meaning of the phrase 'traditional laws and customs' and the continuity of these 'laws and customs' since the assumption of sovereignty. This matter of 'tradition' is at the very heart of repatriation in the register of landed property – and, I suggest, at the heart of repatriation in all registers of cultural property.

Barkan and Bush's tripartite division of cultural property does not, in my view, provide an adequate framework for assessing variety in these registers, mainly because it depends exclusively on a classification of objects. It would be more appropriate, as suggested by Fred Myers (2004b), to think in terms of the relationships that obtain between subjects and objects, between people and things, in the realm of Indigenous cultural property in Australia. It is, after all, axiomatic that property is defined as a relationship between persons and things, and that possession of, and rights in, property are defined in terms of particular conditions of social inclusion and exclusion, out of which the values of things arise. These values are not inherent in the objects themselves, although they may appear so. Moreover, when the values do come across as inherent, objects may seem to take on their own life and be registered as subjects. In marxist terms, they are 'fetishised'. They appear to have their own lives, thereby occluding the lived relationships of production that they embody. However, subjects may also appear as objects – for example, when people are placed in the position of slaves – so that when dealing with the relationship between people and things in repatriation it behoves us to think through the ways in which objects can be fetishised as 'more than objects' and subjects can be dispossessed or 'objectified'. In other words, we need to think through the matter of how people and things are reproduced, alienated and appropriated through social traffic.

In thinking this matter through in terms of nationalism, it is necessary to interrogate the history of both subjects and objects and how they have been possessed, dispossessed and repossessed. In Australian history, we generally tend to think in terms of a threefold transition from the precolonial past, sometimes referred to as 'deep', 'ancient' or 'prehistoric', to the colonial past, often called 'recent', 'modern' or 'historical', leading to the present situation, sometimes called 'postcolonial' or 'postmodern' in which repatriation has become a major issue, both in Australia and internationally. We can view this transition schematically in the following diagram, which connects the sequential timeframes to people and different types of objects: objects *per se* – what Barkan and Bush call 'material and tangible property'; land or 'country' – what one might think of as nonportable property; and stories or 'traditions', which would subsume much of that area which Barkan and Bush refer to as 'representations'.

	POSSESSION: Precolonial past (Deep, Ancient, Prehistoric)	DISPOSSESSION: Colonial past (Recent, Modern, Historical)	REPOSSESSION: Postcolonial present (Postmodern, Future)
Indigenous people	Ancestors ('First Australians')	Appropriated people ('Stolen Generations')	Repatriated heirs ('Indigenous Australians')
Indigenous objects	'Traditional' objects	Appropriated objects (Museum collections)	Repatriated objects
Indigenous land	'Traditional Ownership'	Appropriated land	Land rights and native title
Indigenous stories	'Oral Traditions' (Dreamings)	Appropriated 'Voice'	Writing Aboriginal culture and history

This table elides the complexities involved in the historical trajectory of each category of 'possession' (people, objects, land, stories), but it draws clear attention to a particularly salient feature of the logic of repatriation – namely the manner in which each category is aligned with all others and the way in which the alignment tends towards a notion of 'spirituality' or sacredness. In this, I follow the logic of what Sandra Pannell calls 'the Indigenous (re) appropriation of Indigenous things' (1994: 18–39), particularly in relation to the absolute identity that obtains between sacred objects, country and ancestral beings, making them consubstantial in form – although I extend her categories here by making a distinction between 'people' and 'stories'. Of particular note is the way in which Pannell engages the notion of inalienability in relation to this consubstantial suite since, when relationships of consubstantiality obtain, we are not in the realm of alienable possession, but in the realm of a possessive relationship which points 'to the shared and inalienable nature of that relationship' (Pannell 1994: 33). For me, however, the main reference point for making sense of inalienability in this context is not the Indigenous domain *per se*, which has been forever in question under colonial conditions, but the relationship that was inaugurated on 26 January 1788 when, according to the foundation myth, Australia was authentically possessed by the Crown – although how authentically is the very matter which lies at the heart of the history wars. In other words, it is the Crown's inalienable possession that remains open to questions of authenticity and, as I want to say here, it is in the asking of these questions that we find the unfolding logic of repatriation in all of its registers.

The Road to Nowhere

Identity is the idea or sense one has of oneself – it is being in and for itself. At the same time, identity is also a function of relationships in a changing world, so that to be continuous it must transcend itself. It must become through being with and for others. The table above is simply a sketch of how Aboriginal people's key relationships have changed dramatically in the last two centuries: from being 'self-determining' peoples with 'tribal' identities, to people whose identities were conditioned by impoverishment and exclusion from zones dominated by invaders, to people whose identities largely arise, however problematically, through being citizens of Australia – and thus 'self-determining' once again.

It is possible to expand this sequence somewhat by pointing to four stages along a developmental continuum between exclusion and inclusion. Prior to 1788, Aboriginal people were completely excluded from Australia, for the simple reason that Australia did not exist. Hence Aborigines were quite literally a race apart from Europeans. Inasmuch as this defines a relationship, it is one between being and nothing, since each was defined as being in itself and nothing to the other – a relationship which, through the assumption of sovereignty and the implementation of primitivist logic, was turned into an asymmetry, with Aborigines defined as 'nobody' and Europeans defined as 'somebody' (most critically by the doctrine of *terra nullius*). This logic of exclusion continued in the early stages of colonisation through broad notions of eliminating a 'dying race'.

On the other hand, as it became clear that the 'Aboriginal race' (a concept which made no sense outside of the context of settlement) was failing to 'properly' disappear, there arose a two-stage development of cross-referencing Aboriginality and Euro–Australian identity – the first stage continuing to register difference in terms of race, the second recoding difference exclusively in terms of culture. Here I refer to notions of absorption and assimilation, which, while evidently continuous across time, were nevertheless also marked by rupture. For, while absorption continued the idea of elimination by grafting Aboriginal genes onto European stock, with the desired effect of turning the entire Australian population white, it was nevertheless a first, if minimalist, step towards inclusion. Assimilation, on the other hand, was yet more inclusive in the sense that it was no longer grounded in eugenics, but discursively constructed inclusion in terms of conformity to a national ideal of cultured modernity – habits of mind and comportment typical of good citizens that could be universally articulated irrespective of racial character. At the same time, this period saw a quickening of interest in Aboriginal culture and the idea that this national heritage should be protected 'for all Australians'. Hence, the step from the idea of assimilation or 'integration' to the idea of self-determination was by no means massive. Once it was admitted that Aboriginal culture was something of national worth, it was inevitable that the bearers of this culture would be able to make a stronger discursive claim on the nation for further inclusion in terms of cultural difference. It is this general claim that underpins more specific claims for the repatriation of people, objects, land and voice.

But this was more than a linear historical shift. It has been said by Søren Kierkegaard, and many others subsequently, that 'Life is lived forward but understood backward'. As the present emerges from the past, the past emerges from the present. Kierkegaard actually took his cue from a more elaborate statement by German theologian Carl Daub, who stated: 'The act of looking backward is, just like that of looking into the future, an act of divination; and if the prophet is well called an historian of the future, the historian is just as well called, or even better so, a prophet of the past, of the historical' (Watkin 1996). Aboriginal history and the role of repatriation in relationship to it, I want to suggest, is prophetic in just this sense, as a kind of divine or oracular 'retrodiction'. Hence, just as a prophecy 'foretells' a story that later 'really happens', a 'retrodiction' makes what 'really happened' in the past conform to a contemporary narrative. It is in this retrospective understanding that I believe we should search for a logic of repatriation which is fundamentally a-historical in character.

'Repatriation' suggests the replacement of things in their original and proper place, but this raises the question what this place 'really is'. In reading backwards to the past, we do so from a vantage point where the idea of Australia, or the nation, is taken for granted. In fact, Australia did not exist in the precolonial past, but we now act as if it was 'really there'. Since the very beginnings of self-determination we have continually spoken of an ancient land, with ancient dreamings, an ancient culture and an ancient people – Australian Aborigines; 'the first Australians', 'the first pioneers', 'the original Australians', 'our Aborigines', 'our Aboriginal countrymen' and even 'true blue blackfellas' (Berndt and Berndt 1952, 1978; Abbie 1969; Grenfell Price 1943; Murray 2002). This Aboriginality was forged in the colonial encounter, but only in the sense that it was initially the photographic negative of a positive image of white Australia – progressive, scientific, modern and historical, as opposed to regressive, magico–religious, ancient and timeless ('prehistorical'); these are English descriptors that have become firmly attached to the Aboriginal idea of the 'Dreaming' as a transgressive unconscious (Wolfe 1991: 197–224). This unconscious was, first of all, quarantined and excluded, but it has gradually moved closer and closer to its counterpart so that, the more Aboriginality has moved towards the nation, engaging with and appropriating the latter's characteristic forms, the more non-Indigenous Australia has mirrored the process by appropriating Aboriginality, indulging in fantasies of being black (McLean 1998) and getting in touch with the 'real Australia'. This 'real Australia', originally being a negative reflection, is nowhere, since by definition it is consigned to the past. But we would do well to remember that 'nowhere' is the literal meaning of utopia – which the *Oxford Dictionary of English* defines as 'an imagined place or state of things in which everything is perfect'. Lots of Australians (and others) believe they can travel to this 'no place' – the 'Never Never Land', where Albert Namatjira now strangely rubs shoulders with Henry Lawson and John Williamson (Marcus 1988: 254–74).

By definition, authenticity is a condition of undisputed originality, but the 'history wars' show too well that there is both certainty and uncertainty about

Australian origins and Australian authenticity – certainty on both sides of the trenches, but uncertainty about the outcome of the battles. One might say that behind these battles lie Paul Gaugin's celebrated questions: 'Where do we come from? What are we? Where are we going?'[2] Commentators such as Elizabeth Povinelli (2002) and Patrick Wolfe (1994) have highlighted the way in which state-authored primitivism implicates Aboriginal people in an ongoing process of assimilation in the self-determination era – assimilation in the sense that recognition of Aboriginality implies the incorporation of a domesticated identity, one which is cleansed of savagery and imbued with a communitarian spirit that transforms Aborigines into that rare species which Wolfe tellingly refers to as *Homo superorganicus* (1994: 109). But the 'history wars' are, in fact, a contest about such appropriate designations of savagery. On the one hand, the conservative position is that the savages have been rightly civilised; but the progressive position is that the civilised have been wrongly savage. What is at stake is whether the nation is seen as 'white Australia', and thereby authenticated by a lineage that leads back to Europe and ultimately to the classical civilisations of Ancient Egypt, Greece and Rome, or 'Indigenous Australia', authenticated by a lineage that goes back forty, fifty or sixty thousand years to classical Aboriginal Australia.

Given that repatriation is seen as returning or restoring appropriated things to places they seemingly once occupied, we might be tempted to suggest that we are on a utopian road to nowhere. But of course, that is not how we think. After all, reconciliation marches are couched in terms of us heading somewhere, towards a comprehensively inclusive and unified nation. But the two paths, one backwards and the other forward, are in fact the same. It is simply that the direction of travel is reversed in each case, since the inclusive nation of the future is a reflection of that communitarian ideal which characterises the fantasy of Australia in its authentic and (Ab)original form. Michael Taussig (1993: 217–47) has suggested that the nation state characteristically takes the form of a fetish, a sacred 'thing' said to be inhabited by a spiritual form that would otherwise be unknowable – unknowable because the reified object is taken to be the embodiment of something other than itself, essentially immaterial, but capable of being apprehended in its materiality. In other words, the thing represents an essentialised abstraction: 'the nation'. However, it is also a distraction in the sense that as it is taken as an embodiment of something, seemingly concentrating all its powers, it simultaneously erases the complex, contradictory and concrete forms of interpersonal power that actually create an embodied society. The paradigm case in Australia is 'our' national flag, the type of emblem that Emile Durkheim (1915) compared to Aboriginal sacred objects which, in turn, Taussig analyses in order to illustrate the nature of state fetishism. The scandal of the fetish, Taussig suggests, is that it signifies nothing that actually exists, even though it is the transubstantiation of a real order of relationships that are simultaneously reified in objects and deified as a national spirit, national psyche or 'collective conscience'. I view repatriation in precisely these terms – as the simultaneous retrojection of the national spirit into the deep past and projection of that spirit into an indefinite future. As such it is an aspect of so called 'symbolic reconciliation'; though what the symbolism elides is the altogether more messy and turbulent business of 'practical reconciliation' as an aspect of national governance – not simply as a matter of dealing with health issues and the like, but also in terms of the difficulties involved in all matters where Indigenous Australians are in a position to negotiate with Australian institutions, including museums. Hence, repatriation is embedded in the relationship between myth and history – between the myth of an essential national unity and the ongoing histories of conflict and accommodation in the Australian people's myriad relationships with each other.

Domesticating Tradition

If we now return to the diagrammatic sketch of the relationship between the deep past, the recent past and the ongoing present, we can more precisely identify a general model of repatriation. First of all, in relation to stories, I draw attention to Peter Sutton's revealing remarks about the relationship between Aboriginal myth and Aboriginal history, where he convincingly shows not only how classical myths address historical questions, but also how postclassical history is contained within symbolic forms whose function is to underpin identity formation (1988: 251–68). As he says:

> Written, photographic and taped records are seen as highly useful in history making, no matter how far back in time they go. Archaeological records are also used, and denied, depending on who is using them. For some, radio-carbon dating has established a powerful weapon in the fight to have prior Aboriginal occupancy of Australia recognised. I heard 'the Dreamtime' identified as '40,000 years ago' one day near Kempsey ... Urban Aboriginal history construction is a statement, moral and political, about the suffering, resilience and persistence of a colonised people, but it is also a search for a background and underpinning to what must be assumed to be an indefinite state of future difference. In this sense it is the creation, as much as an explanation, of a separate identity. (Sutton 1988: 261)

Oral traditions, then, are becoming a thing of the past as more and more Aboriginal cultures, histories and identities are inscribed in various locations – something which, paradoxically enough, oral history programs help to achieve. As they come to be inscribed they also reach an audience much larger than the Aboriginal population – and of course, many (perhaps most) contributors to the enterprise are not Aboriginal. We can say therefore that in the precolonial past, oral traditions were an exclusively Aboriginal domain, whereas in the colonial past, writing about Aborigines was exclusively a non-Aboriginal domain which marginalised oral history and, in the postcolonial present, Aboriginal traditions have increasingly taken a written form that is not only decidedly inclusive of Aboriginal input, but inclusive to the point of privileging that input's authenticity. Yet, Sutton's idea of 'an indifferent state of future difference' has to be qualified by the fact that even white histories have become 'black at heart' – sympathetically black, or at least 'black armband'. Moreover, in Aboriginal people's use of written forms of storytelling, Aboriginal stories have likewise 'hybridised', with the master narrative conditioned by reaction against the myth of *terra nullius* through retorts such as 'We were here first' and 'We have survived'. Nevertheless, survival and the repatriation of voice entails a certain fading of the past as oral traditions have increasingly been displaced and 'domesticated' by the written word.

Naturally, land rights and native title are types of repatriation. Furthermore, they are both based on the ideas of 'tradition' (traditional entitlement) and dispossession of land. Part of the apparent paradox of land rights, however, has been the way in which Aboriginal land, in all its forms (protected sites, freehold title and land where native-title rights and interests have been recognised), has never had so many non-Aboriginal people and bureaucratic structures (land councils, prescribed bodies corporate, departments of the environment, etc.) governing it and trying to develop it in various economic directions. Aboriginal land is also a hybridised entity. The extent to which it is under bureaucratic control reflects how Aboriginal storytelling is only privileged when it takes a written form. Indeed, many of the organisations are sponsors of this storytelling – this is hardly surprising since their collective identity depends on exposing the lie of *terra nullius* and they depend entirely on documents to support claims for land and site protection. Of particular note is the way in which this documentation is heavily weighted towards the sacred, as in the preservation of 'sacred sites', the documentation of what the Aboriginal Land Rights (Northern Territory) Act calls 'primary spiritual responsibility', and the requirement in native title proceedings that 'laws and customs' be fully 'traditional' in scope. In this sense, the repatriation of country to Indigenous Australians is also at once replacement and displacement – both the recognition that Crown land is open to claims by 'others' and the domestication of such claims through the implementation of bureaucratic procedures.

Perhaps the best-known Aboriginal story that invokes an indigenised Australia is Sally Morgan's book *My Place* (1987). However, 'place' in this instance invokes a sense of position within an Aboriginal family or community. Whatever else one might say about Morgan's book,[3] the repatriation of her Aboriginality is emblematic of and organically related to both the motif of forced disinheritance in what Bain Attwood calls the 'stolen generation narrative' (Attwood 2001:183–212) and the general resurgence of Aboriginal identity that has been reflected in the Australian census figures over the past twenty years or so,[4] as well as in occasional scandals about people without Aboriginal descent claiming Aboriginal identities.[5] In my view, the repatriation of human remains is part of this same general process of indigenising the Australian population, except that it is specifically the transformation of skeletal material into ancestors who lie beyond the apex of genealogical reckoning. More often than not, skeletal remains are assumed to be the ancestors of particular peoples simply because they have been located at particular places with which those peoples have historical association. There is, therefore, a world of difference between this ancestry and that which can be traced through genealogical and historical records. As we know, the matter of descent – through sociogenetic connection – has been central to some disputes over the return of human remains, with those with a scientific interest in the material sometimes claiming that returns are a submission to some kind of religious fundamentalism.[6] They are not wrong, since the connection between Aboriginal communities and their primordial ancestors is a mystical one, based largely on forms of tradition (some partly new) that transmute ancestral burial grounds into sacred sites, which in turn substantiate mystical links to landscapes. Hence, the practice of claiming skeletal remains depends largely on archaeological knowledge, yet typically denies the validity of that knowledge – a fact that naturally rankles with archaeologists of a more conservative bent. On the other hand, the idea of a mystical connection to Aboriginal ancestry has currency amongst people who both are and are not of Aboriginal descent, with not a few trying to substantiate the 'feeling' of being Aboriginal by extensive genealogical research. Others may simply be satisfied with the feeling of a sacred connection to the land – the land to which skeletal material is ideally returned, but which in principle guarantees all Australians' indigeneity. At the same time, however, that indigeneity is not only a link to the past; it is also a link to an ideal future in which all or most Australians might legitimately claim a domesticated (and domestic) form of Aboriginal ancestry. High and rising rates of intermarriage between Aborigines and non-Aborigines are already edging us towards the dream of a generalised Aboriginal population – a generalised public *Aboriginality* where, in family matters, 'black is the new white'.[7]

Finally, we need to consider the place of tangible objects. It seems to me that secret sacred objects need to be considered as part of the more general inventory of 'traditional' objects found in museum collections and elsewhere. My museum experience at Museum Victoria suggests that 'traditional' objects are classified in three ways. Some, such as pointing bones or 'feather feet' are treated as sensitive and therefore not accessible, although they are not deemed to be sacred. Some, such as weapons or tools, are completely accessible, although it has become a matter of good form to consult with communities before these objects are displayed. The difference between the two, as this difference has been refracted in our consciousness, is between the malignant and the benign – between a history which reflects Aboriginal sorcery, and therefore evil doing, and a history which can be praised as 'ingenious', 'productive' and 'adaptive'. Secret sacred objects are positioned against both of these, as both good and magically powerful, as both benign yet closed to public view – as if to reflect the ambiguity in Durkheim's opposition of the sacred to the profane, the latter ambiguously situated as either 'bad' or 'mundane'. Sensitive objects are censored but, interestingly enough, are never the subject of calls for repatriation, given that they tend towards a noncomplimentary view of Aboriginality; but open objects are not censored, because they enhance the public's view of Aboriginal traditions. Yet secret sacred objects are censored and, by that very fact, enhance our view of Aborigines as keepers of a sacred trust. Never mind that in their original context secret sacred objects were instruments of power and control over women and juniors. Never mind that they were often used in systematic acts of gerontocratic terrorism. Never mind that they were objects that were systematically traded in alliances between those senior men who wielded political control. Never mind that a great many of them in museum collections are 'fakes' as some have labelled them, hurriedly constructed as tokens of exchange relationships with non-Aboriginal people. Never mind that some of the 'genuine articles' were similarly traded to the likes of Baldwin Spencer, Frank Gillen or T.G.H. Strehlow. Never mind, because the valuations of the objects inherent in such transactions are now barely relevant to their principle purpose, which is essentially to signify the restoration of the sacred – the same sacred embodied in Aboriginal land, in Aboriginal ancestors and Aboriginal traditions. This is not a matter of exclusively, or even predominantly, Aboriginal interest. As Pannell remarks in this context, 'the search for authenticity might begin with the Other, or the objects of Otherness, but always ends with ourselves' (Pannell 2005: 119). And 'ourselves' in this context in principle includes every Australian, be s/he black, white or some shade in between.

In this regard there is a formal correspondence between human remains and secret sacred objects. The correspondence, I argue, lies in their respective opposition, in the first place, to 'the dream of a generalised Aboriginal population', and secondly, to a generalised identification with Indigenous objects. European collecting of secret sacred objects, as with other 'traditional' objects, created a massive upsurge in demand, giving rise to periods of intensified production and distribution that coincided with the strongest missionary challenges to classical religion (Jones 2005: 67–96). The making of objects for sale was, as others have intimated (Anderson 2005: 97–107; Jones 2005), the first opening up of the 'Dreaming' for mass consumption, some decades before the current era in which Aboriginal art has been transferred to other media before 'taking the world by storm'. But it is of great interest that the 1970s, and especially the Papunya art movement, is seen as the great watershed in Aboriginal people's revelation of 'sacred objects' to a larger world, even though this process had in fact begun much earlier.[8] My sense is that as the art market has expanded, and with it the growth and hardening of the view that Aboriginal people are only revealing the 'outside meanings' in their canvas, bark and other imagery – thereby retaining the secret 'inside meanings' of their ritual symbolism – the items amassed in the earlier era of collecting have been, as it were, closed down and revalorised as belonging exclusively to the secret and ancient domain of Aboriginal ritual. The relationship between the earliest forms of secret sacred objects and contemporary forms of Aboriginal art is actually one of continuity, but a line has been drawn between, on the one hand, classical commodities with more ancient lineages spanning the pre-European and early colonial era and, on the other, postclassical commodities characteristic of a postmodern, postcolonial world. While modern forms of copyright control and licensing can apply to the postclassical forms, secret sacred objects resist entirely any logic of commodification, even to the point of no longer being consumable in any venue outside of a restricted Aboriginal domain. In spite of having been alienated in the past, secret sacred objects have come to represent the ancient and inalienable core of the 'Dreaming' itself – that which Euro–Australians cannot and should not know, so long as it is understood that the valued secrets are guarded by those who can and should know. Like skeletal remains, these 'ancient' objects are decidedly of the past, entirely and indubitably 'traditional'. And as skeletal remains stand outside of genealogical time in relation to recent and present generations of Aboriginal people, so do secret sacred objects stand as the mysterious *fons et origo* of open sacred objects inserted into recent and contemporary circuits of commodity exchange. Lesser objects that are not 'high art' similarly flood these circuits, consumed by tourists rather than connoisseurs. In these contexts, as in others, it is the open market that acts as the agent of domestication, at the same time calling into being a past when no such openness existed. It is in this past that secret sacred objects ostensibly belong.

Conclusion: Consignments to Oblivion

My argument, then, is a general one. In a nutshell, I maintain that repatriation is, in essence (and I use that word advisedly) a consignment of things into the deep, distant and utopian past. Skeletal remains, secret sacred objects, land and oral traditions thus form a set, marked off from the colonial past, which is in turn, due to the ascendancy of 'black armband' history, essentially construed as an expropriation and objectification of these things; of Aboriginal bodies, Aboriginal objects, Aboriginal lands and Aboriginal voices. The postcolonial present, whose very name suggests an incomplete process which heralds a future rather than a consolidation of a current state of affairs, is a strange hybrid of these utopian and dystopian states, inasmuch as it is a reconciliation of authentic Aboriginality, construed as an independent and wholly different reality returned to its 'natural' state, and the culture of those who were once but arguably no more invaders. My case, then, rests on the view that the postcolonial is not only 'redemptive', but also revelatory. In public Aboriginality (notably the confessional bodies of the stolen generations), in the consumption of Aboriginal objects (notably 'traditional' art), in the spectacle of Aboriginal sacred sites ('protected' areas, often within the confines of tourist venues and national parks) and in the myriad stories of Aboriginal culture and history (too diverse to name), we see positive signs of national unity whose negative correlates are, through repatriation, consigned to oblivion.

I choose my words carefully, given that oblivion is defined as 'the state of being forgotten, especially by the public'. While it is true that I am saying that repatriated things are in some sense 'dead things', it is their very demise – their falling from public consumption, their resistance to commodification, their complete 'disappearance' – which somehow guarantees the authenticity of those 'live things' which are revealed, displayed, bought and generally exposed to all concerned as 'truly', 'genuinely' and 'authentically' Australian. Hence, these 'live things' emerge as the nation's invention of itself 'out of nothing' – that is, out of a country that did not exist on the eve of 26 January 1788. Repatriation, therefore, is the creation of 'no-things', which are the ground from which 'real things' mysteriously emerge. As the dictionary meaning of 'oblivion' suggests, repatriated things are literally made 'un-conscious', unknowable.

I speak in general terms, but that befits my topic. I am aware that many are more concerned with the particulars of repatriation and the specifics of the ongoing development of this phenomenon. I am not, for the simple reason that I am interested in the way repatriation articulates with the logic of nationalism – a logic that is totalising, unifying and committed to singularity ('oneness'), thus requiring a dialectical relationship with 'nothingness'. I am aware that the idea of a 'national interest' always glosses over complex and difficult negotiations whose outcomes are contingent. I am aware, for example, that not all returned skeletal remains are buried, away from the prying eyes of the scientific establishment and that, even when they are, the scientists assisting do so with profound ambivalence (Pardoe 1992: 132–41). I am aware that attempts to return secret sacred objects have, in some circumstances, eventuated in more objects located in museums than were ever there before, and have enhanced the symbolic capital of museums and allied institutions (Anderson 2005), while in other circumstances such return is likely to see secret sacred objects increasingly falling into the hands of private collectors (Batty 2005). I am aware that there are a great many other instances of the complexity and contradictory nature of social relationships and tributaries of power that the idea of 'the nation' simplifies, reduces and essentialises in its name. I am aware that these relationships and tributaries can be difficult and painful, and that they generally place both Aboriginal communities and scientific establishments under a good deal of stress. Nevertheless, my case is that repatriation arises as a public good because, in principle, it moves in the direction of an ideal that is beyond all that. The more exclusive we appear to be with the past, the more inclusive we appear to be in the present.

Notes

1.   For example, the 11th episode of the Australian Broadcasting Commission's Open Learning program, Aboriginal Studies, entitled *Economics: Independence or Welfare*, situates calls for contemporary economic independence in terms of the latter being a return to an 'original affluent society'. On this point see Sahlins (1974: 1–39.)

2.   The title of one of Gaugin's best-known primitivist paintings: *D'ou venons nous? Que sommes nous? D'ou allons nous?* The painting is now in the collection of Boston's Museum of Fine Arts.

3. Much has been said about the book that is pertinent to my theme. See especially Attwood (1993: 302–18), Langton (1993: 29–31) and Morton (1996: 123–24).
4. The official Indigenous population figure in Australia for 1966 was 101,978; in 1986 it was 227,645; in 2006 it was 517,200. Much of this astonishing increase is accounted for by more people self–identifying as Indigenous, plus the fact that Indigenous Australians are recruiting more non-Indigenous spouses, but nevertheless identifying their children as Indigenous. For a relevant discussion see Rowse (2004: 322–24).
5. There have been various instances where the Indigenous ancestry and identity of individuals has been publicly disputed, notably those involving people such as Sreten Bozic (aka B. Wongar), Elizabeth Durack (aka Eddie Burrup), Sakshi Anmatyerre (aka Farley French), Mudrooroo (aka Colin Johnson), Eric Willmot and Roberta 'Bobbi' Sykes. There is also the famous case of dispute over Aboriginality in Tasmania after the 1999 Aboriginal and Torres Strait Islander Commission election, when the Indigenous identity of many Tasmanian voters was called into question (Guilliatt 2002: 18–23) – this being but one specific example of a general phenomenon of problematic identification which dogs many arms of Australian bureaucracy. For a comment on such matters of authenticity and authentication as they relate to the circulation of Aboriginal art, see Myers (2004a: 5–20).
6. 'Regrettably, Australian society faces an anti-intellectual creationism ... It represents an amalgam of Dreaming beliefs and anti-evolutionary Christian fundamentalism'. This was how John Mulvaney described the return of the Kow Swamp human remains (1991: 19). See also Gelder and Jacobs (1998: 86–8).
7. As exemplified most starkly in Germaine Greer's 2003 intervention. Greer's call for an Aboriginal republic of Australia was not as original as it seemed to many at the time of the publication of her essay, since the conjunction of calls for Aboriginal sovereignty and for the renunciation of the British monarchy had been heading in that direction for a decade before. See Morton (1996).
8. For a particularly relevant account, see Bonyhady (2000).

Bibliography

Abbie, A.1969. *The Original Australians*. London: Frederick Muller.

Anderson, C. 2005. 'Museums, Collectors and Repatriation: the Objects of Otherness', in C. Anderson (ed.), *Politics of the Secret*. Sydney: Oceania, pp. 97–107.

Attwood, B. 1993. 'Portrait of an Aboriginal as an Artist: Sally Morgan and the Construction of Aboriginality', *Australian Historical Studies* 25: 302–18.

———. 2001. '"Learning about the Truth": the Stolen Generations Narrative', in B. Attwood and F. Magowan (eds), *Telling Stories: Indigenous History and Memory in Australia and New Zealand*. Sydney: Allen and Unwin, pp. 183–212.

Barkan, E. 2002. 'Amending Historical Injustices: the Restitution of Cultural Property – an Overview', in E. Barkan and R. Bush, *Claiming the Stones, Naming the Bones: Cultural Property and the Negotiation of National and Ethnic Identity*. Los Angeles: Getty Publications, pp.16–46.

——— and R. Bush. 2002. 'Introduction', in E. Barkan and R. Bush (eds), *Claiming the Stones, Naming the Bones: Cultural Property and the Negotiation of National and Ethnic Identity*. Los Angeles: Getty Publications, pp. 1–15.

Batty, P. 2005. 'White Redemptive Rituals: Repatriating Aboriginal Secret-Sacred Objects', *Arena Journal* 23: 29–36.

Berndt, C. and R. Berndt. 1978. *Pioneers and Settlers: The Aboriginal Australians*. Melbourne: Pitman.

Berndt, R. and C. Berndt. 1952. *The First Australians*. Sydney: Ure Smith.

Bonyhady, T. 2000. 'Papunya Stories', *Australian Humanities Review*, December. Retrieved 25 June 2005 from http://www.lib.latrobe.edu.au/AHR/archive/Issue-December-2000/bonyhady2.html

Department of Foreign Affairs and Trade. n.d. 'Indigenous Arts and Culture'. Retrieved 12 June 2005 from http://www.dfat.gov.au/facts/indg_arts_culture.html

Durkheim, E. 1915. *The Elementary Forms of the Religious Life*. London: Allen and Unwin.

Friedman, J. 1990. 'Being in the World: Globalization and Localization', in M. Featherstone (ed.), *Global Culture: Nationalism, Globalization and Modernity*. London: Sage, pp. 311–28.

Gelder, K. and J. Jacobs. 1998. *Uncanny Australia: Sacredness and Identity in a Postcolonial Nation*. Melbourne: Melbourne University Press.

Greer, Germaine. 2003. *Whitefella Jump Up: the Shortest Way to Nationhood*, Quarterly Essay 11, Melbourne: Black Inc.

Grenfell Price, A. 1943. *What of Our Aborigines?* Adelaide: Rigby.

Guilliatt, R. 2002. 'A Whiter Shade of Black?' *Good Weekend* 15 June.

Jones, P. 2005. '"Objects of Mystery and Concealment": a History of *Tjurunga* Collecting', In C. Anderson, *Politics of the Secret*. Sydney: Oceania pp. 67–96.

Langton, M. 1993. '"Well, I Heard it on the Radio and I Saw it on the Television …": an Essay for the Australian Film Commission on the Politics and Aesthetics of Filmmaking by and about Aboriginal People and Things', Sydney: Australian Film Commission.

Lattas, A. 1990. 'Aborigines and Contemporary Australian Nationalism: Primordiality and the Cultural Politics of Otherness', *Social Analysis* 27: 50–69.

———. 1991. 'Nationalism, Aesthetic Redemption and Aboriginality', *The Australian Journal of Anthropology* 2: 307–24.

———. 1992. 'Primitivism, Nationalism and Individualism in Australian Popular Culture', *Journal of Australian Studies* 35: 45–58.

Macintyre, S. and A. Clark. 2003. *The History Wars*. Melbourne: Melbourne University Publishing.

McLean, I. 1998. *White Aborigines: Identity Politics in Australian Art*. Cambridge: Cambridge University Press.

Maddock, K. 1991. 'Metamorphosing the Sacred in Australia', *The Australian Journal of Anthropology* 2: 213–32.

Marcus, J. 1988. 'The Journey Out to the Centre: the Cultural Appropriation of Ayers Rock', *Kunapipi* 10: 254–74.

Morgan, S. 1987. *My Place*. Fremantle: Fremantle Arts Centre Press.

Morton, J. 1996. 'Aboriginality, Mabo and the Republic: Indigenising Australia', in B. Attwood (ed.), *In the Age of Mabo: History, Aborigines and Australia*. Sydney: Allen and Unwin, pp. 117–35.

Mulvaney, D.J. 1991. 'Past Regained, Future Lost: the Kow Swamp Pleistocene Burials', *Antiquity* 65(246): 12–21.

Murray, N. 2002. 'Was True Blue a Blackfella?', *The Age*, 6 July.

Myers, F. 2004a. 'Ontologies of the Image and Economies of Exchange', *American Ethnologist* 31: 5–20.

————. 2004b. Painting Culture: the Making of an Aboriginal High Art. Durham: Duke University Press.

The Oxford Dictionary of English, 2003 Oxford: Oxford University Press.

Pannell, S. 1994. 'Mabo and Museums: "The Indigenous (re)Appropriation of Indigenous Things"', *Oceania* 65: 18–39.

————. 2005.'The Cool Memories of Tjurunga: a Symbolic History of Collecting Authenticity and the Sacred', in C. Anderson (ed.), *Politics of the Secret*. Oceania Monograph 45. Sydney: Oceania, pp. 108–22.

Pardoe, C. 1992. 'Arches of Radii, Corridors of Power: Reflections on Current Archaeological Practice', *Journal of Australian Studies* 35: 132–41.

Povinelli, E. 2002. The Cunning of Recognition: Indigenous Alterities and the Making of Australian Multiculturalism. Durham: Duke University Press.

Rowse, T. 2004. 'Notes on the History of Aboriginal Population of Australia', in A. Dirk Moses (ed.), *Genocide and Settler Society: Frontier Violence and Stolen Indigenous Children in Australian History*. New York: Berghahn Books. pp. 315–25.

Sahlins, M. 1974. *Stone Age Economics*. London: Tavistock.

Sutton, P. 1988. 'Myth as History, History as Myth', in I. Keen (ed.), *Being Black: Aboriginal Cultures in 'Settled Australia'*. Canberra: Aboriginal Studies Press, pp. 251–68.

Taussig, M. 1993. 'Maleficium: State Fetishism', in E. Apter and W. Pietz (eds), *Fetishism as Cultural Discourse*. Ithaca: Cornell University Press, pp. 217–47.

Watkin, J. 1996. 'Kierkegaard Quotations and Questions'. Retrieved 23 June 2005 from http://www.utas.edu.au/docs/humsoc/kierkegaard/resources/Kierkquotes.html

Wolfe, P. 1991. 'On Being Woken Up: the Dreamtime in Anthropology and in Australian Settler Culture', *Comparative Studies in Society and History* 33: 197–224.

————. 1994. 'Nation and MiscegeNation: Discursive Continuity in the Post-Mabo Era', *Social Analysis* 36: 93–152.

Part IV

Repatriation and the History of
Scientific Collecting of
Indigenous Remains

9

The Vermillion Accord and the Significance of the History of the Scientific Procurement and Use of Indigenous Australian Bodily Remains

Paul Turnbull

Henry Atkinson, a senior lawman of the Yorta Yorta people, speaks eloquently in this volume of the bewilderment and anguish caused by the desecration of ancestral burial places. However distressing it has proved, his obligation under customary law has been to secure the repatriation of Yorta Yorta remains lying in collections within various museums and medical schools in Australia, Europe and the United Kingdom.[1] In recalling his experiences in campaigning for remains to be brought back to country, Henry Atkinson reminded us that repatriation has its origins in 'Indigenous people ... demanding control, accountability and recognition of their ownership of the past. It was not something conceptualised by scholars for the good of Indigenous people.' (Pardoe 1991: 16)

As Indigenous Australian efforts to rescue the dead gained momentum through the 1980s many researchers in disciplines such as archaeology, anatomy and physical anthropology were genuinely perplexed as to why Indigenous people should demand the return of skeletal remains and soft tissue that, in many instances, had lain in museum and medical school collections for a century or more. A number of prominent researchers questioned publicly whether repatriation could be anything other than a political stunt, orchestrated by a handful of urban Aboriginal radicals seeking to give new emotive force to long-standing political demands in respect of land rights and the overcoming of social inequalities. In the Australian press, conservative commentators dismissed leading campaigners such as Michael Mansell, Bob Weatherall and Henry Atkinson as men with little or no connection to the life-ways and culture of the people whose remains they sought.

What was new about the repatriation campaigns witnessed in the 1980s was not the motivation of leading campaigners, but their ability to be heard in the public sphere and, moreover, to secure widespread non-Indigenous support for their cause. The desire to see the dead reunited with ancestral country long predates the 1980s. Indeed, the history of Indigenous Australian people's efforts to secure the return of remains from scientific collections can be traced in archival sources back to the late nineteenth century. Evidence of Aboriginal efforts to prevent scientific theft from ancestral burial places can be found in a wealth of historical sources dating from the earliest years of European invasion. Soon after the establishment of the Port Jackson penal settlement in 1788, European colonial officials, convicts and settlers came to be familiar with Aboriginal mortuary ceremonies and cultural obligations to the dead. So much so that, by the late 1830s, the British Crown had formally recognised Aboriginal customary rights to land given over to burial and remembrance of the dead in accordance with time-honoured custom (Turnbull 2002: 63–86).

The Significance of the Vermillion Accord on Human Remains

Considered within the context of this extensive history, the adoption of the Vermillion Accord on Human Remains by the World Archaeological Congress (WAC) in 1989 can be seen as marking an important shift in how repatriation was understood within scientific circles. The accord implicitly recognised that demands by Indigenous peoples for the return of remains reflected the survival and continuing vitality of their cultures and systems of customary law. As such, it was a long overdue attempt to create a framework for negotiations between scientific researchers and communities respecting the legitimacy of both scientific and Indigenous customary interests in the fate of remains.[2]

Looking back on the years that have passed since the adoption of the Vermillion Accord we can see that its principles have been used as the basis for dialogue in numerous cases where continued scientific possession of Indigenous remains has been contested. Negotiations in the spirit of the accord have not always resulted in scientists and Indigenous community representatives finding common ground. However, in respect of Aboriginal Australian remains, there have been numerous examples since the early 1990s of Aboriginal people and scientific personnel in Australian and United Kingdom institutions resolving the fate of remains. In a number of instances, negotiations with museums and medical schools have resulted in acknowledgement of Indigenous ownership and control, but not reburial. Remains have become the focus of new avenues of research aimed at solving questions of mutual interest to researchers and Indigenous communities. Scientific investigation has not ceased, although it is the case that the science being done is different because the research questions asked have been formulated through negotiation with Indigenous communities.

Twenty years after the adoption of the Vermillion Accord, the polarities of outlook that characterised relations between scientific researchers and Aboriginal people in the 1980s have given way to dialogues resulting in the relinquishment of possession and traditional monopolies of interpretation by scientific personnel as envisaged in documents such as the influential 1993 Report for the Council of Australian Museum Associations (Council of Australian Museum Directors: 1993). Yet, there is one dimension to repatriation that deserves more attention than it has gained to date. This is the questions that many Aboriginal Australian Elders, community spokespersons and activists involved in repatriation over the past two decades have asked: why were the dead taken and what was done with them within museums and medical schools?

We owe it to those Aboriginal men and women whose lives have been intimately affected by this disturbing aspect of our colonial past to try and answer these questions. Yet, they are questions also worth asking because the research that might provide answers could help in the task of establishing the provenance of remains whose origins have been presumed to be unclear or unknown. In many instances, institutions have been able to provide communities with meagre information on the provenance of specific items in their collections, but crucial evidence pertaining to where and how remains were procured has been found by examining correspondence in museum archives, the records of various metropolitan and colonial government agencies, private diaries and letters and a diverse range of printed materials. This information has proved of inestimable benefit in the profoundly important task of ensuring that the dead are returned to the right ancestral country in accordance with the appropriate religious ceremonies.

Reconstructing the circumstances in which remains were procured and used may also prove valuable to both Aboriginal communities and scientific researchers for what it might provide by way of vicarious knowledge that could prove helpful in future discussions centred on rights in respect of human remains and other forms of Indigenous cultural property.

Reviewing the reaction of personnel in various museums and medical institutions to repatriation demands during the 1980s, we can see how unhelpful it was that they had only a limited appreciation of how the history of the procurement and scientific uses of Aboriginal remains was understood by Aboriginal people. Not only was there little or no awareness of how knowledge of scientific grave robbing figured in the collective memories of communities, but also no appreciation of the ongoing vitality of religious and cultural affinities with the ancestral dead – even within communities who had experienced the loss of ancestral land and now lived far away in rural towns and metropolitan centres. There was a pronounced tendency to think that history had rendered the cultural heritage of those campaigning for repatriation as ephemeral to their identity. This in turn disposed institutional personnel to think that Aboriginal campaigners could be persuaded to see how radically different contemporary research interests in Aboriginal remains were from the science of the period between 1788 and the 1920s. While readily conceding that this earlier science was bad or pseudoscience because of the existential concreteness it gave to notions of Aboriginal racial inferiority, institutional spokespersons stressed that subsequent science had been instrumental in demolishing the truth claims of these earlier racially biased inquiries, arguing moreover that the capacity of science to detect and refute error made the case for the continued preservation of remains for scientific investigation ethically far superior to that for repatriation and likely reburial. What better way, it seemed to them, was there to redress the ethical outrages of the past than leaving researchers free to use Aboriginal remains to produce new, reliable knowledge about human origins and evolutionary difference that would truly be of benefit to the world's Indigenous and non-Indigenous peoples?

The question of how far the intellectual practices and products of scientific research on Aboriginal remains contributed to the dissipation of the cognitive strength of the concept of race lies beyond the scope of this paper (Barkan 1992; Anderson 2005).[3] Though it is clear that researchers in various disciplines of the biomedical and social sciences between the last years of the nineteenth century and the late 1930s contributed significantly to the demise of race's hold over the European imagination (Barkan 1992).[4] My concern here is with how this inclination to stress the lack of intellectual or ethical continuities between the racial science of earlier generations and contemporary scientific aspirations was interpreted by Aboriginal people campaigning for repatriation during the 1980s.

By entering into negotiations with Aboriginal spokespersons, believing that they could be persuaded to see the history of scientific procurement and use of remains as irrelevant to deciding their future, museum and biomedical personnel seriously misjudged the crosscultural complexities of the situation. As Maori researcher Linda Tuhiwai Smith has argued, scientific researchers '... may see the benefits of their particular research projects as serving a greater good "for mankind"', but '... the ideal that benefiting mankind is indeed a primary outcome of scientific research is as much a reflection of ideology as it is of academic training. It becomes so taken for granted that many researchers simply assume that as individuals they embody this ideal ...' (1999: 2). What was not appreciated was that Indigenous peoples cannot forget how procurement and scientific use of remains was implicated in the worst excesses of colonialism:

> Just knowing that somebody measured our 'faculties' by filling skulls of our ancestors with millet seed and compared the amount of millet seed to the capacity for mental thought offends our sense of who and what we are. It galls us that Western researchers and intellectuals can assume to know all that is possible to know about us, on the basis of their brief encounters with some of us. It appalls us that the West can desire, extract and claim ownership of our ways of knowing, our imagery, the things we create and produce, and then simultaneously reject the people who created and developed those ideas and seek to deny them further opportunities to be creators of their own cultures and their own nations. (Smith 1999: 1)

Faced with demands for the return of ancestral remains, researchers and museum personnel sought to persuade Aboriginal community Elders and representatives that they were sympathetic to their plight and had no intention to deny their aspirations. They pointed to various initiatives by several Australian museums from the mid 1970s to involve Aboriginal and Torres Strait Island people in research, exhibition and educational programs. However, despite these initiatives, the few Aboriginal and Torres Strait Islander people employed in museums by the 1980s found that they were unable to influence engrained modes of institutional thinking about Indigenous cultural heritage.

The bitter controversy over ancestral remains in the Museum of Victoria during the mid 1980s, for example, arose in large part because of the unwillingness of senior staff and associated researchers to listen to the museum's Koori staff concerns about community views regarding the exhibition of remains at an international scientific gathering (Mulvaney 1991: 12–21).[5] Further, when Indigenous community leaders put their case to state and federal politicians, they found the latter generally content to seek advice from non-Indigenous experts who, while sympathetic to Indigenous distress over the continued preservation of remains and secret sacred objects, argued that the conflicting interests of researchers and Indigenous peoples should be judged by the criteria of whether repatriation or continued preservation would serve the greater good. In early 1983, for example, the annual meeting of state ministers with responsibilities for arts and cultural matters endorsed the position of the Museum of South Australia that any decisions taken to deaccession Indigenous items from its collections would be resolved conscious of the museum's responsibility to all sections of the community (Museum of Victoria: 1983). Similarly, the Australian Council of Museum Directors employed Western scientific and ethical criteria when in May 1983 it endorsed the principles that museums should consider the 'disposal' of remains of 'limited scientific value', and that those of known individuals '… should be buried in an appropriate place or otherwise dealt with', but only in accordance with the wishes of those who were 'direct descendants' of the deceased (Museum of Victoria: 1969–1987).

The continuing marginal position of Indigenous Australians in respect of ancestral remains in museum and medical school collections was to be a key theme in one of the most influential documents in the history of repatriation: the paper presented to the 1989 WAC inter-congress at the University of South Dakota, Vermillion, by the Brisbane-based Foundation for Aboriginal and Islander Research Action (FAIRA). In the paper, entitled 'Aborigines, Archaeologists and the Rights of the Dead', FAIRA reminded non-Indigenous delegates that even in the supportive atmosphere of the inter-congress only four of seventeen speakers on Aboriginal heritage at the inter-congress were Aboriginal. Of these speakers, three had been funded through a modest grant from the Institute of Aboriginal Studies that still fell short of covering their expenses (FAIRA 1989: 9).[6]

At Vermillion, FAIRA called on delegates to adopt a code of ethics that recognised the rights of the Indigenous dead to burial in accordance with their cultural traditions, drawing attention to the recognition of communities' right to reclaim the dead from Western scientific institutions in the draft declaration of principles in respects of the rights of Indigenous peoples being formulated within agencies of the United Nations.[7] However, the main focus of the paper was on the failure of Western scientific institutions to acknowledge their complicity in '... the oppression of Australia's Indigenous peoples through acts of cultural terrorism ... [frequently] involving the unsanctioned and indiscriminate excavation of our burial grounds and interference with our dead' (FAIRA 1989: 1).

FAIRA argued that scientific institutions had not only acquired their collections by brutally disregarding the rights of Indigenous Australians to bury the dead in accordance with their religion and customary law, but had also knowingly received remains from individuals killed in frontier violence and, in several instances, actually 'murdered for their bodies' (FAIRA 1989: 3). The plundering of ancestral burial places, moreover, had also had its aftermath, FAIRA maintained, in the bones of Aboriginal men and women being used by leading scientists of the colonial era with a view to proving their inferiority, thus justifying successive racialist policies of protectionism and assimilation (FAIRA 1989: 1). To compound the outrage, ancestral remains had been exhibited in museums in ways that were highly suggestive of the motivation of skeletal collectors and their scientific patrons being not simply to prove the racial inferiority of Indigenous Australians, but to turn their dead into trophies of conquest (FAIRA 1989: 1). In short, as FAIRA was to most provocatively assert, parallels between scientific control of Indigenous Australian remains and the 'continued use of the remains of Jewish victims of the Nazi holocaust in West German medical schools ...[could not] be overstated' (FAIRA 1989: 10).

Though it remains unpublished, FAIRA's paper to the WAC inter-congress has circulated widely over the past fifteen years and been used as a source for numerous conference addresses, press releases and newspaper articles. In this respect it has proved valuable in reminding us that Aboriginal people cannot contemplate the subject of scientific research on remains without being forcibly reminded that the bodies of their ancestors were not only desecrated, but also used to produce knowledge that promoted their colonial subjugation. However, in its uncompromising arraignment of science, the paper presents a conceptually problematic and empirically unsatisfying account of how nineteenth- and early-twentieth-century anatomical and anthropological research was implicated in colonial violence and oppression. It is true that bodily remains were procured after colonial police and settlers killed Aboriginal people, and there is highly suggestive evidence that in several instances Aboriginal people may have been murdered for the sake of their heads and skeletons. But these atrocities were isolated incidents that, had they become widely known within colonial society, would have provoked widespread outrage. It is also true that leading investigators of Aboriginal anatomy and morphology directly influenced the creation of policies and institutions to control the lives of Aboriginal people after the expropriation of their land. However, the ways in which scientific investigation of

Indigenous bodily remains gave cognitive strength to colonialist perceptions of Aboriginal destiny life-ways was often more indirect and at times more subtle – though equally pernicious in its consequences.

My concern in the remainder of this chapter is briefly to outline the case for undertaking a less conceptually rigid and more empirically grounded appraisal of how scientific analysis of bone and soft tissue influenced European thinking about the origins, nature and future of Aboriginal peoples. I want to suggest that while the procurement of ancestral remains by colonists was, in specific instances, actuated by aggression and the desire to inflict terror on Aboriginal people, the portraits of scientific body snatchers and their scientific clientele that emerge on studying surviving archival sources reveal that they were more often benignly disposed towards the Aboriginal people they encountered or interacted with, and often exhibited humanitarian – albeit strongly paternalist – concern for their welfare on their being dispossessed of their land with the spread of pastoral settlement. Their interest in procuring Indigenous remains, moreover, reflected the discursive weight in European intellectual and scientific circles from the era of the Enlightenment onwards of the idea that the pursuit of knowledge illuminating the origins and nature of humanity was a moral obligation, if not a religious duty.

Aboriginal Ancestral Remains and the Natural History of Humanity

We need to see that the meanings and values of Aboriginal remains changed as anatomical and anthropological research was affected by significant shifts in thinking about the nature and origins of humanity during the course of the nineteenth century. Not only this, in the evolution of scientific discourse, the meanings of remains came to be differently interpreted as a consequence of where researchers were located and with whom they interacted. Even with the emergence of transnational anatomical and anthropological networks from the 1850s onwards, how knowledge disseminated by these networks was interpreted was still influenced by intellectual assumptions and practices prevailing within particular institutions and societies. Also, more exclusive forms of interaction, such as patronage relationships between leading metropolitan scientific figures and colonial researchers, influenced the practice, results and perceived usefulness of research on remains.

Not only were remains variously entangled within a complex dynamic web of scientific discourse, the question of how they were implicated in colonial oppression requires the investigation of the historically contingent connections between the production of scientific knowledge and the concerns of a variety of social groups and institutions in both imperial centres and the Australian colonial context. Further, account needs to be taken of the fact that the relative weight of wider cultural forces was also subject to change, and capable of varying in influence as a consequence of the social circumstances and personal outlook of both those involved in researching remains and those who subsequently used the knowledge they produced.

Within the confines of this chapter, there is space to do no more than briefly outline some of the ways in which the scientific meanings and values given to human remains changed during the course of the nineteenth and early twentieth centuries, and to suggest some of the ways in which this evolving body of anatomical and anthropological knowledge became implicated in the colonial oppression of Aboriginal people. Nonetheless, this should be sufficient to underscore that the fate of Indigenous ancestral remains in scientific hands is inadequately explained as having been a violent manifestation of colonialist desire to prove Indigenous racial inferiority, so as to justify the expropriation of ancestral country and the forced resettlement of its owners on mission stations and government reserves. Archival investigation brings into focus a more complex historical landscape, in which the outcomes of anatomical and anthropological research had pernicious consequences, but did so by contributing in more indirect and subtle ways to colonial perceptions of Indigenous inferiority, the rationality of colonial acquisition of ancestral lands and the internment of its inhabitants under protectionist legislation.

Consider, for example, the commonly held assumption that one of the ways in which colonial and metropolitan scientists were fundamentally implicated in the colonial subjugation of Aboriginal people was by giving cognitive strength to European perceptions of Indigenous bodily and mental inferiority. While this is true, it was rarely, if ever, that the primary goal of examining Indigenous bones and soft tissue structures was to prove racial inferiority. Reviewing the wealth of relevant information published in specialist scientific journals and contained in unpublished correspondence, it is clear that generally researchers implicitly assumed Aboriginal people were corporeally and intellectual inferior. What they were looking for in investigating bodily remains was evidence bearing on how and why human populations had come to differ organically to the extent of warranting the hierarchical classification of humanity into different races, or perhaps even different species, as was maintained by some leading scientific figures through the course of the nineteenth century.

The reigning scientific orthodoxy from the last decades of the eighteenth century until well into the 1840s was that humanity shared a common ancestry, but populations had come to exhibit physical and mental differences as a consequence of environmental modification. Where people had come to inhabit parts of the earth characterised by harsh climates and poor natural resources, they had suffered what leading anatomical figures of the time termed 'degeneration'. Those inhabiting places with temperate climates and abundant natural resources escaped degeneration and quite possibly experienced bodily and mental improvements within what most scientific observers assumed were providentially determined limits (Turnbull 1990: 207–19).

A good illustration of how this reasoning came to be empirically grounded through the examination of skeletal material is to be found in the comparative anatomy textbook that Alexander Monro, anatomy professor at Edinburgh University, published in 1825. From the text of one lecture that he gave annually between 1817 and the early 1840s we learn that with the aid of the articulated skeleton of an Eora man, he explained to his students how the natives of the region surrounding the Port Jackson penal settlement established in 1788 were tall and slender as a consequence of inhabiting an environment in which a great deal of their energies were expended on hunting, supplemented by nutritionally poor wild plants. The shape and density of cranial and density bones further suggested to Monro that the dark-skinned native 'New Hollanders' were probably not of African ancestry, but a people who had migrated from the Asian landmass in whom the interaction of vital forces and the rigors of life in the supposedly harsher environment of New Holland had over time resulted in such a state of degeneration rendering them incapable of civilization (Monro 1825: 226).

As Bob Reece has shown in his pioneering study of early colonial perceptions of Aboriginal people in New South Wales, the presumption that typical bodily morphology was evidence of Indigenous corporeal and mental degeneration was commonplace in various books, journal articles and newspapers published in Britain and Sydney prior to the late 1830s (Reece 1974). What is revealed by closer scrutiny of these texts is that comparative investigation of what were presumed to be Aboriginal anatomical peculiarities had its aftermath in contributing to colonial perceptions of Indigenous inferiority. Authorities such as Monro offered what many colonial officials felt was compelling evidence as to why Aboriginal communities had not been found to practice what Europeans understood as agriculture. Indeed, anatomical knowledge appeared to explain Aboriginal resistance to integration within the emerging agrarian economy of New South Wales, raising doubts in the minds of many colonists whether the process of degeneration that was assumed to have affected Aboriginal people had gone beyond the point of being arrested or reversed.[8] Further, we would do well to note that the circulation of anatomical knowledge almost certainly occurred by modes other than print. Amongst the several thousand students who attended Monro's lectures over nearly a quarter of a century were a significant number who established themselves as medical practitioners in the Australian colonies during the first half of the nineteenth century. Many of these men were to play a significant part in the cultural life of the early Australian colonies.

Metropolitan anatomical research during the first half of the nineteenth century also contributed indirectly to the plundering of Indigenous Australian burial places in another respect. Records relating to the collections of the Anatomy Department at Edinburgh University suggest Monro's interest in comparative human anatomy also had its aftermath in past students seeking out additional skeletal remains as gifts for their old professor. Some of these donations, moreover, may have been connected with the fact Monro was one of a number of senior figures in the British medical establishment who became involved in the debates stimulated by phrenology, the radical science of cerebral location that gained credence in progressive middle-class circles in Britain between 1815 and the early 1840s (Cooter 1984).

Monro and other leading university-based anatomists were critical of phrenology, dismissing its core premise that the shape of the outer surface of the human cranium was an accurate indicator of the relative strength within the mind of specific emotions and intellectual qualities, though he and a number of other leading medical critics who subscribed to environmental degeneration nonetheless believed that intellectual capacity could be gauged from the density and shape of cranial bones. In drawing attention to how Indigenous Australian cranial morphology exemplified this, these authorities inadvertently stimulated interest in phrenological circles in acquiring Aboriginal skulls with a view to proving that their typical shape was in fact a reliable indicator of the relative power of emotion and reason in the mind of the 'New Hollander'. As a result, the theft of skulls to augment the collections of British and colonial adherents to phrenology came to be the major cause of Indigenous burial places being desecrated prior to 1850. And while it can be said that the reasoning of phrenology's adherents was such that this desecration could be understood to have been motivated by the desire to prove Indigenous inferiority, that proof was sought by devotees of phrenology primarily because of its perceived weight in refuting the reasoning of their critics. Only in certain instances was phrenological knowledge drawn upon as the basis for proposals concerning the welfare of Aboriginal people, and then generally with little result other than strengthening orthodox environmentalist perceptions of Indigenous inferiority.[9]

By the 1840s, environmentalist explanations of racial difference had come to be challenged by accounts of organic development arising out of the research of prominent Parisian anatomists and their pupils, amongst the latter of whom were numerous British medical students attracted to Paris after 1815 by the greater opportunities in that city's medical institutions to refine their understanding of bodily structures and functions through postmortem anatomy (Desmond 1989). These anatomists regarded all forms of organic life as having been subject to a trajectory of gradual transformation into more sophisticated kinds of being. In the case of humanity they reasoned that racial inferiorities previously attributed to environmental factors were actually due to these races having in time reached the ultimate expression of their type. To some, morphological differences between northern Europeans and the peoples of Africa, Melanesia and Australia were highly suggestive that these different races were descended from separate ancestral organisms.

Within this new discourse of racial transformationism, Aboriginal remains assumed new significance. They were considered objects potentially yielding insights into the organic processes by which human racial differences had emerged, and perhaps confirmation of whether humanity indeed had polygenic origins. This new status is particularly well illustrated by the anatomical collecting and research of Joseph Barnard Davis (1801–81). A surgeon and prominent figure in London anthropological circles during the mid decades of the nineteenth century, Davis was the most energetic collector of Indigenous Australian skulls and skeletons of the Victorian era. The impetus for his collecting Australian remains was his belief that their typical morphology was amongst the most compelling indications that humanity was comprised of the descendants of separately originating humanoid beings.[10]

The influence of transformationism in British scientific circles, however, was limited, and displaced in the early 1860s as a result of the widespread acceptance by younger scientists of Darwin's monogenetic theory of evolution. Darwinism quickly became the intellectual orthodoxy in British scientific circles, with the result that the motivation for procuring remains again changed. Initially, the value of the Aboriginal dead was that they might provide crucial evidence in support of Darwin's theory but, by the 1880s they were seen as a means of resolving questions arising in the course of seeking to reconstruct the course of human prehistory along Darwinian lines.

Regardless of how transformationists and Darwinians hypothesised the origins of humanity, skeletal remains were regarded as important materials for conjecturally recasting human history as essentially a story of racial struggle and supersession. Initially, the focus of this imaginative reconstruction was the deep past of western Europe, but imagining the course of more recent events in terms of racial supersession proved particularly attractive to Australian colonial officials. It provided a cogent explanation of relations between Aboriginal people and settlers during the first half century of settlement. Frontier conflict, however regrettable, was symptomatic of a natural process that would terminate in the extinction of the inferior native race. And it also strengthened the sense of colonial authorities that they had a moral duty to mitigate the worst aspects of this process (Turnbull 2000: 130–40).[11]

Disturbing Continuities

One could continue to trace in outline the cognitive evolution of European scientific thinking and opinion about the nature and origins of human difference from the 1880s into the first decades of the twentieth century – the period in which most Indigenous Australian ancestral remains that are currently the subject of repatriation claims were procured. However, to do so would merely serve to further show that the history of the procurement and scientific uses of Indigenous Australia remains was subject to important conceptual changes, which were variously to inform colonial perceptions of the nature and destiny of Aboriginal people.

Even so, there were continuities in how remains were viewed in scientific circles in several important respects. Firstly, there was the value accorded collecting and comparative analysis of human bodily structures. We can trace this phenomenon from the last decades of the eighteenth century, which witnessed increasing numbers of younger middle-class men seeking an education that would provide entry into a growing market for medical services. The monopoly on medical teaching long enjoyed by universities and more recently constituted bodies such as the Royal Colleges of Surgeons in London and Edinburgh was challenged, resulting in institutional reforms by the 1830s that created the basis of modern medical education. In the process, medical reformists championed the vision of the practitioner of medicine as a man not simply possessing practical knowledge of the body, but imbued by his education with a philosophical commitment to furthering understanding of the laws underlying the growth and reproduction of organic life (Desmond 1989).[12]

Consequently, many nineteenth-century naval surgeons and doctors who practiced in the colonial sphere pursued various scientific activities beyond the routine practice of medicine, and inspired many of their nonmedical peers to do likewise. Indeed, such was the virtue of scientific activity believed to be that it seemed wholly fitting to leading citizens of the rapidly expanding city of Sydney that, in erecting a memorial to John Gilbert, the ornithologist killed in 1845 on Ludwig Leichardt's first expedition, they should adorn it with the Latin inscription, *Dulce et decorum est pro scientia mori* (Sweet and honourable it is to die for science).[13]

Within various archives and publications are numerous accounts by surgeons and doctors describing their involvement in the procurement of Indigenous remains. A number of these tell of attempts to get remains at the risk of death at the hands of outraged communities. What these sources also show is that with the spread of European settlement in Australia, explorers and land surveyors, natural history collectors and also many ordinary settlers were equally ready to risk hardships and personal safety to procure remains from Indigenous burial places (Turnbull 2002: 63–86).

What is also clear from archival sources is that scientific interest in Indigenous remains was not immune to exploitation for extra-scientific ends. Stephen Petrow and Helen MacDonald have recently shown how fierce personal rivalry and hunger to secure recognition in metropolitan scientific circles led to the mutilation in 1869 of the corpse of William Lanne, popularly believed by Europeans to be the last male member of the Tasmanian race (Petrow 1997: 90–112; MacDonald 2005). However, we would do well to see that the Lanne affair was not the only time scientific interest in Indigenous remains was a thinly veiled pretext for personal ambition. From the early decades of European settlement there were instances where remains were sent to leading scientific figures by colonial scientific personnel in order to create or enhance patronage ties. With the establishment of colonial museums and medical schools in the Australian colonies, various personnel associated with these institutions strategically gifted remains to leading figures in metropolitan institutions such as the British Museum of Natural History, the Royal colleges of surgeons in Edinburgh and London, and university medical schools. What they sought to gain by these gifts varied; some aimed to strengthen their chances of election to membership of European scientific societies (Turnbull 1991: 108–21).[14] In several instances they aimed to secure favour for themselves or their sons with leading medical teachers.

Regardless of how the shape and texture of Indigenous bones were scientifically interpreted, there was consensus that comparative osteological collections were a crucial resource for generating knowledge to strengthen or unsettle competing interpretation of humanity's deep past. It thus followed that the most racially interesting specimens – amongst which Indigenous Australian remains were agreed to be – were the most eagerly sought after. Archival sources further reveal that reputation and status were not the only things earned through the theft of remains. From the 1850s onwards, low-paid museum workers, itinerant natural history collectors and bush workers also took advantage of scientific interest in Indigenous remains. They approached colonial and overseas museums offering remains with a view to being hired as collectors, or simply to sell them.

There is a further continuity in how remains were viewed in scientific circles between the early nineteenth and twentieth centuries which deserves particular consideration in view of Indigenous claims that the science produced through examining remains led to their ancestors being subjected to regimes of protection. This is the cognitive strength that scientific interest in remains gave to European perceptions of the inevitability of Aboriginal extinction.

By the 1830s, many British intellectuals, politicians and colonial administrators were gravely concerned that in South Africa's Cape district and the Australian colonies resistance to settler ambition had frequently led to the indiscriminate killing of Indigenous people. Few, if any, commentators believed, however, that settler violence alone explained the collapse of native populations. Rather, a wealth of eyewitness testimony to the impact of diseases, infertility and social anomie on Aboriginal communities was interpreted as highly suggestive that their demise was owing to undetermined natural processes.

Research centred on Indigenous bones appeared to confirm suspicions that racial extinction was a natural process. To many scientific observers prior to the 1850s the peculiarities they saw in Indigenous Australian bones when matched against accounts of population collapse appeared to provide additional empirical confirmation of the theory of environmental degeneration that had prevailed in European medical circles since the late eighteenth century. It also gave rise to debate within and beyond medical circles about whether the degree of degeneration supposedly signified by Indigenous bodily structures could be stabilised or reversed by protective, civilizing ventures such as those envisaged by medically trained Christian humanitarians active in bodies such as the Aborigines Protection Society. Anatomical investigation of Indigenous bodily remains was subsequently seen by believers in the progressive transformation of organisms, such as Joseph Barnard Davis, as proving the extinction of native populations such as the Tasmanians was one instance of an irresistible natural process in which races of unequal physiology and intellect sought to occupy the same territory with the weaker being extinguished. And Darwinians saw in comparative examination of Aboriginal bones and European bones signs of the emergence of 'higher races' through the mechanism of natural selection.

Not only were Indigenous remains seen as illuminating the underlying causes of the decline of Indigenous populations in Australia and other spheres of colonial ambition, the high probability of extinction they appeared to confirm in turn stimulated interest in the procurement of Indigenous remains. As George Bennett, a Sydney-based medical practitioner, naturalist and eventually one of the first trustees of the Australian Museum, argued in 1834, the decline in the Aboriginal population underscored the need to move quickly and systematically to collect ethnographic material, including the '... skulls of the different tribes and accurate drawings of their peculiar cast of features'. Within the context of the museum remains would figure prominently '... as lasting memorials of the former races inhabiting the land (Bennett 1834: 69).

Until well into the twentieth century, Bennett's rationale for collecting remains was to be echoed by many colonial scientists and museum curators, regardless of how they conceptualised the course of human natural history. Some of those who removed remains from burial places who were clearly motivated by racially grounded contempt if not hatred for Aboriginal people. For some, their removal of remains can be most plausibly construed as symbolically affirming their ownership of what had once been Aboriginal land. And there were those who robbed burial sites for money, or to ingratiate themselves with socially influential colonial or metropolitan scientists. However, within metropolitan and colonial archives are many more documents relating to the circumstances in which remains were removed from burial places which suggest that the scientific aspirations which stimulated the procurement of remains gained additional impetus from a desire to memorialise those whose destiny was racial extinction.

This is particularly illustrated by the way in which the articulated skeleton of Truganini was exhibited for over forty years after 1904 in the Hobart Museum. Whereas it has been argued that '... many whites saw her skeleton as the definitive trophy of conquest ...' (FAIRA 1989: 3), surviving photographs of how the skeleton was exhibited together with photographs of Truganini, her necklace and hair cuttings put one more in mind of the photographic *memento mori* of the Victorian era. The exhibit appears less calculated to evoke pride in conquest than to provoke viewers to reflect mournfully upon the passing of traditional Tasmanian life-ways and culture.[15]

Even so, we would do well to see that the nostalgia of George Bennett and subsequent scientists and museum curators was still to have insidious consequences, in that the collecting of remains in effect memorialised the passing of a race. As such it gave additional concreteness to the perception that Aboriginal people surviving the impact of colonialism had little or no affinity or connection with the people whose remains had come to rest in scientific collections.

Conclusions

I began this chapter by reflecting on the significance of the Vermillion Accord, drawing particular attention to how the accord has been instrumental in encouraging scientists with interests in human remains to understand and seek to meet the desires of Indigenous Australians in respect of the future of ancestral remains. However, my major concern has been to suggest how the history of the procurement and scientific use of the Aboriginal dead is a more complex aspect of our colonial past.

It is a history in which the meanings of remains shifted as scientific aspirations changed, though importantly, we can discern continuities in scientific treatment of the Indigenous dead, some of which were to have pernicious consequences for their descendants. While much has been achieved in the twenty years since the adoption of the Vermillion Accord, it seems that there is much to be gained by seeking to understand this distributing aspect of our history in greater depth. For one thing, a more historically informed appreciation of how and why remains were procured and used in the production of scientific knowledge shows the cognitive distance between contemporary researchers and the assumptions and practices of those scientists implicated in the desecration of Indigenous burial places. Contemporary scientific interests in remains have to be judged in the light of what knowledge they might generate. However, the vicarious knowledge afforded by studying how earlier generations of scientists procured and used ancestral remains may also be of value in serving to alert us that while contemporary research involving ancestral remains might be radically different, it remains a process equally pervious to cultural and personal predispositions that could have unjust consequences. To recall Linda Tuhiwai Smith's observation, though non-Indigenous researchers may regard their research to be for the greater good of mankind, they need to scrutinise what they mean by that idea, mindful of how, in previous contexts, what was believed to be research contributing to social and moral progress in fact contributed to some of the worse excesses of colonialism.

Notes

1. See Henry Atkinson's contribution to this volume. The ancestral country of the Yorta Yorta people includes much of what is now known as the Murray-Goulburn region of northern Victoria and southern New South Wales.
2. The Vermillion Accord declared that the following principles should provide the framework for research on human remains:
    1. Respect for the mortal remains of the dead shall be accorded to all, irrespective of origin, race, religion, nationality, custom and tradition.
    2. Respect for the wishes of the dead concerning disposition shall be accorded whenever possible, reasonable and lawful, when they are known or can be reasonably inferred.

3. Respect for the wishes of the local community and of relatives or guardians of the dead shall be accorded whenever possible, reasonable and lawful.
4. Respect for the scientific research value of skeletal, mummified and other human remains (including fossil hominids) shall be accorded when such value is demonstrated to exist.
5. Agreement on the disposition of fossil, skeletal, mummified and other remains shall be reached by negotiation on the basis of mutual respect for the legitimate concerns of communities for the proper disposition of their ancestors, as well as the legitimate concerns of science and education.
6. The express recognition that the concerns of various ethnic groups, as well as those of science are legitimate and to be respected, will permit acceptable agreements to be reached and honoured.

3. The question, however, is explored in the British context by Elazar Barkan (1992) and in the Australian context by Warwick Anderson (2005). Both studies provide contextualised accounts of the interplay of scientific assumptions and wider cultural forces in unsettling perceptions of the empirical validity and usefulness of the concept of race.
4. Barkan focuses on scientific debates in the interwar period, but stresses the importance of Franz Boas's *Mind of Primitive Man* (1911). Ironically, it was the size of collections amassed by earlier generations of scientists who were determined to delineate racial boundaries that contributed significantly to unsettling perceptions of the conceptual validity of race. As Oxford anatomist Arthur Thomson observed in a 1931 lecture: the '... diversity of skull form displayed in the human species is such that hitherto all attempts to classify have failed. It is easy to make broad generalizations, but ... these broad generalizations are in this case somewhat misleading. On the other hand, if you attempt to go into refinements, the complexity becomes so great that practically the system becomes unworkable' (Thomson 1896: 205).
5. While sympathetic to Aboriginal demands for the repatriation of the remains of known individuals and those having died in comparatively recent time, Mulvaney was concerned to stress the enormity of the loss of Pleistocene skeletal material discovered at Kow Swamp. However, what Mulvaney and other commentators on the reburial of these remains have not acknowledged is that Koori elders were hardened in their determination to have them reburied by the refusal of senior personnel within the Museum of Victoria and researchers interested in the material to concede that they should have any say in how they were used or exhibited. The deterioration of relations between Indigenous and non-Indigenous staff of the museum during the mid 1980s is extensively documented in Correspondence Files 15, 17,18, 30 and 33, Indigenous Cultures Section, Museum Victoria.
6. The grant reflects the important role that the institute, renamed in 1989 the Australian Institute of Aboriginal and Torres Strait Islander Studies (AIATSIS), was to play in promoting Indigenous participation in research on their culture and heritage.
7. Sixteen years on, the declaration remains in draft form due to the refusal of various national governments to recognise various Indigenous rights, notably the collective rights in respect of property.
8. See, for example, the views of Barron Field, first Supreme Court Judge of New South Wales, in his 1822 lecture 'On the Aborigines of New Holland and Van Dieman's Land', published in 1825, in his *Geographical Memoirs on New South Wales* (195–229).
9. Especially from the late 1830s onwards, phrenology gained few converts amongst the Australian colonial elite because of its radical religious and political implications.

10. Davis's views on human origins are most evident in his unpublished 'Notebooks' (see also Stocking 1987, especially pp. 66–67).
11. This theme is explored in Turnbull (2000: 130–40).
12. Desmond (1989) addresses this theme in his *Politics of Evolution*, especially chapters one and two.
13. Interestingly, the inscription is an adaptation of Horace's well-known declaration, 'Dulce et decorum est pro patria mori…' in the second poem in the third book of his *Odes*.
14. The ambitions of Edward Pierson Ramsay (1842–1916), curator of the Australian Museum are discussed in Turnbull (1991:108–21).
15. Out of respect for Indigenous Tasmanian religious sensibilities, photographs of the remains of Truganini are no longer reproduced.

Bibliography

Anderson, W. 2005. The *Cultivation of Whiteness: Science, Health and Racial Destiny in Australia*. Melbourne: Melbourne University Press.

Barkan, E. 1992. *The Retreat of Scientific Racism: Changing Concepts of Race in Britain and the United States between the World Wars*. New York: Cambridge University Press.

Bennett, G. 1834. *Wanderings in New South Wales, Batavia, Pedir Coast, Singapore and China: Being the Journal of a Naturalist in those Countries During 1832, 1833 and 1834*, vol. 1. London: Richard Bentley.

Boaz, F. 1911. *The Mind of Primitive Man*. New York: Macmillan.

Cooter, R. 1984. *The Cultural Meaning of Popular Science: Phrenology and the Organization of Consent in Nineteenth Century Britain*. Cambridge; New York: Cambridge University Press.

Council of Australian Museum Associations. 1993. *Previous Possessions, New Obligations: Policies for Museums in Australia and Aboriginal and Torres Strait Islander Peoples*. Melbourne: The Council.

Crotty, M. (ed.). 2000. *Proceedings of the Social History of Eugenics Conference*. Callaghan: University of Newcastle.

Davis, J.B. 1845–1860. 'Notebooks', MS 140/1–6. Royal Anthropological Institute Library: London.

Desmond, A. 1989. *The Politics of Evolution: Morphology, Medicine and Reform in Radical London*. Chicago: University of Chicago Press.

Fforde, C., J. Hubert and P. Turnbull, (eds). 2002. *The Dead and Their Possessions: Repatriation in Principle, Policy and Practice*. London: Routledge.

Field, B. 1825. *Geographical Memoirs on New South Wales*. London: John Murray.

Foundation for Aboriginal and Islander Research Action (FAIRA). 1989. 'Aborigines, Archaeologists and the Rights of the Dead', paper presented at the World Archaeological Congress on Archaeological Ethics and the Treatment of the Dead, Vermillion, University of South Dakota, 7–10 August 1989.

MacDonald, H. 2005. *Human Remains: Episodes in Human Dissection*. Melbourne: Melbourne University Press.

Monro, A. 1825. *Elements of the Anatomy of the Human Body in its Sound State: with Occasional Remarks on Physiology, Pathology, and Surgery*, vol 1. Edinburgh: MacLachlan and Stewart.

Mulvaney, D.J. 1991. 'Past Regained, Future Lost: the Kow Swamp Pleistocene Burials', *Antiquity* 65(246): 12–21.

Museum Victoria. c. 1969–1987. Collections of Human Skeletal Material and Other Remains. Correspondence File 18, Indigenous Cultures Section. Melbourne: Museum Victoria.

Museum Victoria. 1983. Meeting of Ministers with Responsibility for Arts and Cultural Matters. Correspondence File 17, Agenda Item 11, January 1983, Indigenous Cultures Section. Melbourne: Museum of Victoria.

Pardoe, C. 1991. 'The Eye of the Storm: the Study of Aboriginal Human Remains in Australia', *Journal of Indigenous Studies* 2: 16–23.

Petrow, S. 1997. 'The Last Man: the Mutilation of William Lanne in 1869 and its Aftermath', *Aboriginal History* 21: 90–112.

Reece, R.H.W. 1974. *Aborigines and Colonists: Aborigines and Colonial Society in New South Wales in the 1830's and 1840's.* Sydney: University of Sydney Press.

Smith, L.T. 1999. *Decolonizing Methodologies: Research and Indigenous Peoples.* Dunedin: Otago University Press.

Stocking, G. 1987. *Victorian Anthropology.* London: The Free Press.

Thomson, A. 1893–96. 'Lectures on Physical Anthropology'. Oxford: Pitt Rivers Museum Library.

Turnbull, P. 1990. 'A Forgotten Cosmology: William Hull and the Origins of the Aborigines', *Australian Historical Studies* 14: 207–19.

Turnbull, P. 1991. 'Ramsay's Regime: the Australian Museum and the Procurement of Aboriginal Bodies, c.1874–1900', *Aboriginal History* 15: 2. 108–21.

———. 2000. 'Savages Fossil and Recent: Gerard Krefft and the Production of Racial Knowledge, ca. 1869–73', in M. Crotty, J. Germov and G. Rowell (ed.), *A Race for a Place: Eugenics, Darwinism and Social Thought and Practice in Australia: Proceedings of the History & Sociology of Eugenics Conference, University of Newcastle, 27–28 April* 2000. Newcastle: University of Newcastle, pp. 130–40.

———. 2002. 'Indigenous Australian People, their Defence of the Dead and Native Title', in C. Fforde, J, Hubert and P. Turnbull (ed.), *The Dead and their Possessions: Repatriation in Principle, Policy and Practice.* London: Routledge, 2004.

10

Eric Mjöberg and the Rhetorics of Human Remains

Claes Hallgren

In September 2004, human remains acquired in the Kimberley region of Western Australia by members of the Swedish scientific expedition of 1910 to 1911 were returned to Aboriginal community representatives in a ceremony at the Museum of Ethnography in Stockholm. The expedition also collected a large number of artefacts, some secret or sacred, which remain to be repatriated.

In 2003 I published a book on the expedition entitled *Två Resenärer. Två Bilder av Australier* (*Two Travellers. Two Pictures of Aborigines*). My title referred to the attitude of two of the main participants in the expedition, Eric Mjöberg and Yngve Laurell. Mjöberg led the expedition and he described Aboriginal people in very negative terms, informed by the social Darwinist ideas of the time, in his popular account of the expedition *Bland Vilda Djur och Folk i Australien* (*Among Wild Animals and Men in Australia*), published in 1915. He was equally negative in a second book about an expedition in 1912 to 1913 to Queensland that appeared in 1918 under the title *Bland Stenåldersmänniskor i Queenslands Vildmarker* (*Among Stone Age Men in the Wilderness of Queensland*). Yngve Laurell was engaged as a member of the 1910 to 1911 expedition to secure a representative collection of Aboriginal artefacts for the Stockholm Museum. Yet, in stark contrast to Mjöberg, Laurell described Aboriginal life-ways and culture in what, for the time, were remarkably positive terms.

Mjöberg was a zoologist specialising in entomology and he acquired significant collections of zoological specimens for the Swedish Natural History Museum. However, he also collected a large number of human remains, as well as some ethnographical artefacts. Laurell also collected human remains, though not as many as Mjöberg, at the request of the Museum of Ethnography in Stockholm. He did so discreetly, not wishing to cause distress; and in an interview later in life expressed regret at having not fully appreciated Aboriginal obligations in respect of the dead. In contrast, Mjöberg highlighted his efforts to procure remains in gruesome detail in his published account of the expedition.

Mjöberg's vivid descriptions of how he procured remains come as a shock for contemporary readers of *Among Wild Animals and Men in Australia*, yet in 1915 they were thought appropriate to be published by one of the most respected publishing firms in Sweden and, since then, they have been read by thousands of people without arousing an outcry. It is also disturbing to reflect on the fact that his accounts of procuring remains have not been regarded as very shocking until now. Furthermore, we cannot discount the possibility that Mjöberg's descriptions were actually appealing to readers; and in the course of this chapter my concern is to consider how the apparent acceptability of Mjöberg's descriptions of his 'skeleton hunts' at the time they were written continues to be a moral issue. Indeed, it is morally unacceptable not to reconstruct the contextual framework of Mjöberg's skeleton hunts and to consider its implications for us today.

Considering what was normal at the time, one first has to state the obvious fact that at the end of the nineteenth century and beginning of the twentieth century the collection of human remains by explorers and others in so-called exotic parts of the world was almost the rule rather than an exception. Most Western countries have institutions which hold such collections. In fact, the public attention caused by the repatriation of Aboriginal human remains procured by Mjöberg led the Swedish government to commission an inventory of all indigenous human remains brought to Sweden and kept at various institutions – an inventory that was estimated to take several years to complete. In Sweden, and one suspects many other Western countries, little attention has been paid to these remains in many decades. The embarrassing fact is that when interest in the remains connected with Mjöberg was aroused a widespread search was necessary in order to locate them – a search that was by no means easy as the remains were widely dispersed without proper records having been kept of their location.

In the spring of 2004, the Australian anthropologist and archaeologist Kim Akerman and I were assigned to document and investigate the whereabouts and scientific use of the remains that Mjöberg procured. Originally they had been kept at the Museum of Ethnography in Stockholm, but we discovered that some time in the 1960s they had been sent to an osteological institute. There, no one seemed much interested in examining them and they were simply stored away. Indeed, we could find no proof that they had ever been used for any scientific research apart from one instance in the 1940s, when a dentist collected various skulls from different parts of the world to do some research on their teeth (the results of this research could not be located).

Today, these human remains continue to be considered scientifically unimportant. When I contacted the different osteological institutes in Sweden to find out if they had any Aboriginal Australian human remains, my request – somewhat to my surprise – was extremely well received. The scientists that I contacted were very willing to part with remains and eager to see them returned. They were as morally disturbed as anyone else involved in this issue. In fact, the repatriation of these remains seemed to offer an opportunity to those involved to show their moral concern – no-one that we dealt with expressed second thoughts or doubts about the necessity of repatriation.

Of course, this attitude is not very surprising today, but it should be added that very few seemed conscious of why the collection of Indigenous Australian remains had been of any interest at all in earlier days. In the wake of the public attention given to the repatriation of human remains collected by the Swedish expedition, the most common question from the media and others was: 'Why did they do this?' Knowledge of Australian Aborigines, American Indians and other 'exotic' peoples is much more widespread among the general public today, but there was no awareness or understanding of this strange and disturbing activity of our own ancestors less than a hundred years ago.

At the time when Mjöberg's book was published it was taken for granted that physical characteristics had something to tell about people. For a zoologist like Mjöberg, it was part of a new biological outlook caused by the rapid assent of Darwinian thinking about human origins and diversity in scientific circles – an outlook that Mjöberg believed had to be championed against what he dismissed as antiquated humanist and religious values. In his Australian books, missionaries are especially singled out as enemies of the new biological point of view; they are represented as weak-minded and unrealistic people who by their humanism and faith lack insight into the true biological causes of supposed Aboriginal inferiority. Mjöberg was particularly critical of missionaries for being implicated in what he described as the 'degeneration' of so-called 'full blooded wild Aborigines' who, he believed, would be better left in isolation from colonial society. This does not mean that he embraced cultural relativism. He made it quite clear that he considered Australian Aborigines to be on the lowest rung of the evolutionary ladder, hardly distinguishable from animals. In fact he saw so-called 'wild' Aborigines almost as a species in the fauna of Australia.

In his adherence to Darwinian thinking, Mjöberg does not differ from many other contemporary biologists and explorers but, if we look closer at the descriptions of his 'skeleton hunts' in his published accounts of his Australian travels, it is difficult to see his activities in a solely scientific light. Although it is true that accounts of exploration and travel, even when written with scientific pretensions, tend to focus largely on the telling of adventures with the intrepid explorer as the main character, Mjöberg's 'skeleton hunts' are rather strange adventures, compared to typical scenarios where the life of an explorer is put at risk. They suggest more about Mjöberg's personality than his discoveries.

Why did 'skeleton hunting' receive such an important profile in Mjöberg's narrative? Why had such a narrative any attraction at all to Mjöberg and his readers? To answer these questions one has to begin with some examples of the literary style used in describing these episodes. Consider the following episode Mjöberg recounts of coming upon a tree burial for the first time:

The body was sunken down and from the ground one could only see the grinning skull and the feet, projecting outside the bed. One arm had fallen down and its sun-bleached bones were spread on the ground.

The feet slightly crossed turned westwards. The black nails were still there. The skin covered the larger part of the skeleton, the bones shining through big holes. The skin of the face was gone, the skull being quite unusually white and tidy. The teeth were all there, shining like pearls. Only at the top of the head there was some skin left, covered by a tuft of black tangled hair (1915: 274).

This is obviously not a 'dry' scientific reflection but a rather 'picturesque' literary contemplation, somewhat romantic in style despite its gruesome content. This style is also evident in another episode:

A beautiful evening I loaded my browning, rifle on back, a linen sack under the arm, went off to the burial site, situated about two miles from a small well-worn forest path used by the natives.

It turned out to be a lovely moonlit evening. Nature was in deep sleep just disturbed by the indefatigable musicians of the night, the crickets, and some muffled tramples by the kangaroos.

I reached the airy bed of the dead youth. Perspiring after the ride I rested a couple of minutes and was now sitting in the silent night absolutely alone, the memories of the burial ceremony passing by (1915: 295–96).

It should be added here that Mjöberg had, against the will of the Aborigines concerned, participated as an observer at the earlier burial preparations of this particular individual in order to locate the tree burial and subsequently steal the remains. However, to thwart him, the grieving relatives had shifted the body from the original platform.

When he found recently deceased bodies, Mjöberg had to cut the flesh from the bones. His book describes this act in great detail, making a point of the fact that he was mentally tough enough to do it. These descriptions are not always truthful, however. In one of his most dramatic descriptions of this procedure it is very likely that the taxidermist of the expedition was the one that actually carried out the preparation, making it even more obvious that Mjöberg, was anxious to make himself a hero of these desecrations.

Other, similar extracts to those already quoted – including several luridly describing the removal of the flesh – could be reproduced, but these quotations are sufficient to make the point that Mjöberg seems to draw knowingly on the romantic genre of gothic horror popular throughout the nineteenth and into the early twentieth centuries: *Dracula, Frankenstein, The Strange Case of Dr Jekyll and Mr Hyde*, being some of the most famous examples.

Some of the elements evident in gothic horror stories, and which made them popular at the time, were the focus on the grotesque, the aberrant and the frightening: elements that did not just repulse but also attract. To understand how these contradictory feelings could combine one has to say something of the historical context in Europe that fed the gothic horror stories and also, I will argue, accounts of exploration and travel such as those written by Mjöberg.

One important influence in this period was the growing impact of the natural sciences. The consequence of the new rational outlook promoted by the natural sciences was a breaking with conventional Christian beliefs. This resulted in uncertainty and created an anxiety and reaction that fostered an interest in those aspects of life that seemed less available to a scientific outlook. Spiritualism, for example, was widely popular at the turn of the century. Along with other similar ideas, it supplied something spiritual to an existence that seemed to be threatened by a too rational scientific outlook on life. The interest in this less tangible side of life did not just appeal to a general public but in fact also attracted – for different reasons – scientists, some of whom thought that it was just a question of time before seemingly irrational phenomena would be subject to natural scientific explanation thereby bridging the gap between the rational and irrational.

For example, the application of electricity in inventions such as the telegraph, telephones and radios, paradoxically made some ideas like telepathy and the effect of moonbeams, which previously were often rejected as fantasies and superstition, more plausible. Mjöberg exemplifies this attitude. While he saw himself as an enlightened scientist, he too did not demure from speculations that involved non-scientific assumptions – a way of thinking that he unselfconsciously attributed to uncivilised races.

This tension between the rational and irrational also had what one may call a sociological foundation. To put it generally, there existed a European male elite, who saw themselves as the pillars of society and felt threatened by a diverse group of people who somehow could be expected to undermine their leading role. Especially ominous were the Jews (often considered as half Asians), homosexuals, women who rejected the domestic roles assigned to them and of course lunatics and criminals. Such categories of people were seen to be associated with obscure and frightening forces that threatened the rational order of society. The origins of these perceptions partly lay in the fast development of an industrialised and urbanised society. People in the big cities, being anonymous to each other, could not know for certain whether someone next to them in the street was a robber, lunatic or had some evil intent. The evolving phenomenon of 'the crowd', acting in unison without obeying any authority, also evoked the idea of behaviours directed by unconscious and innate impulses betraying any rational understanding. The elite, seeing themselves of course as wholly rational, did all they could to control and distance themselves from such threatening forces; but they were also fascinated by the very 'horror and abnormity' that threatened them – probably out of an uneasy consciousness that their own lives could not be entirely influenced by reason

It is very much these ambivalent feelings – which of course were widely spread due to the hegemony of the ideas of the elite – that explain the attraction of gothic horror stories. Moreover, while the threat was imaginary and found fictional expression in gothic horror stories, fantasy had real consequences.

The people who constituted an imagined threat did not just do so because they could act anonymously in an urban setting. They were given this role also because they were not easily classifiable in the hierarchical societal order in which white European males were at the top. Individuals and groups who were regarded as threatening were seen as such because they did not fufil their given roles and therefore destabilised the natural order. Jews were considered unreliable as they were not real Europeans, women taking an emancipated stance were not real women and homosexuals betrayed a clear division based on gender. This pattern could easily be projected to a colonial situation where it was thought, for example, that 'half-caste' people or 'partly civilised' people could not be trusted if white male power was opposed. As a rule so-called 'full bloods' in this scenario fared better when compared to the former, as their position was evident, On the other hand, 'full blood' people were considered 'savages' and could easily be singled out as indulging in all kinds of vices that had to be exorcised from 'civilised society'; and in this perspective 'half bloods' were upgraded as they were supposed to share capabilities associated with white people.

Just to make the picture complete one should add that if 'full bloods' were not threatening in a direct military sense they could also be romanticised as wearers of virtues lost in an 'over-civilised' society. Mjöberg expresses all these opinions in his books, without any real concern for consistency. He simply uses the available stereotypes when it suits him. But, above all, his narratives illustrate the combination of attraction and repulsion typical of gothic horror stories, and he was by no means alone in this respect.

The most evident example of this attitude is the preoccupation with cannibalism exposed in Mjöberg's and other's writings of the period. It does not need much investigation to realise that cannibalism, almost universally assumed to be practised by so-called primitive people, aroused feelings of both repulsion and fascination. Mjöberg's accounts of cannibalism were lurid fictions, with the exotic contexts in which they allegedly took place reinforcing their occurrence as true. In the case of Mjöberg, the idea of cannibalism had many facets and is clearly related to his descriptions of 'skeleton hunting'. To begin with, his description of how he cuts the flesh from the bones of dead Aboriginals illustrates him as, if not a cannibal, at least behaving in a fashion approaching that of supposed cannibals. Cutting the flesh from the bones is what one expects from a cannibal preparing a meal. There are also several passages where he describes the supposed cannibalism of Aborigines – whereas nothing Mjöberg observed first-hand justifies his claims, let alone representing these acts of cannibalism in a disturbingly approving way. Indeed, for Mjöberg, cannibalism could be seen as a sound and healthy habit, cannibals not being so fussy or weak-minded as missionaries, for example. In other passages, categories of people who compared badly with 'cannibals' were 'civilised' or 'half-caste' Aborigines as well as many whites in Australia from the lower rung of society – all of them in Mjöberg's view degenerate people. Fear of degeneration was a common theme and almost an obsession of the white male 'elite' at the time, and to Mjöberg the ability to cut the flesh from bones as well as to engage in cannibalism was a sign of the toughness necessary to withstand degeneration. One might say that in this sense Mjöberg saw himself as something of a cannibal.

On the other hand Mjöberg clearly identified himself as a man of science far above people who were cannibals and it is cannibalism that supplies a rationale for his reckless behaviour, with Mjöberg often insinuating that the Aborigines would, if an opportunity arose, gladly kill and eat him. The reader is led to understand that it is not the bones of the Aborigines that is the real issue but the bones of Mjöberg. He could be quite explicit on this point. Commenting on his second expedition to Queensland in the foreword to *På Giftets Vingar* (*On the Wings of Poison*), a science fiction novel he published in 1934, Mjöberg writes: 'The struggle for existence is extremely hard there and well formulated in the sentence: eat or be eaten ... the genuine cannibalistic Australian Negro would gladly have left my picked whitened bones as amulets to coming ebony coloured generations' (1934: 14). Clearly, it is not Mjöberg who wants Aboriginal bones but they, the Aboriginals, who are out for his bones. Hence the desecration of graves is represented as a trifling thing from a moral point of view and – to wit – not just a bone for science but also a boon to science.

Furthermore, travelling among so-called cannibals, Mjöberg could easily override conventional moral rules that applied in Europe – the atrocities of which he was guilty were definitely impossible to enact in a Europe without the threat of legal reprisals. In Europe, fantasies about cannibalism and other horrors had to remain just that: fantasies lived out solely as fiction in gothic horror stories. The Australian outback supplied a stage for enacting horrors that could not be experienced in Europe, and Mjöberg was the director of the fantasy, supplying the reader with the idea that the Aborigines were cannibals. Being horrible people they warranted no sympathy and could be treated in horrible ways. In an outback setting, Mjöberg had the freedom to satisfy his fascination with behaviour forbidden to European society, while at the same time defending the existing order and 'civilisation'. It was Mjöberg who was 'a savage' but he had to go to Australia as a scientist to be so.

Later in life, Mjöberg's compulsive interest in the grotesque, the aberrant and the frightening found expression in his very peculiar and fascinating work of science fiction, *På Giftets Vingar*, published four years before he died in 1938. This book deserves consideration at length, but here I will briefly examine its reworking of gothic horror themes.

Mjöberg claims in the book's foreword that it is an exact transcription of hallucinations he had as a result of being incorrectly medicated while suffering a serious disease. The medicine is the 'poison' of the title of the book. He emphasises that these hallucinations contain nothing of his own experiences, indeed that they are totally unrelated to any of the events of his life. However, on reading the book one can make many connections between this story and Mjöberg's experiences in Australia. Indeed, in my study of Mjöberg in Australia, I call this science fiction his third Australia book, even though it is unlikely that he would have acknowledged that this was the case, or maybe even have been conscious of how it drew upon his Australian experiences.

In *På Giftets Vingar*, Mjöberg describes a people living on an invisible planet, Telluna, situated between earth and the moon. The people are strikingly similar to Aborigines, but Mjöberg makes a fascinating inversion in his description of them compared to his descriptions in his two travel accounts from Australia. The 'Aborigines' of Telluna are sympathetically described in contrast to how Indigenous people are represented in his two Australian books. In the latter, the physical traits of Aborigines are always described in racially chauvinist terms as designating a low place in the schema of human evolution. By way of contrast, the more grotesque and animal-like people look on the planet of Telluna, the more intelligent they are, with the most monstrous far surpassing the intelligence of people on earth.

Mjöberg learns from a being from outer space called the 'Golden Lord' about a new way to perceive human evolution, one that rejects the current view as a misconception. This Golden Lord has abilities and characteristics that to a remarkable degree parallel those of Aboriginal healers or 'clever men'. The Golden Lord has supernatural abilities to take an invisible Mjöberg to various places not only on Telluna, but also on the earth. For example, the Lord takes Mjöberg on a guided tour through a part of London riddled with crime and vice. Here they observe an assortment of human 'perversities' that the Lord shows Mjöberg to underscore the importance of the new evolutionary wisdom he offers humanity.

In the depiction of urban vice, fascination and repulsion – typical of the gothic – are recurrent themes. The area of London they visit is nightly the scene of several murders performed for the pleasure of the act. Crowds of perverse people are attracted to the area, having become so asocial that they have lost the means to return to normal lives and the narrative offers several detailed examples of the perverse instincts that draw them to the area. There is, for example, a description of a group of transvestite prostitutes dressed as men who, being unable to do any decent work due to their obsession, prey on innocent people. A group of sadists are also encountered bearing signs of wounds and bruises as a result of fighting with their victims. Yet, rather than enumerating all the examples of the abnormal desires and vices of this 'scum of the earth' as Mjöberg calls them, I will focus on one further especially revealing episode. This is where the Lord and Mjöberg witness one unhappy man committing suicide. Mjöberg writes, 'The corpse was hastily taken aside and brought down into the gruesome cellar basement, where the dead body might the same evening be the object of mistreatment and mutilation' (1934: 119). Most people would have been horrified by an act of such perversity but it was a behaviour that Mjöberg himself was guilty of when desecrating Aboriginal corpses in Australia.

It is quite clear to me that Mjöberg's disturbing accounts of skeletal collecting in Australia reflect fantasies and imaginations that had a primarily European background. In my view, Mjöberg's science fiction novel suggests that his descriptions of the atrocities he committed in Australia were part of a wider

European obsession – an obsession that constitutes a necessary context to consider when discussing repatriation. If things are to be set right again one should not just point out evident wrongs that were done by Europeans, but also try to understand how the most horrible acts could be given a guise of normality in the circumstances of the time in which they took place. The better we understand a man like Mjöberg the better we understand an aspect of European history that has far more ramifications than is evident at first glance.

In repatriation it is crucial to also ascertain as thoroughly as possible the stories associated with the remains or artefacts procured by European scientific institutions. This is not necessary just for Aboriginal people and other people in a similar situation, but it is equally as necessary, if not more so, for Europeans living today if they are to understand the true extent to which science was implicated in the colonial oppression of Aboriginal people . The question encountered in the wake of the repatriation of human remains from Sweden to Australia, 'Why did the Swedish people do this?' must be honestly faced and answered to the best of our ability.

It is all too easy for the Swedish public to feel complacent by just endorsing the repatriation of the human remains stolen by Mjöberg. Yet, if they knew the full story, perhaps they would realise that these human remains carry stories that one cannot dispose of as easily as the concrete remains – remains that may be considered by many Swedish people to be a lot of uninteresting bones, that no one cares much for anyway, and which therefore, are suitable vehicles to express our present moral righteousness. The 'savages' are our own disciplinary precursors and they and their activities must be researched and presented for contemporary consideration.

Notes

* I wish to express my gratitude to Kim Akerman, not only for reading and constructively commenting on this article, but also for his constant encouragement and inspiring support of my ongoing research on the Swedish expedition of 1910 to 1911.

Bibliography

Hallgren, C. 2003. *Två Resenärer. Två Bilder av Australier. Eric Mjöbergs och Yngve Laurells vetenskapliga expeditioner 1910–13*. Uppsala: Kultur i Focus.
Laurell, Y. 1912. 'Etnologiska Undersökningar I Kimberley 1910–11', unpublished manuscript. Stockholm: Museum of Ethnography.
Malchow, H.L. 1996. *Gothic Images of Race in Nineteenth-Century Britain*. Stanford: Stanford University Press.
Mjöberg, E. 1915. *Bland Vilda Djur och Folk I Australien*. Stockholm: Bonniers.
———. 1918. *Bland Stenåldersmänniskor i Queenslands Vildmarker*. Stockholm: Bonniers.
———. 1934. *På Giftets Vingar*. Stockholm: Nordisk Rotogravyr.

Part V

Museums, Indigenous Peoples and Repatriation

11

Scientific Knowledge and Rights in Skeletal Remains – Dilemmas in the Curation of 'Other' People's Bones

Howard Morphy

The repatriation or restitution of cultural property and the return of skeletal material are not only emotive issues that are likely to attract media attention and political opportunism, they are also relevant to the nature of anthropological museums and the relation of anthropological knowledge to the Indigenous subjects of that knowledge. The relationship is one that is mediated through complex political and cultural processes.

Biological anthropologists and archaeologists, in particular those whose main concern is human evolution, may with some justice argue that they have not received the peer-group support, when it came to formulating arguments and articulating the case against the return of skeletal material, that they might have expected from other members of the anthropological community, (Mulvaney 1991). One reason for this lack of support may be that, as anthropological objects, skeletal remains have, to an extent, been marginalised by the historical position of biological anthropology within the discipline. Biological anthropology was for too many years associated with that past era of nineteenth-century evolutionary anthropology, when artefacts, bones and cultural facts were to a certain extent subject to the same body of theory. Social and cultural anthropologists, in particular those from the British tradition, struggled for years to disassociate their discipline from nineteenth-century evolutionary theory but, in so doing, they failed to keep up with the radical changes that took place in the once closely allied discipline of biological anthropology. Biological anthropology had become, through no fault of its own, alienated from much of the remainder of anthropology, and it became a victim of a stereotype that linked it with a positivistic, invasive and, consequently on both accounts, culturally insensitive approach to other cultures.

However, rather than conveniently treating human remains as someone else's problem, anthropologists would be well advised to see them as part of a much wider debate on anthropological knowledge and not as special cases to be sacrificed in the interests of goodwill and ideological soundness. Defence of the validity of anthropological knowledge should be addressed from a broad perspective of common interest and research objectives across the discipline, before making judgements on the particular issues. If the rights and interests of anthropologists and the subjects of their research are both to be recognized, then the rights of Indigenous people cannot be limited to whatever pragmatically emerges as the most politically convenient issue, but must be developed on a broader basis of interaction and exchange of values. Decisions about the return of skeletal materials involve a balancing of different moral issues and different cultural values that are of general relevance to research into other people's histories and lives. From a broader perspective, skeletal remains may no longer appear to be the central issue that they have currently become. In many respects, although this chapter is focussed on the curation of skeletal remains, it could as easily have been on the return of sacred objects and, in principle, on rights in photographic images and on pages of journals of exploration. Although there are fundamental differences between bones, objects, images and writings as sources of knowledge about and representations of other cultures, it is not impossible to envisage circumstances in which the return of photographs, objects and even writings could be as great a political issue as the return of skeletal material (see e.g., Willis 2008).

In this chapter I will begin my analysis by focusing on the kinds of rights that one might envisage being located in museum objects, before considering the way in which competing rights and interests might be ranked or evaluated relative to one another. This way of introducing the subject draws attention from the start to the fact that, as in almost any issue of cross-cultural rights involving minority groups or fourth world peoples, we are dealing with a contradiction, since the institution in which those rights are located or which is set up to determine those rights is likely to be an alien one. The very idea that there might be rights in museum objects reflects changes in the world in which people exist, and in particular their incorporation in a wider universe of discourse.

I will begin by setting up an opposition between the culture that emphasises the rights of the museum user and the culture that stresses the rights of the object originator. This polarisation helps to articulate the issues, though I will argue in the end that it is essentially misleading, since the museum users are also often members of the originating culture: there are Australian Aboriginal museum curators, educators and researchers, just as there are past and present Aboriginal producers of objects that end up in museum collections.

The Rights From the Museum User's Perspective

The issue of the rights vested in museum objects is a complex one and of necessity I must limit myself to the ideology of public and university museums and will not be concerned with the detailed legal position, or with the case of private institutions. Museums are repositories of cultural knowledge in the form of objects. In the charter of most museums the collections are inalienable and, except in special circumstances, objects are intended to be held forever. The collections should be available for research to contribute to the advance of knowledge in a particular field and through exhibitions the museum should contribute to public education. Thus, objects in museums are public objects and at least a major set of rights in them is held on behalf of the community. The community is difficult to define precisely since it is an ideological construct mediated through the curators, trustees and other higher authorities responsible for the management and legislation of the institution. It certainly does not include only those people with a research interest in the collections – if it did then it is unlikely that skeletal materials would ever be returned.

In abstract, the set of rights holders in a 'global' museum is almost limitless in space and time. As far as geographical spread is concerned, although some museums are mainly of local interest or focus on national identity, most major museums have an international dimension. Most natural history and ethnographic museums, apart from showing national and historical biases in the structure of their collection, could be transported to any other museum-possessing culture and be of equal significance. If a British ethnographic museum's collections were exchanged for a French or German museum's collections then the main differences would be ones that reflected the different colonial histories of the countries concerned – reflecting the entanglement of collecting with colonial processes. Museums in this sense are international and the museum curators, in particular, do not limit their services on the basis of the nationality of the client, even if some governments would like them to.

As far as time is concerned, museum curators deal with infinity on an almost routine basis, light levels are set and storage conditions constructed to allow objects a maximum life span; the possibility of microscopic deterioration may be sufficient to prevent a loan or deny a researcher access to an object. Although, in the case of a few chosen objects, scientific storage conditions may well make it theoretically possible for them to outlast the human race, for the most part, the illusion of infinity is a conceit backed up by caution – the likely real duration of most of a museum's collections may be too depressingly short for words. Nonetheless, the infinite perspective influences the view of who the client is, and the rights of the Inuit five hundred years from now have to be considered at the same time as those of the Indigenous Australian living today. This does not mean that the rights are equivalent since it depends on their relationship to the material concerned. A consequence of such a broad perspective on rights, and one that we shall examine later on, may be that it encompasses so many people that it diminishes the rights of the people who have the closest relationships to the objects concerned, or rather gives priority to rights at such a general level – for example, the right to have access to the object concerned – that it diminishes the rights any particular group or person may wish to have. The wish that a group have to destroy an object may be overridden by the rights of five hundred years of future generations of people to have a say in the decision and to have access to the object themselves. In a forthright and important article ironically titled 'Past Regained, Future Lost' John Mulvaney comes to the heart of the matter when he writes 'can custodianship be logically equated with the right to destroy?' (Mulvaney 1991: 18). Without making any judgement at this stage, any moral argument in favour of the destruction of objects should take into account this responsibility for infinity, that museums see as being vested in themselves.

Thus the justification for a museum, and the one without which such institutions would not exist but would be transformed into theme parks or exhibition venues, is that it holds its collections for all times and makes them available for research. Without this basis of understanding, people would not give objects to museums and governments would not contribute to their running costs, even though it turns out that governments are may threaten the tenure of their collections through instigating or supporting the return of objects to their originating cultures. (Clearly the two functions can sometimes be in conflict, for example, in the case of objects that are so fragile that access to them has to be severely limited, or objects that are so politically or culturally sensitive that access has to be restricted to them so as to restrict information about them or in order not to offend people's sensibilities.)

The Rights From the Perspective of the Originating Culture

The other set of rights relevant to the return of skeletal remains and sacred objects are the rights of the descendants and the rights of the producers of those objects, or people who gain acceptance as such. The rights in law of producers of museum objects varies enormously from country to country depending on copyright legislation, moral rights, privacy laws and the protection of intellectual property. The freedom to exhibit an artist's work as the curator sees fit is by no means universal. However, I am not concerned in this paper with detailed legislation but with the general issues of the extent to which the producer's wishes should be part of the curator's agenda: How would they wish their objects to be used and presented by others if their views were known? And increasingly, how should the curator respond to their views when they are known? Such questions are part of the more general issue of the representations of other cultures, groups or persons, and the use of information about them. Until thirty years ago, such issues were not part of the agenda of most museum curators in Britain and were only emerging as important issues in Australia.[1] Museums, in particular ethnography museums, tended to have a positivistic view of knowledge and their collection policies and exhibitions were designed to present information about other cultures, their technology, their place in the history of mankind and the social context of their artifacts in an unproblematic and largely descriptive way.

Two things combined to undermine this traditional basis for or ideology of ethnographic museums and exhibitions: one was the increasing recognition that such exhibitions were theory laden and influenced by underlying ideological assumptions; and the other was an increasing demand from Indigenous people, particularly the encapsulated fourth world representatives in countries such as Australia, Canada and the United States of America, to have a say in the way their cultures were represented (Ames 1992, 2000). These two movements were interrelated, since the Indigenous response was often part of a theoretical critique that originated in the dominant society, yet at the same time the Indigenous response was one of the factors that changed the conception that members of the dominant society had of outsiders. In a country like Australia, the separation of the views of museums into two categories, dominant societies and Indigenous peoples, is likely to be misleading and to result in the perpetuation of myths: that there is a single Indigenous view and that to be Indigenous that view must be the one taken.

There are in reality going to be a multiplicity of Indigenous views, many of which, if not all, are influenced by and are integrated within the political and ideological structures of the dominant society. However, this represents a complicating factor only if it is assumed that what ultimately needs to emerge is a single correct view. The breakdown of a uniform positivist paradigm into a multiplicity of complementary perspectives should result in the recognition of multiple rights holders, or relevant views, that have to be respected and responded to. The universality of the scientific paradigm comes into question and some of its underlying assumptions are questioned but, as a valid approach, it doesn't disappear. As museums confront the reality of multiple audiences with conflicting demands, the rights of the producers join in with the now-fragmented interests of the consumers. This fragmentation reflects the development of an increasingly complex view of culture, in which it is recognised that objects and events are multiply determined and that their meaning varies greatly according to context and the position of the interpreter, whether man or woman, adult or child, aristocrat or commoner. Such a process of opening up the complexity of the world has at times been associated with a kind of radical hermeneutic libertarianism, in which everything is interpretation. I prefer to see it reflecting the relativity of truth to the particular questions that are asked, and the complexity of the universe. But in each case truth has to be demonstrated in relation to the particular sets of assumptions and beliefs that produce it, and the complexity has to be recognised and elucidated rather than be designated as random chaos.

How then do we accommodate the rights of producers or descendants, how do we rank them in relation to consumers, to curators and their audiences? In many cases this can be done by responding to criticism, changing exhibitions, incorporating alternative perspectives within the same exhibition and ensuring that subsequent exhibitions have alternative views represented. The real problem arises in cases where the demands of one set of rights holders are diametrically opposed to those of another, where people say that their ancestors' bones should not only be removed from exhibition but returned to them for reburial.

Rights in Skeletal Material

Most museums could quite happily live with requests not to exhibit skeletal material and other human remains, even though there are many valid reasons for doing so and although they are often among the most popular of displays. The most contentious issue concerns the return of them to descendants, especially if the return is likely to result in their destruction. In the Australian Aboriginal case, Aboriginal activists and local communities have in some cases explicitly rejected compromises such as storing the bones in Aboriginal keeping places, where they can be preserved under Aboriginal custodianship, thereby keeping open the possibility of future research. Human remains are a major source of information to biological anthropologists about past lives, about people's diets, health and the age structure of populations as well as the evolution, dispersal and genetic relations between various human populations. Recent advances in analytic methods have exponentially increased the information potential of skeletal material and there is no reason to suppose that such an increase will not go on. As Macintosh and Larnach noted in the 1970s, Aboriginal materials are of immense significance since they may represent the 'earliest examples of an evolving generalised modern Homo sapiens sapiens to arrive in their ultimate area of migration' (1976: 124). Australian Pleistocene data is making a significant contribution to problems of human evolution in general and in particular to the questions of the origins and dispersal of what are now referred to as modern humans. Recent research based on the analysis of mitochondrial DNA, as well as more traditional morphological analysis, has shown the rapid spread of modern humans and emphasised the genetic closeness of human populations outside Africa (see e.g., Adcock et al. 2001).

In the case of Australian Aborigines, any well-documented skeletal material has the potential to produce useful information. Of particular importance are going to be skeletal materials of known provenance and date. Any material from the immediate post-contact period can potentially provide information about genetic relations across Australia, the biological correlates of particular forms of local organisation, as well as provide data for comparing pre and postcolonial populations on any number of dimensions. Thus the scientific importance of Australian Aboriginal skeletal material cannot be overemphasised.

The 'transcendent value' argument for keeping collections of prehistoric and near-contemporary Aboriginal bones in museum custodianship in order to make them available for future generations of researchers must be a very strong one. Yet, in recent years, many collections have been returned to Aboriginal groups for reburial including, in addition to contemporary material, perhaps the most valuable prehistoric collections, that of the Kow Swamp burials of nine to fifteen thousand years ago. What were the counter arguments that enabled their return? What kind of moral arguments in favour of the rights of a narrow group of people can have the power to override the transcendent interests of science or 'world heritage'?

There are basically three arguments that have been employed: one is that the materials were illegally obtained against the wishes of the people concerned (Mansell 1985: 27). A second is that they are not the kind of objects that should ever be in museums since they are integral to the religious life of the community; their presence in a museum is thus an act of sacrilege. The third argument is that research into skeletal remains is in theoretical terms opposed to the interests and beliefs of Aboriginal people; in the past it was associated with a racist ideology, which was integral to the European colonisation of their land and in the present, such research generates theories of the population of Australia that run counter to the Dreamtime ideology of an autochthonous origin for Aboriginal people (see Mulvaney 1991: 19). Clearly elements of the arguments can run together.

Although, in perhaps the majority of cases, there is no direct evidence that the human remains were obtained against Aboriginal wishes, this may be because the material itself is so badly documented. However it is worth noting that in many other cases the material was excavated from archaeological contexts and, until the last twenty years, its excavation would not have involved consultation with Aboriginal people. There are however a number of notorious cases, such as that of many Tasmanian Aboriginal skeletons, where we know that they were removed against the explicit wishes of the people concerned. Certainly in the case of the Pitt Rivers Museum, the skeletal material from the Kimberley, the most sensitive part of the collection (Hubert 1992: 105) of material that was returned to Australia, was said by the donor to have been 'obtained with difficulty'. However, in most cases we do not have the evidence to indicate forcible removal.

The most difficult argument to counter, yet also – in some ways – to substantiate, is the general one that the colonial nature of the relationship between Aborigines and Europeans meant that anything obtained by museums was inevitably a product of the dominance by Europeans of the Aboriginal population and hence it was not freely given. Such an argument applies equally to skeletal and nonskeletal materials and perhaps to words as well as things. Perhaps all research workers on human history depend on documents that were obtained in morally dubious circumstances, or reflect in themselves relations of domination, suppression and alienation. What in moral terms is the relationship between the photographs, journal accounts and objects taken on the Benin Expedition – all equally images appropriated from the past by an invading army, yet all sources of information for research? It is also possible, however, to exaggerate the extent to which museum objects are the products of domination, indeed, a good argument can be made that in many cases they are the products of Aboriginal resistance. Many of the Aboriginal objects in museum collections are there as the result of attempts to exchange ideas, to develop economic relations and more generally attempts by Aborigines to engage the European other. While this is not the place to fully develop the argument, it is clear that, just as the nature of Aboriginal resistance to Europeans has been reinterpreted in a more active mode by historians such as Henry Reynolds and R.H.W. Reece, so too can ideological relations. No longer are Aborigines viewed as passive victims of colonial process, even though they were victims of the unequal forces directed against them. In entering into exchanges with missionaries and traders and later with the wider international art market, Aborigines were asserting the value of their cultural products to outsiders and attempting to engage them in their own discourse over the nature of things. I have argued elsewhere that in the long-term, this strategy had in a number of cases a successful outcome (Morphy 2007: section 1). By seeing objects in museum collections as signs of the colonial domination of Aboriginal society rather than as assertions of Aboriginal values in alien contexts people are in danger of interpreting the evidence too narrowly.

The argument that the way something was obtained affects moral rights in it is a strong one, though it is clearly not going to be decisive in all cases. The case is almost unanswerable in parts of southern Australia, including Tasmania, where Aboriginal populations were decimated through disease and murder and the generally debilitating conditions of colonisation. The skeletons in the museums must in some cases have been the skeletons of known individuals whose remains were placed there against their wishes. To their descendants, they inevitably became a sign of the colonial encounter and of the domination of Aboriginal people by the colonists, the appropriation of their land and the threat to their identity and continued survival. It is no exaggeration to compare the Aborigines of southern Australia to the Jewish victims of the Nazi holocaust, and the idea of the Natural History Museum in London storing large collections of holocaust victims' mortal remains for research into human evolution on behalf of transcendent scientific objectives would have a somewhat hollow ring.

A key issue that arises is how far back in time such moral rights should be extended. The further back in time that we go, the harder it becomes to know the circumstances of the death or establish relationships with living people. It is in such cases that the issues have become most contested: should the rights in the remains be vested in humanity as a whole as transcendent rights – the skeletal equivalent of world cultural heritage – or should the rights be vested in the Indigenous group local to the area where the bones have been excavated (the most detailed examination of the issues surrounding this has involved the remains of Kennewick Man from Washington State in the United States).[2]

In such contexts it is desirable, if at all possible, for the interests of both sets of rights holders to be recognised and taken into account in any decisions that are eventually made. The relative balance of rights is going to shift over time in two senses: firstly, the time that has elapsed since the death and, secondly, the time the debate between the Indigenous and the scientific communities has had to develop (Dolan 2001). In the case of the bones of known Tasmanian people, this presents prehistorians and anthropologists with the most difficult challenge and one in which it is hard to imagine Aboriginal rights not being given priority; the analogy with the holocaust is a strong one. In the case of prehistoric materials the balance is much less clear. Where there are competing rights, the extent to which sentiments are shared between the competing claimants and the general population is a significant factor in determining the outcome. It is likely that the sentiments of Indigenous and non-Indigenous Australians today will coincide in the case of human remains that can be thought of as being closely related ancestors of contemporary populations. However, it is less likely that this will be the case with human remains that are thought to represent earlier populations. As Mulvaney has argued, the French are proud of their Palaeolithic heritage and would not welcome its destruction.

The second grounds for reclaiming skeletal material are religious beliefs. A wide range of mortuary practices existed throughout Australia but, in many areas, the disposal of the bones of the dead is an integral part of religious practice – in much of northern Australia, burial took place over a number of years and the final return of the bones to the land is taken as a sign of the return of the spirit to the spirit domain – bones are the sacred part of the person and are seen as the foundation of the clan. Even today, when secondary and tertiary burial are rarely practiced, the structure and themes of mortuary rituals remain similar with possessions and memorial posts substituting on occasions for the absent body. The initial and final burial of the body in the grave reflects an adjustment to European customs and sensibilities rather than a radical discontinuity with previous practice. In much of southern Australia, where the demand for the return of skeletal material has been strongest, the change in practice has been greatest, often resulting in a predominantly Christian ritual treatment of the dead. Memories of precontact mortuary practices are in many cases, where they exist, remembered by people from a literate tradition with access to early anthropological accounts. And any continuity with Pleistocene practice is highly improbable.

In many respects, however, such continuities are irrelevant. Anthropologists should be the first to recognise that human societies are in a continual state of change and that continuities are created as much out of the present as out of past practices. Details of immediate post-contact practice are at one level quite irrelevant to the religious sentiments of the present, and there is no reason why people should not believe that the fate of past souls depends on the return of their bones to the land. Many Christian sects, having far more improbable beliefs about the possibility of saving past souls, are protected by the constitution of the United States. Christian influence should not make it less reasonable for Aboriginal people to wish the body to be returned to the grave, even if some Christians believe, as do some people from Arnhem Land, that the bones – once the soul has left – are no longer an integral part of the person. The difficulty that anthropologists face is that, coming from a tradition that is at the same time scientific and relativistic and whose practitioners are trained to suspend their own beliefs and to be generally tolerant of the beliefs of other peoples, they find it difficult to confront fundamentalism in any form, but in particular when it is argued by those whose beliefs they had previously been defending. Ironically, accepting the fact that people will change, and acknowledging people's right to change does not in itself solve the problem of competing rights but, rather, compounds it since the descendants of contemporary populations may hold quite different views to the present generations. From this perspective, it is quite logical that Mulvaney, that most distinguished of Australian prehistorians, should be both outraged by the fundamentalism of Aboriginal advocates of the return of skeletal material and at the same time regret that they are denying themselves or their descendants future possibilities (Mulvaney 1991: 17, 19).

The third set of arguments in favour of the return of skeletal material are arguments against the research itself, either in relation to the history of biological anthropology or its present-day objectives. Much nineteenth-century biological anthropology was concerned with the identification of racial types and with the relationship of those types to human evolution or to parallel developments in human cultural and social organisation. The practice and, perhaps even more so, the style of this nineteenth-century research was one that often appeared to treat both dead and living members of other cultures as inferior objects of research; certainly not as equal partners in the quest for human origins (Hubert 1992: 105). Many of the negative connotations of biological anthropological practice may be a consequence of the natural and cultural symbolism of the human skulls in their ordered ranks in the anatomist's ossuary. Such displays, as well as being signs of the objectification that is one of the consequences of the scientific approach, hint at skulls as trophies held by victors, symbols of the appropriation of the power of others. In the case of the practitioners themselves a certain distancing from the humanity of the subjects, that is achieved by treating the skeletal remains as scientific specimens to be filed in ordered sets according to classificatory principles, may be necessary in order to avoid confronting the question of mortality at every step; to make the enterprise like any other in evolutionary science, man being no different from any other animal. The psychological distancing of the scientist may be a precise complement to the closeness felt by the descendants, the former avoiding the death of the subject the latter focussing on it. To quote Michael Mansell 'For us, these bones aren't just academic objects to be studied under the microscope they are the remains of our relatives and elders and command respect'.

There is of course no reason why the scientist should be the victim of other people's readings of the symbolism of his or her research; nonetheless, it is important to understand the emotional connotations for the subjects of that research and to respect them if a productive dialogue is to be possible. It is particularly frustrating for biological anthropologists to be tarred by the brush of their nineteenth-century predecessors when recent research has often had the effect of disproving racist theoretical assumptions, has provided valuable ammunition for Aboriginal people to use in defence of their rights and has assisted them to achieve recognition for their cultural heritage. Archaeologists and biological anthropologists have demonstrated the antiquity of people in Australia, their contribution to human cultural development and their genetic closeness to, for example, the populations of Northern Europe – in other words they have demonstrated both their uniqueness and their equality, two of the essential points that Aboriginal people themselves have been making.

Against this, Aborigines have argued that the requirement to make defences in such terms is in itself a consequence of colonialism and that even by putting forward positive arguments within that framework, anthropologists and archaeologists are acting as agents of the colonial process. It is in this context that some have argued that any demonstration of the common origins of human kind is against Aboriginal beliefs. Many of the Aboriginal activists who are demanding the return of skeletal material argue, at least in public, for a Dreamtime or independent origin for the Aboriginal population. (There is of course no reason why some Aboriginal theologian or theological process should not make a belief in a common origin for humanity and a unique origin through spirit conception compatible.)

According to myth, the genesis of the different Aboriginal groups was in the different parts of Australia where they live today. They were created by the Dreamtime ancestors who created their land. This process of Dreamtime creation continues into the present. The present and the past are linked in a cyclical process whereby each child is the product of spirit conception that directly links him or her with the Dreaming. Very often this process of Dreamtime creation also involves the recycling of the souls of the dead, which is accomplished largely through correct burial practice. From this perspective, and combining concern for the fate of the individual's soul with the requirements of group survival, people could feel deep unease at the thought of skeletons of relatives, however distant, remaining forever in museums. People may feel deep sorrow for the person whose sacred journey has been deflected, suspended for a millennium or so while their skull remains locked behind a succession of glass showcases or joins the ranks of the many on the shelves of the museum basement, and they could also feel the loss of a spiritual resource.

I do not intend this to be anything more than a story of how a group of Aboriginal people might feel, as something that could flow logically out of some sets of Aboriginal beliefs. Again, to quote Michael Mansell: 'Laying our ancestors bones to rest is like breathing life into our own.' Many people are not going to have this reaction. Certainly I have no evidence that the people of north-east Arnhem Land, who hold most of the beliefs that I have outlined above, were in any way deeply concerned about relatives whose skeletal remains were deposited in Australian museum collections, though they would undoubtedly be concerned if mortuary rituals were interrupted by the removal of bones and would be unlikely to give permission for their graveyards to be excavated. However, once the mortuary cycle has been completed and the bones have ended up broken into a hollow log coffin, they tend to be viewed as relatively inert and spiritually neutral objects.

What I hope I have shown is not how the request for the return of skeletal remains comes out of a common set of Aboriginal beliefs, which is certainly not the case, but how a whole variety of factors operates together to make it likely that the return of skeletal material, in some cases and in some contexts, will strike a strong chord among many different groups of Aboriginal people depending on their particular history, the history of the skeletal material concerned and contemporary political context. I hope I have shown why arguments directed towards countering particular factors cannot easily work when what one is concerned with is a whole climate of opinion. Arguments in particular cases may even be counterproductive. For example, the argument has been put that traditional Aboriginal attitudes to skeletal material in south-east Australia included regarding skulls as perfectly mundane raw materials, to the extent that they were used as water vessels by their descendants. Putting aside the fact that we know little about the extent of such usage or the cultural context – they may for example have been enemies skulls or the carrying of the skulls could have been part of an extended mortuary practice – the argument may be irrelevant to the real reasons people want the material returned and to contemporary religious beliefs about them.

Arguments Against the Return of Skeletal Material

What then are the strongest arguments that can be employed in favour of the retention of skeletal material? Essentially they are the arguments that we have summarised already and the arguments of general principle that have been put forward by the scientists. Mulvaney's argument against fundamentalism is a strong one, as is the implicit argument in favour of academic freedom and against the censorship of history. Essentially, however, they are arguments from the point of view of the transcendence of science and, in order to be accepted, they require persuasion – for they are up against the beliefs, the grievances and the emotions of the present and the rights of particular individuals and groups. It is clearly vital that arguments be put forward in favour of the research objectives, even while conceding the moral argument in favour of the return of skeletal material in the particular case; it is necessary to challenge the misconceptions about the nature of the research, its objectives and the moral and ethical stance of the scientific community. It is important to disabuse people of the idea that the present objectives are closely allied to the idea of nineteenth-century racist theorists. The danger of returning material without clarifying the basis on which it is being returned is that it may be taken as a tacit acceptance that all of the arguments were correct, thereby supporting a system of argument that can be applied just as easily to many other areas of anthropology.

If we are holding things on behalf of science and humanity the solution must be to involve the producers, owners and descendants in the curation of the collections and in the decision-making process. This doesn't mean that control is handed over but that a partnership develops – since the ideology of a museum is that there are multiple audiences and multiple rights holders, and a museum is conserving things for science as a record of human creativity and the history of the world. But just as this provides a moral justification for the appropriation of other people's products, it also creates a moral obligation to include them among the body of decision makers.[3]

The arguments over the return of skeletal materials are largely arguments over the value that objects have to people and in interactions among people. It is inevitable that objects are going to be of different value to people according to their relative positions in historical process and where in their trajectories through life the particular objects are placed. If we are part of a world community then it has to be in spite of this conflict over values, it cannot mean that we all think the same way since that would almost inevitably mean the imposition of hegemony of values onto a world system. It means that we must allow for the existence of fundamentalist views, yet it also means that those views exist in the context of a discourse in which other people have rights. We are all actively involved in an engagement over the value and meaning of objects, laying claims over them for purposes that are often temporary in the case of objects whose future is unknown and whose potential largely untapped. As Anderson (1990: 54–5) has written 'there can be neither moral nor political content in a relationship between groups that do not know each other, which has therefore no social substance. If we want to do things according to Aboriginal tradition, then it is not simply a moral and political response, which is required in cases of repatriation. An alternative way of looking at such transfers is to consider objects as part of a dynamic social/ceremonial/political and economic system, in which objects circulate, and create sets of rights and obligations between individuals and groups or institutions. In other words the objects act as social currency.' While it could be argued that this is simply involving Aborigines in the culture of the museums as a means of subverting their resistance, it could also be seen as a transformation of the concept of the museum through its incorporation of Aboriginal concepts (Morphy 2006). It is certainly the case that Anderson sees such developments as resulting, in the long term, in the mutual understanding of each other's motives and objectives, and in a forum being created for the exchange of value. One of the ideas communicated will clearly be the concept of the transcendent value of particular categories of museum object. The justification of preservation for future populations is a very strong one, but is not an absolute one. And at least for moments in time, the value of holding an object in a museum may become so negative, that the pressures to release it are overwhelming.

Dolan (2001) in an article examining the response to a Museums Australia policy document pointed out the sense of powerlessness felt by many museum professionals when faced with government and institutional policy. All things being equal the struggle over the value and destiny of human remains and some other museum 'objects' is likely to be a tough one, punctuated by disputes where neither side is prepared to give way and by confrontations where each side is considered authoritarian by the other. But the two sides are not equal; they are unequal in different ways and at different times. Irony takes centre stage. On the one hand, the history of domination and the present poverty of much of the

Aboriginal population make it likely that many Aboriginal political activists will reject the universalistic and transcendent arguments of the European Australian scientist as a matter of principle. On the other hand, the European Australian politicians will support Aboriginal demands on pragmatic grounds – regarding the return of human remains and other objects as a relatively uncontroversial recognition of Indigenous rights. Aborigines have relatively little power but the same is true of museum curators. In the latter part of the twentieth century, museums moved from a time in which their collections were largely disconnected from the populations of origin to one in which these populations had the power to legally resume human remains. The movement that enabled this transformation was located in museum discourse as much as in the world outside, and was associated with changes in the relationships between museums and the communities they answered to.

The dialogue between Aboriginal Australians and museums and their associated professions has developed productively over the past thirty years. Involvement of Aborigines in research has become substantial. Permission of relevant groups is sought before any excavations are carried out, Aboriginal interests are considered in developing research proposals and many Aborigines have become professionals in anthropology, archaeology, heritage and museum curation. Aboriginal involvement in the management of collections and in collection policy, and the development of keeping houses in local communities has created the possibility for Aboriginal groups to hold sensitive materials under their own custodianship. These very processes of dialogue and exchange, together with the acknowledgement of an increasingly broad range of interests in museum collections, are themselves part of value creation processes that change understandings of the world. They set the basis for understanding Indigenous perspectives on museum collections and equally the different ways in which those collections are valued and perceived in society more generally. That dialogue and the increased representation of Indigenous people in the work of museums is likely to change understandings of the value potential and connotations of museum collections. It is also going to expose Indigenous communities to the motivations of contemporary curators as opposed to the motivations that shaped the past histories of those collections. The fear among many curators is that the instrument of the law, set up in an atmosphere of conflict and mutual distrust, cuts across dialogues that may need time to evolve productively. The law may intervene to call a halt to processes of persuasion that are ongoing and that are achieving successful outcomes in more local arenas. The boundaries between the unanswerable cases for the return of skeletal material and the cases where the demand has not even been articulated may be blurred. In the blurred boundary zone, the variety of opinions among contemporary Aboriginal populations and the potential choices of future generations of Aboriginal scientists are disregarded just as much as are the rights of contemporary non-Aboriginal scientists.

Notes

1. It is easy to exaggerate the role that ethnographic museums played in separating objects from their producers. Museums played a significant role in arguing for the value of Indigenous cultures in a world that was often dismissive of them. And many other factors, including geographical distance, contributed to lack of connection between museums and producers. However, globalisation and an increasing consciousness of the rights of Indigenous people contributed to significant paradigm change in ethnographic museums beginning in the 1970s (Karp and Levine 1991), in particular in settler colonial societies (Ames 1992). In the 1980s, the repatriation of cultural property and, in particular, skeletal remains – which had long been a concern – in some cases became a major issue of debate (Fforde, Hubert and Turnbull 2002).
2. Interestingly the US National Parks Service web site on Kennewick Man almost implies the recognition of divergent rights or claims over the human remains of Kennewick Man is in itself rhetoric. Their reply appears to ignore the consideration of Native American interests if they differ from those of the scientific investigators: 'Some commentators and reporters have described the legal controversy swirling around the Kennewick remains in rather super-heated rhetoric pitting the interests of "science" against those of traditional Native Americans. This characterisation ignores the detailed, intensive, and wide-ranging scientific investigation of the Kennewick remains undertaken to determine the facts relevant to the questions in the case and report them' (National Park Service 2004)
3. This position was clearly articulated by the path-breaking report by the Council of Australian Museum Associations, *Previous Possessions, New Obligations: Policies for Museums in Australia and Aboriginal and Torres Strait Islander Peoples.*

Bibliography

Adcock, G.J., et al. 2001. 'Mitochondrial DNA Sequences in Ancient Australians: Implications for Modern Human Origins', *Proceedings of the National Academy of Sciences of the USA* 98(2): 537–42.

Ames, M.M. 1992. *Cannibal Tours and Glass Boxes.* Vancouver: UBC Press.

Ames, M. 2000. 'Are Changing Representations of First Peoples in Canadian Museums and Galleries Challenging the Curatorial Prerogative?' in R.West (ed.), *The Changing Presentation of the American Indians: Museums and Native Cultures.* Washington: National Museum of the American Indian, Smithsonian Institution, pp. 73–88.

Anderson, C. 1990. 'Repatriation of Cultural Property: a Social Process', *Museum* 165(1): 54–5.

Council of Australian Museum Associations. 1993. *Previous Possessions, New Obligations: Policies for Museums in Australia and Aboriginal and Torres Strait Islander Peoples.* Melbourne: The Council.

Dolan, J. 2001. 'Making Policy Practice: Previous Possessions, New Obligations in Western Australian Community Museums', *Open Museum Journal* 3: 1–27.

Fforde, C., J. Hubert and P. Turnbull (eds). 2002. *The Dead and Their Possessions: Repatriation in Principle, Policy and Practice.* London: Routledge.

Hubert, J. 1992. 'Dry Bones or Living Ancestors? Conflicting Perceptions of Life, Death and the Universe', *International Journal of Cultural Property* 1(1): 105–28.

Karp, I. and S.D. Levine. 1991. *Exhibiting Culture: the Poetics and Politics of Museum Display*. Washington: Smithsonian Institute Press.

Macintosh, N.W.G., Larnach, S.L. 1976. in R.L. Kirk and A.G. Thorne (eds), *The Origin of the Australians*. Canberra: Australian Institute of Aboriginal Studies, pp. 113–26.

Mansell, M. 1985. 'Tasmanian Aboriginal Bones', *Anthropology Today* 1(6): 27.

Morphy, H. 2006. 'Sites of Persuasion: Yingapungapu at National Museum of Australia', in I. Karp et al. (eds), *Museum Frictions: Public Cultures/Global Transformations*. Durham, NC: Duke University Press, pp. 469–96.

———. 2007. *Becoming Art: Exploring Cross-Cultural Categories*. Oxford: Berg.

Mulvaney, D.J. 1991. 'Past Regained, Future Lost: the Kow Swamp Pleistocene Burials', *Antiquity* 65(246): 12–21.

National Park Service. 2004. Retrieved from http://www.cr.nps.gov/archeology/kennewick/

Willis, E. 2008. 'The Law, Politics, and "Historical Wounds": The Dja Dja Warrung Bark Etchings Case in Australia', *International Journal of Cultural Property* 15(1): 49–63.

12

Despatches From The Front Line? Museum Experiences in Applied Repatriation

Michael Pickering

Like most Australian museums, the National Museum of Australia has been active in the return of ancestral remains and sacred objects. Repatriation exercises have generally proceeded without incident, attesting to the effectiveness of the methods and procedures applied by Australian museums in the repatriation process. This chapter describes the applied activities of the National Museum of Australia in repatriating ancestral remains and sacred objects. It then considers what has been learned through this work and to identify what might be required for the future development of the repatriation process. My argument is that, while applied repatriation proceeds as a practice, there is still a strong need for the process to be better informed by multidisciplinary debates that address the philosophical and theoretical considerations of repatriation.

Repatriation is a fascinating topic. The issues and considerations that arise when it is discussed can attract contributions from many different interests. The topic easily accommodates questions of ethics, law, anthropology, archaeology, history, philosophy, religion, politics and museology. Sometimes, however, conditions apply, such as time constraints, which limit a professional's, or an institution's, balanced engagement with these broader themes.

In recent years, Australian museums have been meeting the challenges of applied repatriation in Australia, with many notable successes and remarkably few problems. This is the direct outcome of increased federal and state funding that has allowed concerted efforts towards proactive repatriation. The Return of Indigenous Property Program (RICP) has been operating since 2001. An initiative of the Cultural Ministers' Council, using combined federal, state and territory funding, and administered by the Department of Environment, Water, Heritage and the Arts (DEWHA), this program has provided much needed support to both museums and communities (see DCITA n.d.). Individual state and territory museums also occasionally receive support funding through other agencies. The National Museum of Australia's repatriation program has been greatly supported by funding from the Department of Families, Housing, Community Services and Indigenous Affairs.

However, due to a number of considerations, including the expected limited life of external funding, contractual responsibilities and obligations to supply repatriation services to potential custodial communities within socially and administratively acceptable time-frames, the focus of participating Australian museums has necessarily been on actual and prompt physical repatriation, with quantifiable results, over a limited time. As a result, museum staff engaged in repatriation can rarely dedicate the time and resources necessary to carry out pure research into the 'companion' issues associated with repatriation and, thus, they are often reliant upon the work of external researchers to inform repatriation exercises. Similarly, however, such external debates need to be informed by knowledge of the actual practice of repatriation.

To this end, this chapter describes the applied repatriation process as practiced by the National Museum of Australia, the considerations relevant to its application, some of the issued raised in its practice and, finally, makes a plea for greater multidisciplinary involvement.

Repatriation and the Australian Museum Industry

The return of Aboriginal and Torres Strait Islander human remains and sacred objects is now a key principle in the Australian museums industry. Museums Australia, the peak industry professional body, released a document entitled *Continuous Cultures, Ongoing Responsibilities*. This document states explicitly:

> Repatriation
> 1.4.3 The community from which the ancestral remains originated needs to be involved in deciding what will happen to remains repatriated by museums.
> 1.4.4 Museums are to seek out the rightful custodians of ancestral remains and ask them whether they wish the remains to be repatriated to the community or held by the museum on behalf of the community.
> 1.4.5 If rightful custodians ask for the return of ancestral remains museums should agree. All requests for the repatriation of Aboriginal and Torres Strait Islander ancestral remains should be promptly and sensitively dealt with by museums, who must at all times respect the materials' very sensitive nature.
> 1.4.6 Museums must not place conditions on communities with regard to the repatriation of ancestral remains, (Museums Australia 2005:18)

Similar wording applies to secret sacred objects. While not binding on museums, the document both derives from and enshrines the philosophies and principles expected from practitioners in the Australian museum industry. All state and territory museums now have either policies or protocols that commit each museum to the repatriation of Australian Indigenous remains and sacred objects (e.g., National Museum of Australia 2005).

Repatriation at the National Museum of Australia

Australian state and territory museums have been returning ancestral remains and sacred objects to Aboriginal and Torres Strait Islander people for over twenty-five years (although with varying degrees of willingness in the early years). Most repatriation exercises were responses to unsolicited requests from Indigenous groups. Repatriation events were few and far between and handled on a case-by-case basis. Since the late 1990s however, federal, state and territory museums have had the opportunity to be more proactive in repatriation exercises through the provision of extra state and federal funding programs.

Since its inception in 1980, the National Museum of Australia, like most Australian museums, had been returning remains and secret sacred objects to Aboriginal and Torres Strait Islander people upon request. The returns were slow but consistent over twenty years. In 2001, the Museum established a Repatriation Program Unit to manage the return of Indigenous remains and sacred objects. This was facilitated by support funding to repatriate remains returned from Edinburgh University in 1991 and 2000, and by RICP funding for domestic repatriations. Since then, the Museum has become an industry leader in the repatriation of human remains and sacred objects.

The Museum's own holdings of human remains and sacred objects derive from many sources. Most of the remains are from the old Australian Institute of Anatomy collections that were transferred to the Museum in 1985 following the institute's closure. The institute was established in the 1930s and established large collections of human and animal biological specimens, as well as an enviable collection of other cultural objects that are now held by the Museum.

The Museum has also become the unofficial repository and repatriation service provider for some collections from overseas. For example, collections from Edinburgh University, the Royal College of Surgeons, Manchester and Horniman Museums, all in the United Kingdom; the Bishop Museum and Michigan University in the United States and from the Museum of Ethnography in Sweden, amongst others, are held by the Museum while they are awaiting repatriation. While all of these remains have been temporarily deposited with the Museum, the advocacy that resulted in the returns was primarily carried out by Indigenous representatives and Indigenous representative bodies. These include the former Aboriginal and Torres Strait Islander Commission (ATSIC), Aboriginal and Torres Strait Islander Services (ATSIS), the Office of Indigenous Policy Coordination (OIPC), the Foundation for Aboriginal and Islander Research Action (FAIRA) and the Aboriginal Legal Rights Movement (ALRM).

The Museum's holdings of secret sacred objects similarly derive from the Institute of Anatomy's ethnographic collections, collections that were held by the federal government pending the establishment of a national museum, collections that were subsequently acquired by transfer or purchase and by donations.

Process

The operations of the Museum's Repatriation Unit are guided by the Aboriginal and Torres Strait Islander Human Remains Policy (National Museum of Australia 2005) and the *Policy on the Aboriginal and Torres Strait Islander Secret/Sacred and Private Material*. The most significant characteristics of these policies have been, firstly, that they require the unconditional return of remains and secret sacred objects to traditional owners and custodians upon request and, secondly, that any other external access to the remains or secret sacred objects collection is only permitted with the approval of the relevant community.

The Museum has also stored and returned remains from overseas under contract initially to the OIPC and currently to FAHCSIA. This contract imposes conditions of security that, again, are aimed at protecting Indigenous authority over remains.

The Museum does not have an Indigenous committee to oversee repatriation. There are a number of reasons for this. The first and most significant being that the most important authorities and advisors remain, of course, the identified custodians themselves. There is little advantage in imposing another level of management between the museum and the primary custodial community. Secondly, if other advice is required, there are a number of eminent Indigenous people on staff, in the adjacent Australian Institute of Aboriginal and Torres Strait Islander Studies (AIATSIS), at the Australian National University, and within the wider community who provide advice to the Museum on important issues as required.

Identification of Custodians

The Museum's repatriation process is proactive. The work begins with the identification and documentation of remains or objects by geographical or cultural origin. The provenance is then located. The next stage is preliminary consultation with relevant state and territory heritage authorities to assist in the identification of formally recognised representative organisations and/or individuals. The primary reason for this approach is that the National Museum of Australia is as accountable as any other organisation that spends from the 'public purse'; it is expected to show evidence of due process and it is expected that its activities will accord with the laws of the state or territory jurisdictions in which the repatriation activities occur. This responsibility encourages engagement with state and territory government Indigenous heritage management departments, and Indigenous representative bodies such as land councils, native title representative bodies and legal aid services.

Secondly, Indigenous representative bodies, established by legislation or supported by state, territory, or federal funding, themselves have a responsibility to represent custodians, traditional owners and native title holders. The identification of such individuals and groups based on cultural, anthropological, as well as legislative, criteria is their day-to-day business. Access to this information – achieved through their endorsement of a repatriation claimant, not by disclosure of personal and private particulars – assists the Museum in fast tracking the repatriation process to the benefit of custodians. At the same time, such engagement provides some protection for museums when they are required to describe whom they dealt with and the basis for their accepting that individual or group as being the appropriate custodians for repatriated items. As, for example, through government audit, discovery of documents for legal process (native title), enquiries by other Indigenous representatives and senate inquiry.

Put simply, the Museum recognises and uses the local knowledge that such organisations provide in order to assist with identification of prospective custodians or their representatives. The effectiveness of this method is demonstrated by the lack of major opposition to the Museum's repatriation activities by other majority groups.

Once a prospective custodian, custodial group or representative body has been identified, they are advised in writing of the nature of the remains or objects available for return to them. Correspondence includes a statement of 'Advice to Applicants' that details how to apply for the return of material. This statement asks prospective custodians for any information that may assist in supporting their application for repatriation, including:

- The identities of the persons, groups, or community on whose behalf the application is made.
- The specific remains/objects requested.
- Letters of support for the application from local representative organisations such as land councils, native title representative bodies, legal services, government Indigenous or heritage bodies, or other community organisations.
- Where an organisation is making the application, a statement of support from members of the relevant group.
- A statement that the applicants are entitled by the traditions and customs of their community to make application for the remains/objects.
- The relationship of the applicants to the remains/objects requested.
- Contact addresses for other groups or organisations that support the application.
- Any other issues or information that may assist in the application (e.g., specific geographic locations).

Despite what appears to be a rigorous list, the aim is not to make custodians sit an exam for the return of remains or secret sacred objects. Provision of such information is not mandatory and, in the majority of cases, the Museum itself accepts the potential claimant group's rights of ownership based on information gained in the initial process of identification. For example, local Aboriginal land councils in New South Wales and regional heritage organisations in South Australia, and land councils in the Northern Territory, are endorsed by federal, state, and territory governments and by relevant heritage departments. In other cases, certain individuals and local community groups may have an extensive history of recognition, by federal, state, and local government authorities, as the appropriate people to deal with over the care of ancestral remains. Such organisations, groups and individuals are not required to provide extra information in support of their claim – indeed the rule of precedent facilitates future repatriations. What this basic criteria does do, however, is discourage frivolous or vexatious claims by people who may not be acknowledged or authorised, by the majority of the community, to make claim for repatriation. A critical issue when it is remembered that any repatriation is an empowering event.

An officer of the repatriation team then consults further with the applicants and other parties with potential interests. The return of the remains or objects, or alternative management, proceeds in accordance with instructions from the custodians. With the exception of signing a receipt for remains, the return of remains and secret sacred objects is currently unconditional. On their return, custodians may do with the remains or secret sacred objects as they see fit.

Aided by extra government funding, the Museum has also been able to offer some logistical and financial support. This includes:

- Assistance with travel for applicants to view the remains and to collect the remains or objects.
- Visits to the community by repatriation program officers to discuss the process or deliver remains and objects.
- Assistance with funding for ceremonies associated with the final disposal of the remains or culturally appropriate management of secret sacred objects.
- Assistance with obtaining more detailed advice into the characteristics of remains.
- A plain English community report on human remains describing the remains and providing such information as the age, sex and health of the individual, and what is known of the history of collection.

The future of external funding is always uncertain. Nonetheless, the Museum will continue to return remains and objects and provide such support as resources allow.

Where groups do not have the resources to take receipt of remains or objects, the Museum offers to either return them to a designated repository or store them temporarily on their behalf. The remains or objects are considered the property of the community/custodians and the Museum claims no authority over the remains or objects beyond keeping them safe and secure.

In terms of identifying and consulting with custodians, this process has worked well. The philosophy throughout is that the obligation is on the Museum to return remains and objects, not to put custodians through extensive tests and trials.

Research

The National Museum's repatriation unit is, in simple terms, primarily a service provider as opposed to an independent research unit. It is charged with achieving the prompt repatriation of remains and sacred objects to custodians. This is an ethical as well as contractual obligation. Thus, the Museum's repatriation unit does not do 'pure' biological anthropological research. In-house investigations are carried out when necessary in order to facilitate provenancing, reunification of separated bones in order to return individuality to the deceased and repatriation of remains and secret sacred objects. However, such inquiry is usually focused in its aims and restricted in its circulation. Access to any community reports requires the approval of the community concerned.

This protocol annoys some researchers who feel that they should have independent access, particularly to remains, or that a repatriation unit should be generating research articles on Indigenous remains from within the unit. However, in order to maintain the trust and confidence of Indigenous communities, it is important to demonstrate that the unit has no vested personal research interests in the remains or objects that might be seen as delaying or otherwise compromising the prompt return of remains or objects, or the right of the relevant custodial group to control, and participate in, research. Thus, where a community requests further research beyond that required for facilitating return, the unit attempts to put them in touch with suitable external professionals. The professionals are encouraged to engage with and provide services (hopefully free of charge) to communities in the belief that such direct engagement is beneficial for both sides.

Such an approach is not unique to the Museum. Ethical research on Indigenous remains and sacred objects is tightly controlled by government, industry, institutional and professional policies, protocols and ethics and community approval is required before research can begin (for example, Museums Australia 1993, 2003; AIATSIS 2000: Australian Archaeological Association 2004; Australian Anthropological Society 2003; Australian National University 2004 and relevant state and territory Indigenous heritage legislation). The outcome is that, today, no Australian museum will allow access to its holdings of Indigenous remains without the approval of the community socially associated with those remains or sacred objects.

Results

Over the four years of the Museum's repatriation unit's operations, and at the time of writing, the remains of approximately 642 individuals have been returned to Aboriginal communities across Australia. A further fifty-four have had title returned but are held at the Museum by the request of communities until resources become available for final treatment and repatriation. Appropriate communities are being consulted over a further 114 provenanced remains.

The unit has also returned 308 secret sacred objects to communities of the Pilbara and Kimberley in Western Australia. Consultations are in train over a further two hundred provenanced sacred objects.

The Museum also provides repatriation-related advice and assistance to federal, state and territory cultural heritage institutions, Indigenous communities and representatives, and to the media and public.

What Have We Learned?

One generic outcome of the intensive repatriation of remains and objects over the past five years is that experiences, issues, problems and considerations that might previously have arisen only occasionally – say every two or three years – now arise regularly. Australian museums are rapidly accumulating considerable experience that is helping guide subsequent repatriation exercises. Some of the more significant observations are:

- *The Value of Complementary Community Resourcing*
  Proactive repatriation has always been seen as a positive action. However, in initially committing to financially support the return of remains and objects, little consideration seems to have been given to supporting the receipt of remains and objects. Communities need the resources to receive, house or finally inter repatriated material. The repatriation process is slowed considerably when communities simply cannot receive items within an 'administratively preferred' time-frame (such as a financial year).

- *Appreciation That There is No 'One-Size-Fits-All' Approach*
  Despite strong advocacy at a political level for the prompt return of remains and objects, many local groups and communities have specific cultural values that affect the speed and characteristics of any repatriation. For example, there have been concerns that the spiritual power of the remains or objects could be too powerful for safe return into the community. There are also concerns that the appropriate ceremonies for receipt and reburial are performed. In both cases, being informed of a precedent often assists custodians in choosing a path of action. Communicating the experiences and actions taken by other groups in similar situations has thus proven to be a great facilitator of repatriation.

- *The Importance of Consultation at the Local Level*
  Indigenous organisations and representatives operating at a state or national level have managed much of the advocacy for return of remains and objects. This advocacy has been important and its contribution should not be belittled. However, it is also clear that local custodians may have different perspectives

and agendas as to how remains and objects are to be managed. It is also the case that sometimes representative bodies, including government heritage offices, may not be communicating to the wider custodial community. Thus, there is a need for thorough liaison at the local level if a repatriation-related activity is to reflect the wishes of the receiving community.

- *Recognising Repatriation as the Return of Authority*
  When it first started, the focus of repatriation was the physical transfer of remains and objects to relevant communities. However, experience shows that assessment of success based on simply counting numbers of remains and objects physically returned is an inadequate expression of the progress or success of the repatriation process. Of more significance is assessing the level of communication with, and empowerment of, custodial groups. Are they receiving full and fair information? What assistance is being provided? What concerns do they have and are they being addressed? Are they content with the way discussions over repatriation are proceeding? Is it clear that they are now acknowledged as having the authority to decide on the fate of remains and objects? Repatriation is, after all, as much the return of authority over remains and objects as it is the physical return of those remains or objects themselves. Indeed, there will be times when a refusal to accept remains or objects must be seen as a successful outcome in a repatriation event (see also Pickering 2002, 2003).

- *Potential Conflicts between Indigenous and Non-Indigenous Cultural Heritage Values and Practices*
  One particularly interesting concern for museums is the potential for conflict between Indigenous and non-Indigenous philosophies of rights in heritage. Australian museums, amongst other heritage institutions, generally recognise that rights in cultural heritage exist independent of a detailed knowledge of that cultural heritage. Further, they recognise that people have a right to be identified as moral, if not legal, owners of items of their culture. However, this philosophy may at times be at odds with Indigenous custom. For example, under this philosophy, remains and sacred objects could be returned to a group or person of the correct corporate identity – as with a duly authorised representative of a language group – but of an inappropriate social grouping, or sex or age. This person might have legitimate authority, and a commensurate claim, to remains or objects under a Western, legally defined heritage authority code, but a less important status under a customary authority code. The return of remains and sacred objects is a major empowering act – the recipient takes control of very powerful and influential items. It would be easy to artificially empower someone who has a legitimate right to an object under a Western heritage policy structure but less of a right under a customary structure. Fortunately, the Museum, has not been in a position where it has been necessary to make a determination based on these considerations.

- *The Legitimacy of Museum Collections*
  Many, if not all, remains and objects were acquired without the free and
  informed consent of the original custodians, and in violation of tradition or
  custom – they were stolen or traded without authority. However, it must be
  recognised that a number of items, both secret sacred objects and human
  remains, were acquired legitimately in accordance with the cultural protocols
  of both giver and receiver, particularly those acquired over the past sixty years.
  Records and personal accounts clearly show that some researchers, both male
  and female, were occasionally given remains and secret sacred objects with the
  free and informed consent of the giver and not in violation of tradition. On
  several occasions, the Museum has received instructions from Indigenous
  custodians informed of the full history of collection, that the researcher who
  received the object should also be consulted over its future care, management,
  or disposal.

Nonetheless, the Museum is committed both to the return of both remains
and secret sacred objects regardless of the circumstances of collection. Those
remains and objects for which there is no desire for return are consequently
subject to culturally informed procedures of care and management.

Conclusion: Where To From Here?

This chapter has provided a simplified summary of applied repatriation processes
as currently practised by the National Museum. Its processes and protocols do not
differ much from other Australian state and territory museums. It is hoped that
such descriptions of applied repatriation will inform more abstract
multidisciplinary debate, just as it is hoped that the engagement of other
disciplines will inform the applied repatriation process.

As noted at the beginning, however, as an exercise in applied repatriation the
process is subjected to a number of administrative, financial, institutional,
industry and cultural considerations that require prompt and proactive action
towards return. As a result, other areas of interest – topics that will inform applied
repatriation – are sometimes neglected. Such topics reflect the breadth of interest
and expertise present at this conference, and include:

- History, including questions such as: Who made the collections and what
  were their motivations in doing so? Where did they collect from and what was
  their methodology? What happened to the collections? Should the attributes
  of collection affect the nature of repatriation? There is an immediate need, and
  an immediate audience, for parallel research into the history of collections.
- Law: Was the collection legal at the time? What Indigenous legal title might
  still exist in collections? What current laws might affect repatriation? Are
  collections currently housed legally? What are the ethics of law that might

affect repatriation of Indigenous remains and sacred objects? (For example, Department of Culture, Media and Sport 2003; Palmer 2000).

- Anthropology: What is the cultural context of items collected? What is the ethnography of use and the ethnography of the collection? We know many remains and sacred items were collected by theft. However, we also know that many more recent researchers were given objects, and sometimes remains, with the free and informed consent of the custodian. We need to know these stories in order to fully inform custodians.
- Ethics and philosophy: What ethical considerations apply to repatriation? What might be the arguments for or against repatriation? Can the issue be subject to impartial, politically neutral debate and consideration?
- Voices of Aboriginal and Torres Strait Islander people: Last, but perhaps, most importantly is the need for the process to reflect the desires of prospective Indigenous custodians. There is no single opinion amongst custodial groups as to what is required in repatriation. Some groups want remains and items returned, some do not; some want research into remains and objects, some do not. What is important, however, is that every opinion – every exercise – informs the repatriation debate and practice.

Although they will greatly inform applied repatriation, such discussions are not critical preliminaries to success in applied repatriation as practiced by museums. As stated earlier, many successful returns have already taken place. Discussions of related issues will, however, not only inform and complement the practice and the politics of repatriation but contribute to knowledge of the humanities and social sciences in their own right (For example, Palmer 2000; Turnbull 1991; 1994, 1997, 1998, 1999, 2001; Fforde 2004; Department of Culture Media and Sport 2003).

To this end, I conclude with a plea for greater participation by other disciplines. In so doing, a not-so-secret agenda must be admitted to. Practitioners in applied repatriation are often challenged as to why repatriation of remains and sacred objects should occur, and why it should be unconditional. In most cases, this opposition to repatriation is based on personal opinion, rather than through reference to informed debate. I believe that serious discussion of historical, anthropological, theoretical and ethical issues will ultimately both advance the case for repatriation as well as prove a valuable contribution to knowledge and, by extension, the understanding of museum audiences.

Bibliography

Australian Anthropological Society. 2003. 'Code of Ethics'. Retrieved October 2008 from http://www.aas.asn.au/docs/AAS_Code_of_Ethics.pdf

Australian Archaeological Association. 2004. 'Code of Ethics of the Australian Archaeological Association'. Retrieved October 2008 from http://www.australianarchaeologicalassociation. com.au/ethics

Australian Institute of Aboriginal and Torres Strait Islander Studies. 2000. *Guidelines for Ethical Research in Indigenous Studies*. Retrieved October 2008 from http://www.aiatsis.gov.au/ _data/assets/pdf_file/2290/ethics_guidelines.pdf

Australian National University. 2004. 'Australian National University Human Research Ethics Committee Application Form'. Retrieved October 2008 from http://www-dev.anu.edu.au/ro/ORI/Human/Brewer-Protocol-Package.pdf

Department of Culture, Media and Sport (DCMS). 2003. *The Report Of The Working Group On Human Remains*. London: DCMS.

Fforde, C. 2004. *Collecting the Dead: Archaeology and the Reburial Issue*. London: Duckworth.

Museums Australia. 1993. *Previous Possessions, New Obligations: Policies for Museums in Australia and Aboriginal and Torres Strait Islander Peoples*. Retrieved October 2008 from http://www.history.sa.gov.au/history/about_us/collections_policy/Appendix1cJuly05.pdf

————. 2003. *Continuous Cultures, Ongoing Responsibilities: 2003 A comprehensive policy document and guidelines for Australian museums working with Aboriginal and Torres Strait Islander cultural heritage*. Museums Australia, Canberra.

————. 2005. *Continuous Cultures, Ongoing Responsibilities: 2003 A comprehensive policy document and guidelines for Australian museums working with Aboriginal and Torres Strait Islander cultural heritage*. Museums Australia, Canberra.

National Museum of Australia. 2005. *Aboriginal and Torres Strait Islander Human Remains Policy*. Retrieved October 2008 from http://www.nma.gov.au/shared/libraries/ attachments/corporate_documents/policies/atsi_human_remains_policy/files/18357/POL -C-011_Aboriginal_and_Torres_Strait_Islander_human_remain_-2.0_(public).pdf

Palmer, N. 2000. *Museums and the Holocaust*. Leicester: Institute of Art and Law.

Pickering, M. 2002. 'Repatriation, Rhetoric, and Reality: the Repatriation of Australian Indigenous Human Remains and Sacred Objects', *Journal of the Australian Registrars Committee* June 2002, pp. 15–19, 40–41.

————. 2003. 'Define Success: Repatriation of Aboriginal and Torres Strait Islander Ancestral Remains and Sacred Objects, *Museum National* February 2003, pp. 13–14.

Turnbull, P. 1991. 'Ramsay's Regime: the Australian Museum and the Procurement of Aboriginal Bodies, c.1874–1900', *Aboriginal History* 15: 2. 108–21.

————. 1994. '"To What Strange Uses": the Procurement and Use of Aboriginal Peoples Bodies in Early Colonial Australia', *Voices* 4 (3): 1–27.

————. 1997. 'Ancestors, not Specimens: Reflections on the Controversy over the Remains of Aboriginal People in European Scientific Collections', *Electronic Journal of Australian And New Zealand History*. Retrieved from http://www.jcu.edu.au/aff/history/articles/turnbull.htm

————. 1998. '"Outlawed Subjects": the Procurement and Scientific Uses of Australian Aboriginal Heads, ca.1803–1835', *Studies in the Eighteenth Century* 22 (1): 156–71.

————. 1999. 'Enlightenment Anthropology and the Ancestral Remains of Australian Aboriginal People' in Alex Calder et al. (eds). *Voyages and Beaches: Pacific Encounters, 1769–1840*. Honolulu: University of Hawaii Press, pp. 202–25.

————. 2001. '"Rare Work for the Professors": the Entanglement of Aboriginal Remains in Phrenological Knowledge in Early Colonial Australia', in J. Hoorn and B. Creed (eds), *Body Trade: Captivity, Cannibalism and Colonialism in the Pacific*. Melbourne: Pluto Press, pp. 3–23.

13

'You Keep It – We are Christians Here': Repatriation of the Secret Sacred Where Indigenous World-views Have Changed

Kim Akerman

For many non-Aboriginals and some Aboriginals within institutions involved with the repatriation of secret sacred material, knowledge of the subject is either very limited or based on a set of premises derived from the work of such anthropologists as Baldwin Spencer, T.G.H. Strehlow, C.P. Mountford, Mervyn Meggitt or Ronald Berndt. The work of these men has led to a 'central Australian' interpretation of the nature and function of certain classes of objects (plain or engraved tablets of wood or stone of various sizes that are generally known as *jurunga* or *churinga*) that does not necessarily hold true for similar types of objects that are found elsewhere in Aboriginal Australia. Historical references and an involvement in the repatriation of sacred objects that extends back to the early 1970s convinces me that, while maintaining connotations of secret and sacred, these types of objects have been present within the last century or so in many parts of Western Australian and do not necessarily fulfil the same roles in traditional religious life as their central Australian counterparts.

Repatriation of these objects is consequently a more complicated issue than simply returning them to a local group in the area from which they were first removed. Further complications in the process of repatriation arise from historical circumstances that saw migrations of many different groups of Aboriginals to centres of settlement and also the acceptance of Christianity by many Aboriginal peoples.

Knowledge of both the nature of the historical processes and the dynamic changes that have affected Indigenous religious life, together with ongoing consultation, is required prior to any physical transfer of such sensitive and potentially, because of the power believed to be inherent in them, dangerous objects into an Indigenous milieu.

Before proceeding further I wish to draw attention to the volume *Politics of the Secret*, edited by Chris Anderson (1995). The various papers within this book, apart from two essays by Erich Kolig and myself respectively, address the notion of secret sacred objects from a Central Australian perspective. However all of the papers are particularly relevant to the consideration of the concepts of tradition, the secret sacred and the notion of repatriation.

Collecting, History and Questions that Need to be Considered when Contemplating Repatriation

Repatriation is not a recent concept in Western Australia. Until the early 1970s, many objects that had been collected in one way or another were held at the head office of the then Department of Native Welfare. In 1972 one of my first assignments with that department was to investigate the possibility of repatriation of objects with senior men from Indigenous communities who were members of one of the departmental advisory bodies.

Through the process of consultation, it became apparent that for some of these 'Elders' the repatriation exercise was to an extent an embarrassment. As one man, a most respected Kimberley identity and a man after whom a room at the Australian Institute of Aboriginal and Torres Strait Islander Studies (AIATSIS) was named, whom I had known since the mid 1960s, said, 'Some of these things are things we no longer follow. We can take them back and keep them at the community or you can put them in the special place at the museum'. He was referring to the repository for such objects that was maintained by the Western Australian Museum. In many cases his response was repeated by lawmen from other parts of Western Australia.

In September 1964, anthropologist John McCaffrey was taken by a number of men from Fitzroy Crossing to Cherabun Station to visit a cache of objects. One of the men selected a number of these objects, which he said were his, and described the symbolism of the iconography to McCaffrey; another object, which he owned but had not made, he was unable to interpret. According to McCaffrey, 'He said he did not know what it meant even though it looked much like the ones he had done. Only the man who had made it knows its meaning he said' (nd: 31).

Later on in the excursion these objects were offered to and accepted by McCaffrey:

He asked if I would take the pieces. I said that I would. He thanked me profusely, taking his bible out of his shirt pocket saying that he follows this way now and that the old way was past. He had put it behind him. He seemed very grateful that I would take the pieces. I had the impression that my taking them allowed him to go on to other concerns. He said he no longer 'read this fellow (the boards)' but that now he read 'Bible'. There is a similarity in function – boards and Christianity are both religions. The boards he 'reads' the imagery. Christianity he 'reads' the words. (nd: 31)

At a later stage in his Derby fieldwork, one man (who would within a few years become a most respected leader, lawman and composer) told McCaffrey:

> That his generation refused to follow the law of his father. He talked of refusing the sacred sticks, as symbolic of refusing their rule and way of life. When offered the sticks they simply refused. Would not accept. Before the coming of missionaries and police as their protection they could not stand against the elders. To do so would have meant death (nd: 71).

This same man was to add:

> the elders are not unhappy with their refusal to accept old ways. 'They happy anyway.' When the old generation has passed they will get rid of the sacred sticks by sending them away or preferably by selling them. They are done with them (nd: 71).

By the end of his fieldwork in the Kimberley in 1966, McCaffrey had amassed a considerable collection of sacred objects from people who believed that they had no further purpose for them. These objects were later confiscated by the Commonwealth, when McCaffrey sought to export them, and lodged in the Institute of Anatomy. The National Museum of Australia now administers those collections. Unfortunately, since their confiscation, all records that may have accompanied them are missing; although, I was able to identify several pieces from descriptions in the McCaffrey notebooks. This collection forms part of a greater collection that is now in the process of repatriation to relevant Kimberley communities.

This is not to say that all people or all communities decided to or were prepared to surrender these types of cultural objects so readily, or abandon the ceremonial life in which they played a part. One of Western Australia's first land excisions for cultural purposes was made at Fishermen's Bend at Broome in the 1960s. This reserve was created specifically at the request of the law leaders of that town, to protect important cultural objects from both the weather and from theft. In the early 1970s, police and the Aboriginal Affairs Planning Authority (which had replaced the Department of Native Welfare) were involved in tracing and returning objects stolen from a cache at Liveringa Station on the Fitzroy River.

When dealing with repatriation issues in the Kimberley region alone, it is clear that these types of objects mean different things to different cultural groups. In a much earlier paper (Akerman 1979: 234–42), I described how the contemporary Kimberley region can be viewed as broadly embracing five cultural blocs, each with their own specific sets of traditions that are generally maintained, regardless of the constant and varied interaction – including some aspects of ceremonial life – that exists between them.

These groups are as follows:

1. Dampierland Peninsula.
2. Central and Northern Kimberley – The Plateau.

3. Ord Basin.
4. The Djaru lands and the south-east Kimberley.
5. The southern region incorporating the southern drainage basin of the Fitzroy
   River and the adjacent Great Sandy and Tanami Deserts. There is a very strong
   desert-derived influence over the whole Fitzroy River Basin.

Examination of historical and ethnographic records from about 1900 on, show
large-scale ebbs and flows of cultural activity both within and between these
various blocs.

J.R.B. Love (1930, 1936), Helmut Petri (1954) and Andreas Lommel (1997)
all address the nature of religious practises in area 2, the northern and central
Kimberley, and the changes that they witnessed occurring there during the first
half of the twentieth century. Berndt (1974: 11–12, 14–15) addresses some of the
externally derived religious activity that has impacted upon this area. Kolig has
succinctly addressed the place of sacred objects in the Fitzroy Crossing and other
areas of the Kimberley Region in the late twentieth century (1995: 27–42). Kolig
notes that change is constant. He uses the production of contemporary fine art by
both men and women at Fitzroy Crossing as an example of how indigenous
compromise permits the secret to be created and displayed in ways that would
have been unthinkable a decade or two earlier (Kolig 1995: 39).

E.A. Worms details one particular travelling ceremonial cycle, the *Kurangarra*
which, introduced into the Kimberleys in the late 1920s, had influenced many areas
of Western Australia by the 1950s but which was in decline by the 1960s (1942:
207–35; see Wilson 1954). The importance of the *Kurangarra* in terms of the
repatriation of secret sacred objects to the northern Kimberley cannot be overemphasised. It was this ceremonial cycle that introduced carved and painted
churinga-type boards to the region. These boards and the activities associated with
them circulated through the northern region along the reticulated pathways of the
wunan ceremonial exchange cycle that, blending in with other adjacent, similar
systems, traverses the entire Kimberley. It is evident that boards that have been
collected in the central Kimberley were originally derived from desert-oriented
communities to the south-east and south of the Kimberley and were not created at
the point of location. Consequently, while being regarded as secret sacred/dangerous,
they did not possess the same totemic/clan/country affiliations that they may have
possessed, in the manner of sacred Arrernte *churinga*, at their point of origin.

Transmission of these objects also appears more casual in this area. Individuals
rather than corporate groups owned many of these objects and they were able to
decide to whom, along the many branches of the *wunan* web to which they were
immediately responsible, they would transfer custody of the boards. Each
individual who received such an object could do what they willed with it, until he
decided to present it to a specific individual. According to McCaffrey:

> They said that (the objects) came in with name of X and Y. They keep them unnamed
> for a while – perhaps a year. Unnamed in sense that they are not designated for the next

men and the next site – at Kalumburu or Z. Before being named by the custodian they are 'free, unnamed' and may be sold to anyone. (nd: 109–10)

With the demise of *Kurangarra* activity in the north Kimberley, ceremonial life became more oriented to celebration of life-stages, particularly male initiation, and there was no longer the same degree of participation in religious life that involved the types of ceremonial objects under discussion. This situation continues to the present day, even though some of their southern neighbours, with whom the people of the northern Kimberley share initiation ceremonies, continue to participate in religious activities that focus on the production and display of such objects.

In the northern area today such objects, while still regarded as secret sacred/dangerous are not considered necessarily vital to the maintenance of religious life. These objects are still items of exchange, but ultimate disposal is made by personal choice rather than by group consensus.

Travelling cults such as the *Kurangarra* that have been recorded moving through the south Kimberley in more recent times include the *Worgaya* and the *Juluru,* often better known as the Balgo Business (Petri and Petri-Odermann 1970: 270–6; Kolig 1981,1995: 49–67). Both ceremonial cycles also traversed the north Kimberley in the early 1970s but without the same degree of impact as occurred in the southern areas (Akerman 1979: 235–6).

Historical Change, Christianity and Refusal to Accept Introduced Religious Activity

Moving further south to the Pilbara, discussions with ceremonial leaders throughout the region show that there exists a similar range of cultural diversity that requires consideration when establishing repatriation protocols. In 2003, meetings that I held in one town established that members of the local group were adamant that while the return of ancestral remains was desired, the return of religious objects was not. They had long accepted Christianity and were quite happy for the objects, that may have been associated with the religious beliefs of their ancestors, to remain within the museum environment.

Further investigation, particularly focusing on objects that had been collected in this town over the last seventy years or so, showed that they had probably originated with immigrant groups – resident for many years in the town – but who had in the last decade or so returned to reside within their own homelands. It was clear that the whole concept of the immigrant group had to be taken into account when determining who could speak for certain objects, and that a simple locational reference did not necessarily mean that the traditional owners of that place were in fact the custodians of a particular object or suite of objects.

At another Pilbara town, a further point was driven home when Ngaluma lawmen, refused to consider all but one class of sacred object, provenanced to them, for repatriation. They explained how in the 1940s and 1950s, their senior lawmen had not only rejected the religious activity associated with the other pieces, but also had forbidden the ceremonial leaders who were intent on transmitting the Kurangarra ceremonial cycle across a wider field through Ngaluma territory. I was given a different perspective on the matter in talking to men who had been involved in spreading this ceremony when they explained that, while journeying to a group of people who had expressed a desire to learn and adopt the ceremony, they showed respect for the Ngaluma lawmen by taking a significant detour to avoid their territory. This later group then took responsibility for the further transmission of the cycle.

The Pilbara and Kimberley Repatriation Process – the Situation Today

While these pitfalls need to be considered in any repatriation process, the repatriation program that began in 2000 has seen the return of several hundred objects to people deemed by their peers to be the appropriate custodians. An extensive consultation process has ensured that the widest possible and most appropriate body of senior lawmen or their delegates has been consulted. Objects, belonging to groups as far north as Bidyadanga (La Grange), as easterly as Jigalong and south to Mount Newman and Onslow, have now been returned to their custodians. In late 2005, ancestral remains that had been gathered from every state and federal museum within Australia, were transported back to the Pilbara to rest in an approved repository until local groups determine their final disposition. Consultation about objects in the southern Pilbara and adjacent Gascoyne–Murchison districts commenced in 2006

As a result of early consultations in the Kimberley and the Pilbara, relevant senior custodians have forwarded requests to state and federal institutions asking them to prepare collections of ancestral remains and cultural materials identified for repatriation and to forward them to the Western Australian Museum. The intention of this action was to limit the pressures on individuals to travel interstate and make unilateral decisions about the disposition of the repatriated material. It was made clear during consultation that such travel, particularly when it involved such sensitive cargoes, was extremely stressful. The Museum was seen to be an appropriate interim holding body given that it was located closest to the ultimate destinations of the material concerned. Communities would then either directly or through their agents make the appropriate arrangements for the final leg of the journey home.

Part of this repatriation process involved my examining museum collections and separating open or mundane objects that through lack of knowledge had been incorporated or placed within the secret sacred repositories. This process had been discussed with senior custodians prior to being undertaken. While some may think this was presumptuous, it was undertaken with approval and personal knowledge of my own prior involvement in Aboriginal religious matters. It was clear that for many institutions there were a number of objects about which there was little information or knowledge but which did not belong within the domain of those artefacts considered for repatriation. Consequently, at one institution, a Cape York shark tooth knife (minus the teeth) had been classed as a bullroarer.

In most collections, very beautifully engraved, spatulate slats of wood had been, for want of better knowledge, classed as secret sacred. Although similar to some smaller varieties of *churinga,* these objects were in fact a form of ceremonial hairpin. While having an important ceremonial function as denoters of status, they were regarded as completely open; they could be made in a public situation, were displayed publicly and could be seen and handled by individuals of either sex.

These ceremonial hairpins are probably the most common esoteric artefacts obtainable in many parts of the northwest today. I am aware that one institution in New South Wales flew members of a remote desert community to Sydney to collect several hairpins under the impression that they were *churinga.* The community chairman remarked that they would put them on public display when a proposed cultural centre is completed – 'So that people can see how beautiful the engraving is'. He considered a suggestion that other, more recent examples be sent back to the institution from which the early examples had come in order 'that people in Sydney could see that such engraving was still practised in his community'. While keen to reciprocate in this manner the proposal was, unfortunately, not followed up.

The repatriation process in the Pilbara has been actively supported and to an extent directed by the Wangka Maya Pilbara Aboriginal Language Centre. Staff from the centre staff have assisted with vehicles, support staff and logistics and, through the lawmen and women who make up their board, directed and facilitated contacts with relevant communities. A number of respected senior men, including Bruce Thomas, David Stock and James Wally were delegated at meetings conducted with senior Law leaders to, accompany me throughout the consultation process. Peter Coppin and Teddy Allen ensured that the process flowed smoothly and allowed the repository at Warralong to be used as a general holding place for all the objects returned to the Pilbara. Objects from other areas of the Pilbara would remain there until the appropriate custodians determined where their own particular suites of objects should be kept.

In the Kimberley the process has been facilitated by the Kimberley Aboriginal Law and Culture Centre (KALACC). Due to staff changes at KALACC, the process has been delayed to a degree, although wide consultation with senior Law leaders has been undertaken by me over the past four years. A significant repatriation exercise that was carried out in 2003 saw the return of the ancestral remains of twelve individuals to the Kimberley from Sweden.[1] These remains had been removed from the Kimberley in 1911. Three other sets of remains also located in Sweden were returned to Indigenous communities in Queensland, New South Wales and Victoria. The repatriation of both cultural objects and ancestral remains from the repositories of the Western Australian Museum has been substantially achieved.

Conclusions

I hope in this brief report that attention has been drawn to some of the potential pitfalls of which one needs to be aware when involved with the repatriation of secret sacred materials. While I have drawn on my own experience in two large areas of Western Australia, I believe the points raised are relevant elsewhere on the continent; I have only focused on some of the more immediate issues. Other more complex problems can also occur that would require a more detailed presentation to do them justice. These include the questions such as who would take custody of sacred material when individuals of an appropriate ceremonial status no longer remain within a group? Also, what happens when it is felt that possession of such materials may be seen as advantageous in competing Native Title Claims? And finally, will other Indigenous parties accept a decision made by traditional custodians that sees secret sacred material retained within a museum repository, albeit one that ensues access is controlled by those custodians?

Notes

1.   See the chapter by Hallgren in this volume.

Bibliography

Akerman, K. 1979. 'The Renascence of Aboriginal Law in the Kimberleys', in R.M. Berndt (ed.), *Aborigines of the West: Their Past and Their Present*. Nedlands: University of Western Australia Press, pp. 234–42.

Anderson, C. (ed.). 1995. *Politics of the Secret*. Oceania Monograph No 45. Sydney.

Berndt, R.M. 1974. *Australian Aboriginal Religion*, vol. 3. Leiden: Brill.

Kolig, E. 1981. *The Silent Revolution: the Effects of Modernisation on Australian Aboriginal Religion*. Philadelphia: ISHI.

———. 1995a. Darrugu – secret objects in a changing world. In Anderson, C. (ed). *Politics of the secret*. Oceania Monograph No.45. Sydney, pp. 27–42.

———. 1995b. 'A Sense of History and the Reconstitution of Cosmology in Australian Aboriginal Society: the Case of the Myth Versus History', *Anthropos* 90: 49–67.

Lommel, A. 1997. *The Unambal*. Sydney: Takarakka Publications.

Love, J.R.B. 1930. 'Rock Paintings of the Worrora and Their Mythological Interpretation', *Journal of the Royal Society of Western Australia* 16: 1–17.

———. 1936. *Stone Age Bushmen of Today*. London: Blackie.

McCaffrey, J. n.d. 'The Field Notes of John McCaffrey. Kimberley 1964–1966'. Unpublished manuscript. Transcribed by Kim Akerman.

Petri, H. 1954. *Sterbende welt in nordwest-Australien*. Braunschweig: Limbach Verl.

——— and G. Petri-Odermann. 1970. 'Stability and Change: Present Day Historic Aspects Among Australian Aborigines', in R.M. Berndt (ed.), *Australian Aboriginal Anthropology*. Nedlands: University of Western Australia Press, pp. 249–76.

Wilson, J. 1954. 'Kurangara: Aboriginal Cultural Revival', *Walkabout* 20: 15–19.

Worms, E.A. 1942. 'Die Goranara – Feier im Australischen Kimberley', *Annali Lateranari* 6: 207–35.

14

The First 'Stolen Generations': Repatriation and Reburial in Ngarrindjeri Ruwe (country)

Steve Hemming and Chris Wilson[1]

> All those Old People and the people we got here, [they are] all our family.
> We know where they were taken from, illegally taken from their burial grounds;
> their resting places and we know that they are our ancestors, we are connected
> to them. They were taken away from us. Where they've been and what has
> happened to them, we don't know, we can only guess, but we've got a good
> idea that they've been taken, they've been looked at, they've been studied,
> they've been examined, all those things have happened to them. We know
> that their spirit has been at unrest. We believe that the things that happen
> around us, our lands and waters, is all connected. It's part of it, and what's
> happening here is part of the healing process, when we bring our
> Old people home ...
> (Tom Trevorrow, Chair, Ngarrindjeri Heritage Committee,
> Welcome Home Ceremony, Camp Coorong, 28 August 2004)

Introduction

In this chapter, we consider some of the social, cultural, political and economic
implications of repatriating Old People (human remains) to an Indigenous
community. Our focus is the return of Ngarrindjeri Old People from museums
within Australia and the United Kingdom to Ngarrindjeri Ruwe (country) in the
lower Murray region of South Australia. This issue is part of the global repatriation
debate which often excludes serious consideration of the consequences of
repatriation for Indigenous people. We seek to expand understandings of the
impacts of repatriation on Indigenous communities as well as to provide an anti-
colonial reading of the practice of archaeology from the perspective of an
Indigenous archaeologist and a non-Indigenous academic (see Smith 1999;
Hemming and Trevorrow 2005; Wilson 2005; Hemming 2006). We argue that

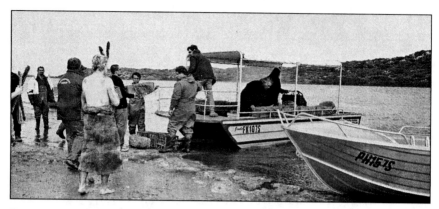

Figure 14.1. *Ngarrindjeri family members transporting Old People across the Coorong in South Australia during the first Ngarrindjeri reburials at Parnka Point. Photograph by Naomi*

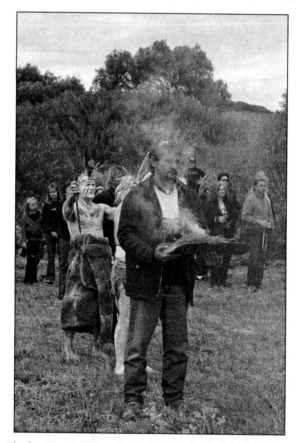

Figure 14.2. *The first Ngarrindjeri reburial ceremony at Hacks Point, along the Coorong in South Australia. Photograph by Toni Massey.*

non-Indigenous governments and 'collecting' institutions, such as museums, have a responsibility to compensate for the damage caused by their actions. We also argue that these same governments and institutions have a longer-term duty, requiring significant resources, to support Indigenous communities in the difficult and overwhelming process to care for and rebury their Old People.

For several years, Ngarrindjeri leaders have been requesting the return of their Old People from museums and collecting institutions. In April 2003, one of the largest 'collections' of Ngarrindjeri Old People consisting of over three hundred individuals, and referred to as the Edinburgh collection, made the final return to the Ngarrindjeri nation (see Fforde 2004). In 2004 Museum Victoria repatriated a further seventy-four Old People and signed an historic Kungun Ngarrindjeri Yunnan (Listen to what Ngarrindjeri people are saying) (KNY) agreement with the Ngarrindjeri nation which formally acknowledged the removal of Old People as well as recognised Ngarrindjeri rights and connections to *ruwe* (see Hemming and Trevorrow 2005; Wilson 2005). More recently the Ngarrindjeri nation has negotiated further repatriations from UK institutions including the University of Edinburgh and the Royal Albert Memorial Museum in Exeter.

As a result of the original theft and the subsequent repatriation of Old People, Indigenous communities such as the Ngarrindjeri face a series of complex issues, which need to be better understood by non-Indigenous interests so that a just approach to repatriation can be developed. At present, few resources have been provided through federal or state government programs to address these needs for Indigenous communities; this results in increased stress on Indigenous Elders, leaders and communities and is an additional drain on scarce resources. This lack of resources persists even at a time when there has been a growing recognition of the disadvantage in Indigenous communities (see Altman and Hinkson 2007).

Under the former Howard government, Ngarrindjeri leaders could not obtain the necessary resources from the federal government to collect their Old People's remains from overseas institutions in a culturally appropriate manner. In response to this lack of national goodwill in a matter that should be a national responsibility, support was sought from international organisations and other Pacific rim First Nations (see Hemming, Rigney and Wilson 2008). In 2005, for example, the World Archaeological Congress (WAC) formally supported Ngarrindjeri leaders in their efforts to negotiate, oversee and conduct the repatriation of Old People from overseas institutions such as those in the United Kingdom (see WAC 2005). Since the election of the Rudd government, the situation has improved and repatriation from UK institutions is being resourced and federally sanctioned in a culturally appropriate manner.

The history of institutional and state benefit from the theft of Ngarrindjeri Old People is what Ngarrindjeri Elder Uncle Tom Trevorrow refers to as the 'First Stolen Generations'. This history places a moral responsibility on the shoulders of present state museums (and their associated state governments) to provide ongoing financial support for Indigenous communities grappling with repatriation and reburial issues. This is a process that requires sensitive, culturally appropriate apologies, public recognition of the injustices of the past and an ongoing commitment from 'collecting' institutions for repatriation and reparation which includes repairing the social, cultural and spiritual damage that has occurred to Indigenous communities. The 'First Stolen Generations' were torn from their country and resting places in much the same way as Indigenous children were stolen from their families (see Trevorrow et. al. 2007). For Ngarrindjeri people, the pain and suffering caused by these acts of racialised power has been handed down through generations. Only through government support and culturally appropriate funeral ceremonies can the healing begin.

Pethamuldis: Looting and 'Collecting'[2]

Ngarrindjeri burial grounds were often very large, associated with particular *lakalinyeri* (local descent groups) and easily identified. Early watercolor paintings by non-Indigenous artists such as George French Angas depict Ngarrindjeri platform burials in the lower Murray lakes region (see Hemming, Jones and Clarke 2000). These burial grounds were targets for looting and desecration by early settlers, scientists, and other 'collectors'. William Ramsay Smith, an Adelaide coroner, with a close association with the South Australian Museum, played a key role in the theft of Ngarrindjeri Old People's remains from their burial sites. Many of the remains that were stolen by Smith were sent overseas to collecting institutions, including the Royal College of Surgeons in London and the University of Edinburgh (see Fforde 2004). Smith was also responsible for the theft of the writings of the Ngarrindjeri scholar and inventor David Unaipon (see Smith 1930; Unaipon 2006).

In the late-nineteenth and early twentieth centuries, Indigenous burial sites became a systematic target for looting and 'collecting', as there was a growing demand for the remains of 'Aboriginal people' inspired by the belief that Indigenous people were a 'dying race' (see Fforde, Hubert and Turnbull 2002). Many of these Old People were stolen from their resting places or hospital morgues and distributed to museums and other collecting institutions overseas and in Australia. The South Australian Museum, for example, still has the majority of its collection of Indigenous human remains and a significant proportion of these are Ngarrindjeri Old People.[3] The scientific interest in Indigenous human remains was driven by changes in European explanations for the history of 'mankind'. Tom Griffiths writes about this shift towards scientific racism in his book, *Hunters and Collectors: the Antiquarian Imagination in Australia*:

> By the middle of the nineteenth century, the monogenist, ethnographic, diffusionist, environmentalist tradition represented by [James Cowles] Pritchard was under attack. The influence of racialism on scientific enquiry strengthened. The change in scientific outlook can be characterized as a shift from 'monogenesism' to 'polygenism', from a belief that humanity was one species descended from a single pair, to a view that

humanity consisted of several separate 'types' or species with independent histories and different moral, intellectual and biological capacities. (1996: 39)

Not only were the skeletal remains of the Old People stolen from burial sites but also whole bodies and body parts were 'collected' for science. Hemming (2007: 156) has highlighted some of his experiences in relation to the collection and storage of Indigenous human remains while working at the South Australian Museum:

> When I started working at the South Australian Museum in the early 1980s, there was a black, wooden, coffin-like box ... I was told that it contained the bodies of Aboriginal people 'collected' by the Museum in an attempt to preserve 'specimens' of the so-called 'extinct full-blooded Aborigines' of south eastern Australia ... This story turned out to be largely true.

Cressida Fforde (2004: 43) reported that 'this box contained two adults, a young child and a stillborn baby preserved in fluid'. Ngarrindjeri leaders such as Trevorrow and Uncle Matt Rigney have publically expressed their disgust at the practice of 'collecting' body parts and the difficulties their repatriation presents when negotiating with Ngarrindjeri community members (see Wilson 2005).

During the twentieth century, burial grounds were not 'looted', as had occurred in the past; however, there was growing academic research interest in such sites. Major excavations of burials occurred under the auspices of the South Australian Museum at places on the Murray River such as Swanport, Tartanga, Devon Downs, Fromm's Landing and Roonka. Early anthropological and archaeological research was seldom conducted with the approval of local Indigenous people (see, for example: Stirling 1911, Hale and Tindale 1930, Mulvaney 1960 and Pretty 1977). In recent years, archaeologists have excavated Ngarrindjeri burial sites if Indigenous human remains have been exposed at surface level, eroding out of embankments or disturbed during new developments. In addition, Old People's remains were often stored in local police stations until they were 'deposited' in the South Australian Museum. As a result of this history of theft, removal, excavation and storage, many Indigenous human remains are still located in a diverse set of institutions, which are not easily accessible to Indigenous peoples. Importantly, the authors of this paper have worked with Ngarrindjeri leaders such as Uncles Tom and George Trevorrow, to develop a collaborative approach to heritage conservation and research, bringing Flinders University researchers such as Lynley Wallis into a partnership that supports Ngarrindjeri care for burials and burial grounds (see Hemming and Trevorrow 2005; Wallis, Hemming and Wilson 2006; Hemming et al.2007; Wallis, Domett and Niland 2007).

Ngarrindjeri leaders have begun to point out that the removal of Old People from their resting places contradicts the instructions of the British Government during the establishment of South Australia as a British colony (see Ngarrindjeri nation 2006; Rigney, Hemming and Berg 2008). In 1837, instructions were issued by the Colonial Secretary's Office, which should have protected the burial grounds of Indigenous people:

Colonial Secretary's Office
11th August 1837
OFFICIAL INSTRUCTIONS TO WILLIAM WYATT, ESQ., AD INTERIM PROTECTOR OF THE ABORIGINES.
In taking upon you the office of *ad interim* Protector of the Aborigines, to which office you have been appointed, His Excellency the GOVERNOR desires to acquaint you with his views of the course which he wishes should be adopted towards the Aborigines of this Province, with a view to their peaceful residence among us, and their instructions in the arts of civilised life ...

If on becoming acquainted with the habits and customs of the Aborigines, you should find that in any part of the country they are in the practice of making use of land for cultivation of any kind, or if they have a fixed residence on any particular spot, or if they should be found to appropriate any piece of land to funeral purposes, you are required to report such fact to the Colonial Government without loss of time, in order that means may be taken to prevent its being included in the survey for sale.

It is essentially necessary that the natives should be convinced that on all occasions they will meet with full and impartial justice.

(*South Australian Government Gazette* 1837)

This instruction was soon ignored and, by the end of the nineteenth century, Ngarrindjeri people had suffered the theft of *ruwe* and the desecration of many of their burial grounds. Ngarrindjeri people on several occasions protested against the theft of their Old People and thus made many requests for repatriation. In 1903, Ngarrindjeri people at Raukkan (formerly Point McLeay Mission) complained to the secretary of the Aborigines' Friends Association, W.E. Dalton, about the theft of 'skeletons' from Kumarangk and sought their return (*Adelaide Advertiser*, 25 September 1903). In the early 1940s, complaints were made to anthropologists Ronald and Catherine Berndt about the disturbance of burials by archaeologists from the South Australian Museum (see Berndt, Berndt and Stanton 1993: 16). Prior to the late 1960s, however, Indigenous people had no access to justice in Australian society so these protests were unsuccessful. Furthermore, Ngarrindjeri had no power to protect their burial grounds and cultural sites from desecration until the introduction of state and federal Aboriginal heritage legislation in the 1980s (see Trevorrow and Hemming 2006; Kartinyeri 2008). Given the fact that there has never been a prosecution under the South Australian *Aboriginal Heritage Act 1988* (SA) it appears that legal powers to protect important sites are still limited.

Repatriation: the Return of the Old People

Repatriation may be characterised as the return of someone or something to its original place of origin and it may include the remains of a person, associated grave goods, secret sacred objects or other cultural property. Repatriation also refers to the return of power, authority, ownership and control – issues that are equally important for many Indigenous communities (see Langford 1983, Wilson 2005). The repatriation of Indigenous human remains is a global issue for First Nations who have experienced the violence and control of European imperialism and colonisation (see for example: Smith 1999; Simpson 2001; Smith 2004; Thomas 2001, Fine-Dare 2002; Watkins 2000, 2003). In the United States the federal *Native American Graves Protection and Repatriation Act* (NAGPRA) was designed to facilitate repatriation of Old People's remains. In recent times this legislation has been embroiled in controversy via the tragic struggle by the Confederated Tribes of the Umatilla Indian Reservation (CTUIR) to rebury the Ancient One (referred to by some as Kennewick Man) (see Thomas 2000; Watkins 2003; Smith & Wobst 2005). In South Australia the Ngarrindjeri nation's heritage sites and 'human remains' are 'protected' by the *Aboriginal Heritage Act 1988* (SA) and this legislation, along with its federal equivalent, was found wanting in the 1990s, in the Kumarangk (Hindmarsh Island) issue (see Bell 1998; Hemming 2000), when Ngarrindjeri cultural traditions and sites were desecrated as the result of developments in the lower Murray region (see Saunders 2003; Trevorrow 2003).

In the 1980s, following many years of storage, research and display of human remains, institutions within the United Kingdom were reluctant to repatriate the Indigenous human remains that were held within their collections. However, throughout the 1980s the Tasmanian Aboriginal Centre (TAC) campaigned for the return of William Lanne's skull from the University of Edinburgh. Although the request to repatriate the skull was refused due to its research potential, in 1990, following ongoing communication and struggle, the skull was returned (Fforde 2004:123–24). In 1991, the University of Edinburgh developed its repatriation policy, which enabled further repatriation events to occur. In August 2003, with the assistance of the National Museum of Australia's Repatriation Unit, over three hundred Old People, initially returned from Edinburgh and housed in Canberra, made their final journey home to Ngarrindjeri Ruwe.

Following the repatriation of the Edinburgh collection, Ngarrindjeri people continued to negotiate for the return of the Old People still held in collecting institutions. In 2004, Museum Victoria used funding obtained through the Return of Indigenous Cultural Property (RICP) Program to enable seventy-four Old People held within their collections to be repatriated. One of the authors, Chris Wilson, traveled to Victoria as part of the Ngarrindjeri delegation sent to bring the Old People home (Wilson 2005). This repatriation event led to a formal KNY agreement and the issuing of a public apology by Museum Victoria (see Figures 1 & 2). Institutions such as Museum Victoria have supported the

Ngarrindjeri nation's efforts to create a culturally appropriate repatriation process. Similarly, the authors of this paper share a commitment to supporting the Ngarrindjeri nation in the just resolution of the 'repatriation' issue.

More recently, private collectors and landowners have been repatriating smaller numbers of individuals to the Ngarrindjeri nation. Voluntary repatriation of Old People by individuals and their families is an important form of local reconciliation and has been encouraged by the programs offered at Camp Coorong: Race Relations and Cultural Education Centre. During the same period, Ngarrindjeri leaders have continued to negotiate the repatriation of Ngarrindjeri Old People from UK institutions such as the Royal Albert Memorial Museum, the local South Australian Museum and the Aboriginal Affairs and Reconciliation Division (now part of The Department of Premier and Cabinet). Some of the issues emerging from these negotiations which have been expressed by Ngarrindjeri elders include: funding for repatriating institutions who are not eligible through the RICP; the need for formal agreements between government and museums and Indigenous communities and a formal process of apologies; and the reinstatement of funding for international repatriation between Australia and the United Kingdom that would allow traditional elders to travel overseas to reclaim their ancestors.

Ngarrindjeri have sought support from key international organizations, and travelled widely to share their concerns with other First Nations. In November 2005, a Ngarrindjeri delegation attended the World Archaeology Congress' (WAC) second inter-congress, The Uses and Abuses of Archaeology for Indigenous Populations, that was held in Auckland, New Zealand. Tom Trevorrow, during a speech at the conference, stated that:

> The spirits of the Old People are not at rest because their bodies have been removed from country and interfered with. We don't want any evil spirits that have entered our Old People's remains to accompany them home to Australia. We must conduct a cultural spiritual cleansing ceremony at the places where Old People's remains have been held (see WAC 2005).

On 15 November 2005, WAC formally supported the Ngarrindjeri nation's 'right to have their Old People returned to country and to have full control over this process both nationally and internationally' (see WAC 2005). What needs to be better understood by governments, collecting institutions and the wider community is that, during repatriation and reburial, Indigenous communities are utilising complex Indigenous knowledge, expertise and skills to appropriately care for the ancestors whilst sustaining important cultural traditions. This process provides space for young Ngarrindjeri people to learn more about Ngarrindjeri culture, to revitalise traditions, to share history with non-Indigenous peoples and, as a consequence, to contribute to a creative and living Ngarrindjeri culture.

Added to this local strategic approach, Ngarrindjeri leaders have been actively seeking partnerships with Indigenous nations from around the Pacific rim. In

2004 the Ngarrindjeri nation supported a proposal to the National Congress of American Indians (NCAI), made by the CTUIR, to consider the establishment of a Pacific Rim Treaty of First Nations. In 2007, the United League of Indigenous Nations (ULIN) was formed and the Ngarrindjeri nation was a founding signatory (see ULIN 2007). This international body, as a principle, supports Indigenous repatriation and has the capacity to bring significant resources to negotiations, research, training, legal cases and community contexts.

Despite the limited government resources available for reburials, the Ngarrindjeri were funded by the federal Department of Families, Housing, Community Services and Indigenous Affairs (FaHCSIA) for further international repatriations conducted in July 2008. This involved repatriation handovers at Edinburgh University, the National Museums Scotland and the Royal Albert Memorial Museum, as well as negotiations with the Natural History Museum in London. Repatriation for the Ngarrindjeri nation continues to be discussed on a daily basis as the elders prepare and negotiate for the growing numbers of Old People to be reburied back into Ngarrindjeri Ruwe.

Tentative Footsteps: Resistance, Transformation and Reburials

Currently there are over four hundred Old People housed at Camp Coorong whilst extensive research, planning and discussion takes place within the Ngarrindjeri nation in relation to reburials. Ongoing research support from Finders University-based scholars such as the authors of this paper, Lynley Wallis, Daryle Rigney and Katrina Niland has been critical in assisting with preparations for reburials and the complex negotiations required with local and state government agencies. It is clear that governments need to take more responsibility for funding Indigenous community research. Ngarrindjeri leaders such as Tom Trevorrow, Matt Rigney and Uncle Major Sumner have stressed the need for significant funding to support: community meetings, the administrations of Ngarrindjeri organisations taking responsibility for repatriation, additional research, negotiating land for reburials, community negotiations about appropriate ceremonies for Old People from different times and different parts of Ngarrindjeri Ruwe, the management of reburial sites, community training and the capacity to settle community disputes emerging from these issues (see Wilson 2005).

The possibility of developing an extensive Ngarrindjeri reburial program has emerged at a time when Ngarrindjeri Ruwe is being subjected to new forms of colonialism produced by the rapid development of a myriad of management reports and plans (see Hemming 2006). For Ngarrindjeri leaders this has meant a struggle to resist and manage this new invasion of Ngarrindjeri space. Overnight, Ngarrindjeri leaders have had to develop the political literacy to engage with a complex system of interrelated planning interests including: heritage, local council planning, Natural Resource Management (NRM), water-catchment boards, tourism, fishing and irrigation (see Hattam, Rigney and

Hemming 2007; Hemming, Rigney and Pearce 2007). These new management regimes have also placed increased stress on Ngarrindjeri burial grounds. For Ngarrindjeri people to protect existing burials and to organise reburials in a newly mapped and managed country, leaders have had to develop strategies for negotiating their reburial needs in these new management spaces. This complex colonial context creates economic, social, political and spiritual stresses.

International environmental values flow into Ngarrindjeri Ruwe with the new NRM regimes. For example, in 1971 eighteen nations including Australia signed a treaty known as the Ramsar Convention on Wetlands that was designed to protect wetlands of international importance. One of these wetland areas is the Coorong and Lakes Alexandrina and Albert Ramsar Site – a central part of Ngarrindjeri Ruwe. The first Ramsar plan for the region controversially omitted a Ngarrindjeri position paper on Ngarrindjeri values and the management of the Ramsar site (see Department of Water, Land and Biodiversity Conservation (DWLBC) 2000; Hemming, Trevorrow and Rigney 2002). The Ngarrindjeri working group argued that:

> The Ngarrindjeri lands – in particular the River, the Lakes and the Coorong are crucial for the survival of the Ngarrindjeri people. They have a spiritual and religious connection with the land and the living things associated with it. The fish, birds, and other living things are the Ngartjis (totems) of the Ngarrindjeri people. Many Ngarrindjeri people have a strong spiritual connection to their Ngartjis and a responsibility to protect them. Without their Ngartjis they believe they cannot survive (NRWG in Hemming, Trevorrow and Rigney 2002).

Although, severely hampered by limited financial and human resources, Ngarrindjeri leaders have continued to engage with the developing systems of NRM. They have recognised that the reburial of repatriated Old People, and the protection of existing burial grounds, must be coordinated with the growing planning and legislative requirements of NRM. In 2006, the Ngarrindjeri nation launched the *Ngarrindjeri Nation Yarluwar-Ruwe Plan: Caring for Ngarrindjeri Sea Country and Culture* (2006) as a strategic response to new government planning regimes. The Yarluwar-Ruwe plan is formally acknowledged as a foundational document for all government NRM planning documents for the Ramsar site (see MDBC 2006). It identifies amongst its strategies and priorities the need to: 'Negotiate secure burial grounds for repatriated Old People throughout Ngarrindjeri Ruwe. [and] Work with all levels of Government to determine the most appropriate legal method for protecting burial grounds in perpetuity' (Ngarrindjeri nation 2006: 28). Building Ngarrindjeri expertise, capacity and employment opportunities is fundamental to recent Ngarrindjeri planning aimed at developing a just approach to resolving issues such as the repatriation and reburial of the Old People. The recently formalised Ngarrindjeri Regional Partnership agreement between the Ngarrindjeri Regional Authority and the state and federal governments, aims to support the further development of a Ngarrindjeri Caring for

Country Centre which will have responsibility to oversee and coordinate issues such as reburial programs (see Hemming and Rigney in press).

Warnung (Hacks Point) and Parnka Reburials: the 'First Step'

In September 2006 the Ngarrindjeri Heritage Committee (NHC) organised the first two major reburial ceremonies of Old People at Warnung (Hack's Point) and Parnka along the Coorong. Warnung is managed by Coorong Wilderness Lodge (a Ngarrindjeri tourism enterprise) and the land at Parnka is part of the Coorong National Park. Preparation for the reburials took several months and was coordinated by the NHC. A team of Ngarrindjeri community members, university researchers and members of the National Museum of Australia's Repatriation Unit worked on documentary research, government negotiations, final identification of the Old People, and preparation of burial sites and a range of other issues. Although a total of sixteen Old People were identified for reburial back into their country, the number increased to twenty-two people following further investigation by the team. The documentation and research already carried out on these 'collections' was extensive, but it still took support from experienced researchers and community leaders to clarify identifications for the reburial.

The reburial ceremonies were attended by many Indigenous community members, non-Indigenous supporters, and local government representatives. A Flinders University archaeology field school was carried out in conjunction with the reburials and staff and students assisted with preparation and participated in aspects of the reburial ceremonies. Students were invited to assist with the ceremonial signal fires along the Coorong which cleansed the area and let the community and the ancestors know what was taking place. The field school was directed by community leaders (George Trevorrow and Tom Trevorrow) and staff from Flinders University (Hemming, Wallis and Wilson). Students conducted excavations and surveys on Ngarrindjeri Ruwe at the request of Ngarrindjeri leaders and they assisted with reburying Old People back into their burial grounds. Ngarrindjeri have supported and conducted cross-cultural education for many years and Camp Coroong was part of the field school program. Feedback from students was very positive and the following excerpt from a student journal provides an example of the life-changing experience:

> I also felt incredibly honoured to be a part of this repatriation process – to be able to help with the lighting of the cleansing fires, to helping out with the surveying of the site. But most of all I felt incredibly honoured to have been given the opportunity to attend the reburial.

The Warnung and Parnka reburials, although resource intensive and emotionally draining, began the healing process for the Ngarrindjeri nation. Ngarrindjeri leaders supported the filming of the reburial ceremonies and preparations, and the development of a documentary to raise public awareness. Ngarrindjeri filmmakers David Wilson, Albert Lovegrove and Chris Wilson are ensuring that the journey of the Old People is told to a national and international audience.

With regard to future reburials the authors, in collaboration with archaeologist Lynley Wallis, have been working with the Ngarrindjeri nation on long-term heritage research, teaching, research and management planning (see Wallis, Hemming and Wilson 2006; Hemming et al. 2007; Wallis, Domett and Niland 2007). This research supports the continuing Ngarrindjeri reburial program and the management and proper care of existing burials and burial grounds in the region. The legal status of existing Ngarrindjeri burial grounds continues to be an issue that the NHC is pursuing and, once the Old People are reburied, Ngarrindjeri leaders want to ensure that they will never again be disturbed from their resting places. Ngarrindjeri leaders continue to develop their understanding of the complexities associated with a long-term reburial program. Without the support of Ngarrindjeri and non-Ngarrindjeri researchers, dedicated Ngarrindjeri community members and other supporters, the reburial process would be potentially chaotic, disrespectful and damaging for the Ngarrindjeri nation.

In 2007, Hemming worked with Ngarrindjeri leaders to prepare an initial funding proposal to the South Australian government to support the proposed Ngarrindjeri Repatriation and Reburial Program and the appointment of a designated Ngarrindjeri repatriation officer within the developing Ngarrindjeri Caring for Country Program. It was estimated that it would take ten years to complete the existing reburials, if four reburial ceremonies could be organised annually, and that the cost per annum would be approximately $250,000. These costs were based on long-term experience with the reburial issue and the first major reburial ceremonies held at Warnung and Parnka. At present, the Ngarrindjeri Land and Progress Association bears almost all of these costs. This proposal followed recommendations made in the Yarluwar-Ruwe plan. While there is to date no action on this proposal, it is likely that through continuous negotiations, the raising of public awareness and support from various groups these broader goals will be achieved.

Conclusion

In April 2005 officials returned soil from the grave of Ngarrindjeri First World War veteran Rufus Gordon Rigney from Belgium to his people and his *ruwe* on the Coorong in South Australia. Ngarrindjeri held a solemn 'connecting spirits' ceremony for the return of this sacred soil. This event was the idea of 2003 Mount Barker High School student Donna Handke. She was inspired by a visit to Camp Coorong and a commemoration plaque in the Raukkan Church. This plaque was designed by the late Ngarrindjeri artist Kerry Kurwingie Giles and inspired by the book *Ngarrindjeri Anzacs* by Doreen Kartinyeri (1996). The continuing work of

Ngarrindjeri elders in the grassroots reconciliation movement produces moving collaborations like the 'connecting spirits' ceremony. Events like these will help to heal Ngarrindjeri Ruwe.

The 'First Stolen Generations' are returning back to Ngarrindjeri Ruwe following decades of removal from their *ruwe*. Their theft has cause spiritual, social and cultural damage to the Ngarrindjeri nation. Although this process has begun, it will take time, planning and resources to assist with community healing. In the past, the repatriation debate has often failed to consider the complex issues faced by Indigenous nations when the Old People are finally returned to country. In comparison with repatriation and reburial issues for Indigenous communities, the Australian Government and, more widely, the Australian public, have been very concerned with the protection of burials at sacred places such as Anzac Cove in Turkey. This site is viewed as a sacred place which is presently being desecrated by tourism-related development. Will Indigenous people receive similar support for the return of their Old People?

There is only so much that can be done at the community level without support from governments and major institutions. Significant resources need to be made available to Indigenous communities, particularly by Australian federal and state governments, to begin to repair this enormous cultural, spiritual and social damage. This will in turn ensure that Ngarrindjeri leaders can refocus their attention to related matters of health, housing, employment and youth without the continuing burden of 'history' on their shoulders. Ironically and tragically, it should be remembered by Australian and British Governments that in 1837 the British Government instructed the South Australian Protector of Aborigines to ensure that Indigenous burial grounds were preserved from 'settlement' by the colonists. It is time for the Australian and British Governments to take responsibility (as many Indigenous communities have in caring for their Old People) to ensure that the repatriation and reburial process is completed and that the First Stolen Generations are finally laid to rest.

Notes

1. This chapter draws on a presentation at the 2005 Museums Australia – National Conference, Sydney, entitled 'Returning the "Old People": The First "Stolen Generations"'. The phrase 'First Stolen Generations' is borrowed from Tom Trevorrow and was used by him in negotiations with Museum Victoria.

2. *Pethamuldi* is the Ngarrindjeri term for someone who is prone to stealing.

3. Ngarrindjeri leaders have attempted to negotiate a Kungun Ngarrindjeri Yunnan agreement with the South Australian Museum to establish a foundation for resolving the repatriation issue and other issues to do with the museum's historic activities.

Bibliography

Altman, J. and A. Hinkson. 2007. *Coercive Reconciliation: Stabilize, Normalize, Exit Aboriginal Australia*. North Carlton: Arena Publications Association.

Bell, D. 1998. *Ngarrindjeri Wurruwarrin: a World That Is, Was, and Will Be*. North Melbourne: Spinifex.

Berndt, R.M., C.H. Berndt and J. Stanton. 1993. *A World That Was: the Yaraldi of the Murray River and Lakes. South Australia*. Melbourne: Melbourne University Press.

Department of Water, Land and Biodiversity Conservation (DWLBC). 2000. *The Coorong and Lakes Alexandrina and Albert Ramsar Management Plan*. Adelaide: DWLBC.

Fforde, C., J. Hubert and P. Turnbull (eds). 2002. *The Dead and Their Possessions: Repatriation in Principle, Policy and Practice*. London: Routledge.

———. 2004. *Collecting the Dead: Archaeology and the Repatriation Debate*. London: Duckworth.

Fine-Dare, K. 2002. *Grave Injustice: the American Indian Repatriation Movement and NAGPRA*. Lincoln: University of Nebraska Press.

Griffiths, T. 1996. *Hunters and Collectors: the Antiquarian Imagination in Australia*. Cambridge: Cambridge University Press.

Hale H. and N.B. Tindale. 1930. 'Notes on Some Human Remains in the Lower Murray Valley, South Australia', *Records of the South Australian Museum* 4: 145–218.

Hattam, R., D. Rigney and S. Hemming. 2007. 'Reconciliation? Culture and Nature and the Murray River', in E. Potter, et al. (eds), *Fresh Water: New Perspectives on Water in Australia*. Melbourne: Melbourne University Press, pp. 105–22.

Hemming, S. 2000. 'Ngarrindjeri Burials as Cultural Sites: Indigenous Heritage Issues in Australia', *World Archaeological Bulletin* 11: 58–66.

———, P. Jones and P. Clarke. 2000. *Ngurunderi: a Ngarrindjeri Dreaming*. Adelaide: South Australian Museum.

———. 2006. 'The Problem with Aboriginal Heritage', in G. Worby and L.-I. Rigney (eds), *Sharing Spaces: Indigenous and Non-Indigenous Responses to Story, Country and Rights*. Perth: API Network, pp. 305–28.

———. 2007. 'Managing Cultures Into the Past', in D.W. Riggs (ed.), *Taking Up the Challenge: Critical Race and Whiteness Studies in a Postcolonising Nation*. Adelaide: Crawford House, pp. 150–67.

———, D. Rigney and M. Pearce. 2007. '"The Meeting of the Waters": Towards a Just Partnership in the Use, Management and Enjoyment of Ngarrindjeri Ruwe (Lands and Waters)', in E. Potter, et al. (eds), *Fresh Water: New Perspectives on Water in Australia*. Melbourne: Melbourne University Press, pp. 217–33.

——— et al. 2007. 'Caring for Ngarrindjeri Country: Collaborative Research, Community Development and Social Justice', *Indigenous Law Bulletin* 6(27): 6–8.

———. 2007. Ngarrindjeri Cultural Heritage Project (2006–2007). Fourth Quarterly Activity Performance Information Report to the Ngarrindjeri Heritage Committee, the Ngarrindjeri Land and Progress Association and the Department for Environment and Heritage (National Indigenous Heritage Program).

——— and D. Rigney. In press. 'Unsettling Sustainability: Ngarrindjeri Political Literacies, Strategies of Engagement and Transformation', *Continuum, Journal of Media and Cultural Studies*.

————, D. Rigney and C. Wilson. 2008. 'Listening and Respecting Across Generations and Beyond Borders: the Ancient One and Kumarangk (Hindmarsh Island)', in H. Bourke et al. (eds), *Perspectives on the Ancient One*. Walnut Creek, Ca.: Left Coast Press, pp. 260–67.

———— and T. Trevorrow. 2005. 'Kungun Ngarrindjeri Yunnan: Archaeology, Colonialism and Reclaiming the Future', in C. Smith and H.M. Wobst (eds), *Indigenous Archaeologies: Decolonising Theory and Practice*. London: Routledge, pp. 243–61.

————, T. Trevorrow and M. Rigney. 2002. 'Ngarrindjeri Culture', in M. Goodwin and S. Bennett (eds), *The Murray Mouth: Exploring the Implications of Closure or Restricted Flow*. Adelaide: Department of Water, Land and Biodiversity Conservation, pp. 13–19.

Kartinyeri, D. 1996. *Ngarrindjeri Anzacs*. Raukkan: Raukkan Council and South Australian Museum.

———— and S. Anderson. 2008. *Doreen Kartinyeri: My Ngarrindjeri Calling*. Canberra: Aboriginal Studies Press, AIATSIS.

Langford, R. 1983. 'Our Heritage – Your Playground', *Australian Archaeology* 16: 1–6.

Mulvaney, D.J. 1960. 'Archaeological Excavations at Fromm's Landing, on the Lower Murray River, South Australia', *Proceedings of the Royal Society of Victoria* 72: 53–85.

Murray-Darling Basin Commission (MDBC). 2006. *The Lower Lakes, Coorong and Murray Mouth Icon Site Environmental Management Plan 2006–2007*. ACT: Murray-Darling Basin Commission.

Ngarrindjeri nation. 2006. *Ngarrindjeri Nation Yarluwar-Ruwe Plan: Caring for Ngarrindjeri Sea Country and Culture*. Prepared by the Ngarrindjeri Tendi, Ngarrindjeri Heritage Committee, Ngarrindjeri Native Title Management Committee, Ngarrindjeri Land and Progress Association, Camp Coorong, South Australia.

Ngarrindjeri Ramsar Working Group. 1999. 'Ngarrindjeri Perspectives on Ramsar Issues', in *Draft Coorong and Lakes Alexandrina and Albert Ramsar Management Plan*, appendix 8. Adelaide: South Australian Department for Environment, Heritage and Aboriginal Affairs.

Pretty, G. 1977. 'The Cultural Chronology of Roonka Flat: a Preliminary Consideration', in R.V.S. Wright (ed.), *Stone Tools as Cultural Markers*. Canberra: Australian Institute of Aboriginal Studies, pp. 288–331.

Rigney, D., S. Hemming and S. Berg. 2008. 'Letters Patent, Native Title and the Crown in South Australia', in M. Hinton, D. Rigney and E. Johnston (eds), *Indigenous Australians and the Law*, 2nd ed. Sydney: Routledge-Cavendish, pp. 161–78.

Saunders. S. 2003. 'Are they going to pull it down?' *Overland*, 171: 60–62.

Simpson, M.G. 2001. *Making Representations: Museums in the Post-Colonial Era*. London: Routledge.

Smith, C. and H.M. Wobst (eds). 2005. *Indigenous Archaeologies: Decolonising Theory and Practice*. London: Routledge.

Smith, L. 2004. 'The Repatriation of Human Remains – Problem or Opportunity?' *Antiquity* 78(300): 404–13.

Smith, L.T. 1999. *Decolonising Methodologies: Research and Indigenous Peoples*. London: Zed Books.

Smith, W.R. 1930. *Myths and Legends of the Australian Aborigines*. Sydney: George Harrap.

South Australian Government Gazette. 1837. Adelaide: Government Printers.

Stirling, E.C. 1911. 'Preliminary Report on the Discovery of Native Remains at Swanport, River Murray With an Enquiry into the Alleged Occurrence of a Pandemic Among the Australian Aborigines', *Transactions of the Royal Society of South Australia* 35: 4–46.

Thomas, D.H. 2000. *Skull Wars: Kennewick Man, Archaeology and the Battle for Native American Identity*. New York: Basic Books.

Trevorrow, T. 2003. 'A shocking insult', *Overland*, 171: 62–63.

———— and S. Hemming. 2006. 'Conversation: *Kungun Ngarrindjeri Yunnan* – Listen to Ngarrindjeri People Talking', in G. Worby and L-I. Rigney (eds), *Sharing Spaces: Indigenous and Non-Indigenous Responses to Story, Country and Rights*. Perth: API Network, pp. 295–304.

————, et al. 2007. *They Took Our Land and Then Our Children: Ngarrindjeri Struggle for Truth and Justice*. Meningie: Ngarrindjeri Land and Progress Association.

Unaipon, D. 2006. *Legendary Tales of the Australian Aborigines*. S. Muecke and A. Shoemaker (eds). Melbourne: Miegunyah Press.

Wallis, L.A., K. Domett and K. Niland. 2007. 'The Hack's Point Burial Site Project: Recording, Understanding and Protecting an Old People's Place at the Kurangk, South Australia. A confidential report to the Ngarrindjeri Heritage Committee, Ngarrindjeri Native Title Management Committee and Ngarrindjeri Tendi.

Wallis, L., S. Hemming and C. Wilson. 2006. 'The Warnung (Hack's Point) Old People's Place Project: a Collaborative Approach to Archaeological Survey, Research and Management Planning'. Unpublished report prepared for the Ngarrindjeri Heritage Committee, Ngarrindjeri Native Title Management Committee and Ngarrindjeri Tendi.

Watkins, J. 2000. *Indigenous Archaeology: American Indian Values and Scientific Practice*. California: Altamira Press.

————. 2003. 'Beyond the Margin: American Indians, First Nations, and Archaeology in North America', *American Antiquity*, 68(2): 273–85.

Wilson, C. 2005. 'Return of the Ngarrindjeri: Repatriating Old People Back to Country', BA Honours thesis. Adelaide: Flinders University.

World Archaeological Congress. 2005. 'Ngarrindjeri Nation Obtains Support of World Archaeological Congress'. Retrieved 11 September 2006 from http://www.worldarchaeologicalcongress.org/site/news/Ngarrindjeri_NZ%20I-C.pdf

Notes on Contributors

Kim Akerman has been involved in Australian Aboriginal studies since 1967, and involved with repatriation issues since 1988–9. In 2001 he worked with the Western Australian Museum to develop protocols for the repatriation of ancestral remains and religious materials to Aboriginal communities in the Pilbara and Kimberley regions. In 2008, he co-authored with Greg Wallace the report *For Now and Forever: An Analysis of Current and Emerging Needs for Aboriginal Cultural Stores and Repositories in Western Australia.* He is currently a consultant on the Return of Indigenous Cultural Property scheme administered by the South Australian Museum, and is a member of the Scientific Advisory Committee of the Kimberley Foundation of Australia.

✦

Henry Atkinson is a Wolithiga Elder and spokesperson for the Yorta Yorta Nation Aboriginal Corporation Council. He has been a life-long campaigner for Indigenous Australian land and cultural rights, and has been actively involved in securing the return of ancestral human remains for over thirty years.

✦

Liz Bell is a Postgraduate Research Student in the International Centre for Cultural and Heritage Studies (ICCHS) at Newcastle University. Her research focuses on the ethical issues involved in dealing with human remains and the effects that changing perceptions have on their treatment by museums and biomedical institutions. She has conducted the first England-wide survey of human remains in museums in order to ascertain which hold human remains, and to establish the provenance and number of remains within their collections.

✦

Elizabeth Burns Coleman is a Lecturer in Communications and Media at Monash University. She has previously lectured in moral and political philosophy (La Trobe University), philosophy of law (Wollongong University) and aesthetics (Australian National University). Her books include *Aboriginal Art, Identity and Appropriation* (Ashgate 2005) and three edited collections: *Negotiating the Sacred: Blasphemy and Sacrilege in a Multicultural Society* (ANU E-press 2006, co-edited with Kevin White), *Negotiating the Sacred II: Blasphemy and Sacrilege in a Multicultural Society* (ANU E-press 2008, co-edited with Maria-Suzette Fernandes Dias), and *Religion, Medicine and the Body* (Brill 2010, co-edited with Kevin White).

Franchesca Cubillo is a member of the Larrakia, Bardi, Wadaman and Yanuwa Nations from the 'Top End' region of Australia. She is currently Senior Curator of Indigenous Art at the National Gallery of Australia. Awarded a Churchill Fellowship in 2006, she has held the positions of Senior Curator of Aboriginal Art and Material Culture at the Northern Territory Museum and Art Gallery, and Cultural Director at Tandanya, National Cultural Institute in Adelaide. She has been involved in the repatriation of Indigenous Australian ancestral remains and cultural property as Curator of Aboriginal Anthropology at the South Australian Museum for eight years, and has also worked as a Manager within the Repatriation Unit of the National Museum of Australia.

Claes Hallgren is a Social Anthropologist at Darlana University. He has been closely involved in the identification and repatriation of Aboriginal skeletal remains from Sweden, and providing copies of early twentieth-century ethnographic research by the Swedish naturalist, Eric Mjöberg, to Indigenous communities in Western Australia. His publications include *Två Resenärer. Två Bilder av Australier. Eric Mjöbergs och Yngve Laurells vetenskapliga expeditioner 1910–1913* (kultur i fokus 2003).

Steve Hemming is a Senior Lecturer and Coordinator of the Australian Studies program at Flinders University. He has been Curator in Anthropology and History at the South Australian Museum. His research and publications span the fields of Indigenous cultural heritage and natural resource management, and Indigenous anthropology and archaeology. With Dr Doreen Kartinyeri, he established the South Australian Museum's national Aboriginal Family History Project. He is presently working on a number of government-based and community research projects focusing on water and natural resources management.

Howard Morphy is Director of the Research School of Humanities and the Arts at the Australian National University. He is an anthropologist and curator. He has published widely in the anthropology of art, aesthetics, performance, museum anthropology, visual anthropology and religion. His books include *Becoming Art: Exploring Cross-cultural Categories* (Berg 2008) and *Aboriginal Art* (Phaidon 1998).

John Morton is a Senior Lecturer in Anthropology at La Trobe University. He has conducted extensive ethnographic research with Aboriginal people in the Northern Territory, South Australia and New South Wales, largely in relation to land rights, native title and heritage protection. He has written on Aboriginal land tenure, religion, public Aboriginality (including indigenous representation in museums) and indigenous links to Australian environmentalism. He has prepared many reports for Aboriginal organisations and related public bodies. His numerous publications include the jointly edited book, *The Photographs of Baldwin Spencer* (2005).

Virginia Myles is an Archaeological Resource Management Policy Analyst at Parks Canada. She obtained her degree in Anthropology and Art History from Carleton University in 1976. For the past 34 years she has worked for Parks Canada in the field of archaeology and collections as a Cataloguer and Supervisor of Archaeology Field Labs, Material Culture Researcher, Archaeological Collections Manager, and Policy Analyst. She addresses issues and develops policy tools relating to Parks Canada's archaeological collection and the management, protection and disposition of objects. She also provides advice regarding archaeological collections to other Canadian Federal Land Managers.

Michael Pickering is the Director of the Aboriginal and Torres Strait Islander Program and Repatriation Program of the National Museum of Australia. He has worked extensively in Australia as an anthropologist and archaeologist. His research interests and publications include studies on material culture, cannibalism, hunter-gatherer anthropology and archaeology, heritage management, and repatriation. He was Senior Curator of the 2009 Darwin and Australia exhibition at the National Museum of Australia.

Martin Skrydstrup is a Postdoctoral Research Fellow in the Department of Anthropology, University of Copenhagen. He has been a Fulbright scholar and holds a doctorate in Cultural Anthropology from Columbia University. For his doctoral research on cultural property, he conducted ethnographies in Hawaii, Ghana, Iceland and Greenland exploring various repatriation cases on a comparative scale. In the field of cultural resource management, he has worked as an expert consultant for the Nordic Africa Institute and the UN World Intellectual Property Organization. He serves on the Board of the International Committee for Museums and Collections of Ethnography and was appointed a special advisor to the Ethics Committee of the International Council of Museums.

Paul Turnbull is Professor of eHistory within the School of History, Philosophy, Classics and Religion at the University of Queensland. Besides his interests in making history in digital media, he is also well known for his research and writings on the history of racial science and the theft and scientific use of

Indigenous Australian Bodily remains. His recent publications include 'British Anthropological Thought in Colonial Practice, 1860–1880', in B. Douglas and C. Ballard (eds.), *Foreign Bodies: Race in Oceania* (2008).

Kathyrn Whitby-Last is a Senior Lecturer in Law at the University of Aberdeen. Her research interests are in domestic and international law relating to cultural and natural heritage. She has written extensively on the law relating to the protection of wildlife habitats, the implementation of the European Community Habitats Directive in the UK, and claims for the repatriation of cultural property. She is a member of the Observatoire Juridique Natura 2000. Her recent publications include: 'Great Britain', in Christopoulou, Haidarlis and Durousseau (eds.), *La gestion des sites Natura 2000, la mise en place des cadres nationaux* (University of Thessaly Press 2009), and 'Town and Country Planning and Natura 2000 in Great Britain', in Cedoua (ed.), *Amenagement de territoire, urbanisme et reseau Natura 2000*, Volume II (Almedina 2009).

Chris Wilson is a Ngarrindjeri man from the Lower Murray Lakes and Coorong in South Australia and Lecturer in Indigenous Studies in Yunggorendi First Nations Centre at Flinders University. He has an honours degree in archaeology and is currently investigating Holocene occupation and subsistence of the Lower Murray in South Australia as part of his Ph.D. research. He is working with Ngarrindjeri Elders and community leaders on cultural heritage and archaeological issues, including the repatriation of Ngarrindjeri Old People (human remains) from Australian and British museums and scientific institutions; and he has advised government on repatriation and reburial issues.

Index